"In a time when it's needed more th███████████████████████n effective program that not only offers to ease the stress and emotional ██████ ir children, but also provides a recipe to begin healing our world."

> —**Elisha Goldstein, PhD**, author of *The Now Effect* and coauthor
> of *A Mindfulness-Based Stress Reduction Workbook*

"With wisdom, kindness, and inspiring clarity born from years of mindful living and teaching mindfulness, Amy Saltzman guides us through the research-proven, practical steps of how to help young people learn the fundamentals of resilience, focus, and compassion. Science-supported, clinically-sound, and educationally brilliant, this book will provide essential tools for all who wish to learn from a master about how children and adolescents can discover *A Still Quiet Place*, a source of emotional and social intelligence and a lifelong center of inner peace."

> —**Daniel J. Siegel, MD**, author of *Brainstorm: The Power and
> Purpose of the Teenage Brain* and *Mindsight: The New Science
> of Personal Transformation*; clinical professor at the University of
> California, Los Angeles, School of Medicine; and codirector
> of the UCLA Mindful Awareness Research Center

"With great clarity and uncommon attention to detail, Amy Saltzman gives us much more than a first-rate mindfulness program. *A Still Quiet Place* is a portrait of a master teacher at work."

> —**Richard Brady, MS**, cofounder and president of the Mindfulness
> in Education Network and coauthor of *Tuning In: Mindfulness in
> Teaching and Learning*

"Amy Saltzman has produced a highly illuminative and extremely practical mindfulness-based program for children and adolescents. *A Still Quiet Place* provides step-by-step instructions for facilitators to administer the program in whole or in part. It is a must-have for mental health professionals, educators, and parents wishing to teach children and adolescents mindfulness and social and emotional learning. Highly recommended!"

> —**Sam Himelstein, PhD**, director of the Mind Body Awareness
> Project and author of *A Mindfulness-Based Approach to Working
> with High-Risk Adolescents*

"Amy Saltzman's authoritative book provides the wisdom and building blocks you'll need to share mindfulness with children and teens. Far more than a workbook, it's a curriculum that you can pick up and use to teach a class, written by someone who has been instrumental in the movement to bring mindfulness to youth since its inception."

> —**Susan Kaiser Greenland, JD**, author of *The Mindful Child*

"A *Still Quiet Place* is exactly the guide that parents and professionals have been waiting for to take the mystery out of the practice of mindfulness. We all know that our children are too stressed, and we want it to change. A *Still Quiet Place* is an essential antidote and accompaniment for the stressed lives that our children lead today. This crystal-clear program teaches children exactly how to bring thoughtful, calming awareness to their day-to-day experiences and struggles, not only reducing pressure and strain but enhancing their quality of life. Filled with child-friendly explanations and exercises, every child will benefit from finding their still quiet place within. Amy Saltzman is the perfect guide to lead them there."

—**Tamar Chansky, PhD**, author of *Freeing Your Child from Anxiety: Powerful, Practical Solutions to Overcome Your Child's Fears, Worries, and Phobias*

"In this clear and compassionate guide, Amy Saltzman offers a joyous path for leading children to peace and self-discovery through mindfulness."

—**Christopher Willard, PsyD**, author of *Child's Mind*

"Amy Saltzman makes teaching mindfulness widely accessible with this wonderful book. It is a brilliant distillation of years of experience teaching mindfulness to children kindergarten through twelfth grade. Saltzman's passion and experience flow through these pages. A *Still Quiet Place* is a must-read for anyone who desires teaching valuable life skills. It is one of the best and most complete books on teaching mindfulness that I've read."

—**Brian Despard**, author of *You Are Not Your Thoughts: Mindfulness for Children of All Ages*

"What our busy modern world needs is for more adults to introduce more children to A *Still Quiet Place*. Finally, we have a step-by-step guide to building vital skills for children like kindness, resilience, attention, and stress management. Saltzman offers practical, everyday guidance to support children of any age and has created an irreplaceable resource in the field."

—**Mark Bertin, MD**, developmental pediatrician and author of *The Family ADHD Solution*. Learn more at www.develop mentaldoctor.com.

"A *Still Quiet Place* is a smart, thoughtful, and encouraging guide to bringing mindfulness to children. Amy's warmth and experience shine through her words, and her invitation to explore the world with kindness and curiosity is exactly what I would want for my own daughter. My teaching, and my parenting, will be better for having read this book."

—**Jennifer Cohen Harper**, author of *Little Flower Yoga for Kids*

a still quiet place

A Mindfulness Program for Teaching Children and Adolescents to Ease Stress and Difficult Emotions

Amy Saltzman, MD

New Harbinger Publications, Inc.

Publisher's Note

Distributed in Canada by Raincoast Books

Copyright © 2014 by Amy Saltzman
        New Harbinger Publications, Inc.
        5674 Shattuck Avenue
        Oakland, CA 94609
        www.newharbinger.com

Excerpt from EVERYDAY BLESSINGS by Jon Kabat-Zinn and Myla Kabat-Zinn. Copyright © 1997 Myla Kabat-Zinn and Jon Kabat-Zinn. Reprinted by permission of Hyperion. All rights reserved.

"Autobiography in Five Short Chapters" reprinted with the permission of Beyond Words/Atria Books, a division of Simon & Schuster, Inc., from THERE'S A HOLE IN MY SIDEWALK: THE ROMANCE OF SELF-DISCOVERY by Portia Nelson. Copyright © 1993 by Portia Nelson. All rights reserved.

Cover design by Amy Shoup; Text design by Michele Waters-Kermes; Acquired by Catharine Meyers

Library of Congress Cataloging-in-Publication Data

Saltzman, Amy, 1958-
  A still quiet place : a mindfulness program for teaching children and adolescents to ease stress and difficult emotions / Amy Saltzman ; foreword by Saki Santorelli.
     pages cm
  Summary: "Today's children and adolescents face intense pressures--both in the classroom and at home. A Still Quiet Place presents an eight-week mindfulness-based stress reduction (MBSR) program that therapists, teachers, and other professionals can use to help children and adolescents manage stress and anxiety in their lives. The easy-to-implement practices in this guide are designed to help increase attention, learning, resiliency, and compassion by showing children how to experience the natural quietness that can be found within. The book also includes links to helpful audio downloads"-- Provided by publisher.
  Includes bibliographical references and index.
  ISBN 978-1-60882-757-2 (pbk.) -- ISBN 978-1-60882-758-9 (pdf e-book) -- ISBN 978-1-60882-759-6 (epub)
1. Emotions in children. 2. Emotions in adolescence. 3. Stress management for children. 4. Stress management for teenagers. 5. Educational psychology. I. Title.
  BF723.E6S25 2014
  155.4'189042--dc23
                2013050525

Printed in the United States of America

16   15   14

10 9 8 7 6 5 4 3 2 1   First printing

contents

foreword

Our children are our greatest treasure. Yet their treasures are hidden to them, desiring to be known. As parents, teachers, and human beings, our job is to lead them into the discovery of their innate, imperishable richness and radiance.

If you care about children reclaiming their deep inheritance—developing their inborn capacity for understanding directly their bodies, minds, and hearts; learning to make wiser choices; and cultivating the resources that will allow them to stand more fully in the world—then plunge into this book and taste directly what Dr. Amy Saltzman is transmitting to all of us.

By all accounts, childhood stress is on the rise in the United States. Much of this stress is toxic, robbing our nation of its greatest wealth: vital, engaged young people. The data unambiguously reveals that American children are worse off in 2010 than they were in 1980. According to the 2010 Children's Defense Fund report entitled *The State of America's Children*, the United States ranks first among industrialized countries in gross domestic product, health expenditures, and number of billionaires. In parallel, it ranks very poorly in fifteen-year-olds' math and science scores and absolutely last in childhood poverty, gun violence, and adolescent birthrates. Once every second, a child is suspended; every eleven seconds, a high school student drops out; every twenty seconds, a student is corporally punished; every three hours, a child or teen is killed by a firearm; every five hours, a child or teen commits suicide; and every six hours, a child or teen dies of abuse or neglect.

We can deny these facts, or feel overwhelmed and paralyzed by them; or we can begin to act. As a mother, physician, scientist, and teacher, Amy Saltzman has chosen to act wisely. She has done the hard labor required to birth a pioneering perspective and methodology that teaches our children to pay attention on purpose, to be present and kind toward what they see and feel and come to know. Like great educators before her, Amy is committed to engaging our children in the adventure of life: a growing ability to live more mindfully.

Amy defines mindfulness as "the universal human capacity for paying attention with kindness and curiosity." Notice *with kindness and curiosity*. I suspect that for most of us, when our parents or teachers exhorted us to "pay attention," they didn't include "with kindness and curiosity." Yet these four words can make all the difference. Here is an interchange between Amy and a fourth grader (following a week of exploring unpleasant events) that exemplifies Amy's kind, curious approach and the subtlety needed to engage skillfully in this work.

Amy: Yes, Angela. What was your unpleasant event?

Angela: I wanted to go play with my friend, and my mom made me clean my room first.

Amy: Yes, not being able to do what you want to do when you want to do it can be unpleasant. What were your thoughts?

Angela: I hate my mom. My mom is mean. She *never* lets me do what I want to do. She is *so* unfair.

Amy: Excellent mindfulness; you noticed a lot of thoughts. And how about feelings?

Angela: I felt mad and sad.

Amy: Anything else?

Angela: Yeah. Actually, I was mad at myself, too, because my mom had told me to clean my room before, and I forgot.

Amy: Again, very mindful. Sometimes it is much easier to be mad at someone else than to be responsible for our choices. And what was happening in your body when all these thoughts and feelings were swirling around?

Angela: Um… My arms and hands were kind of tight, and my face was a little squinched and grumpy.

Amy: Thank you, Angela, for your brave sharing. Anyone else want to share an unpleasant event?

As you can see, there's a lot going on in this exchange that might be helpful to Angela (and her classmates) now and in the future. Amy has helped Angela unpack the bare actuality of her experience by helping her attend closely and caringly to the range of thoughts, emotions, and bodily sensations she was experiencing.

Why does this matter? Because research now suggests that impulse control and the ability to manage emotions have a tremendous impact on our children's ability to choose their behaviors. Scientific studies suggest that self-regulation seems to have a stronger association with academic achievement than IQ or entry-level reading or math scores, and that self-regulation training may be an effective means of reducing school failure.

Mindfulness appears to improve executive function (that is, self-regulation) and enhance emotional intelligence, while encouraging perspective taking and choice, thereby fostering empathetic and compassionate action.

While more scientific investigation is required to help us understand the role of mindfulness in the lives of our children, preliminary evidence now points strongly to its positive benefits.

And let's remember that mindfulness is not a religion. It is a universal human capacity that is strengthened through deliberate education. In fact, mindfulness training is very American. Our great American educator John Dewey said, "An ounce of experience is better than a ton of theory," and Amy knows this. Her lessons and commentary underscore this point over and over again. In essence, Amy is urging the children she teaches to be present to the unfolding of their lives by moving from the conceptual to the embodied. The story Angela recounts is a real-life experience. Becoming a student of her experience, Angela now has the opportunity to understand her actions more closely and, as a consequence, to begin to shape a range of new possible responses. What better motivator for any of us than meeting and shaping our own lives?

This book is an expression of profound respect for our children, a deep bow to their treasured lives, and a road map for bringing mindfulness more fully into the classrooms, community settings, and homes our children inhabit. Despite our best intentions, we are at risk of betraying the trust our children have placed in our hands and hearts. We know better. We are better. We are up to this task. The radiance and beauty they *are* awaits our sustained nurturance.

Amy is offering us a way.

—Saki F. Santorelli, EdD, MA
Professor of Medicine
Director, Stress Reduction Clinic (MBSR)
Executive Director, Center for Mindfulness in
Medicine, Health Care, and Society
University of Massachusetts Medical School

acknowledgments

The simple truth is, this offering would not be possible without the foundational and pioneering work, and loving support, of the following people—and in turn, all those who have supported them.

Georgina Lindsey, transformational coach, mentor, colleague, partner, and friend for the last twenty-five years. Her distinct and extraordinary combination of wisdom, grace, rigor, and compassion lives inside of me and inspires all aspects of my life. Her passionate studying, sharing, and living of a vast variety of ancient and modern wisdom teachings has been of immeasurable benefit to me and everyone she serves. Her devotion to truth, love, and freedom has had a profound influence on me, and permeates every aspect of my work and life. She has coached me to be responsible for my tendencies toward arrogance and ambition, nurtured what is truest in me, and called forth the offerings described in these pages. She is the sunshine for this blossom.

Eric, my husband, who has supported me and encouraged me in simple, quiet ways to pursue this work. We have loved each other despite, and perhaps because of, our foibles and idiosyncrasies, for twenty-nine years.

Jason and Nicole—my children: great sources of joy, and occasional aggravation, who are the impetus and inspiration for doing this work, and who sometimes reveal the discrepancy between who I am as a parent and who I intend to be.

Jon Kabat-Zinn, Saki Santorelli, Florence Melo-Myer, Ferris Urbanowski, George Mumford, Elana Rosenbaum, and the other pioneers at the Center for Mindfulness, who created one of the primary foundations upon which this work is built.

Amishi Jha, PhD, who generously offered the precious gift of her time and scientific discernment in reviewing the preliminary data on this curriculum.

The children, parents, teachers, counselors, physicians, and allied professionals who have participated in, and helped to refine, the offerings presented in this book.

Susan Kaiser Greenland; Gina Biegel; Wynne, Midge, and Rick Kinder; Megan Cowan; Betsy Rose; Chris McKenna; Sam Himelstein; Deborah Schoeberlein; Richard Brady; Heather Sundberg; Cator Schachoy; David Forbes; Teah Stozer; Robert Wall; Laurie Grossman; and Chris Willard, who all committed to doing this humbling and rewarding work *in the room* with children and adolescents, and who have generously shared their creativity, wisdom, challenges, and laughter.

Margaret Cullen, Nancy Bardake, and the "old-timers" in the Northern California mindfulness-based stress reduction (MBSR) teachers community who gathered in local living rooms, and newer friends from around the world, for embodying mindfulness and providing inspiration, clear seeing, and treasured companionship.

Bob Stahl and the Mindfulness Program at El Camino Hospital; Gil Fronsdal and the IMC family program; Kris Goodrich and Josetta Walsh at the Child and Family Institute; Jon Kulhaneck, Claire Ward, Beth Passi, Principal Kimberly Attell, and Steven Murray at Henry Ford Elementary School; Ceil Kellogg, Karen Clancy, and Theresa Fox at Oak Knoll Elementary School; Susan Brochin, James Green, Laura Delaney, and Amy Methenia at Hillview Middle School; and Principal Matt Zito and Julie Brody of Menlo Atherton High School, for their support of, and faith in, this work.

Jess Beebe and the entire team at New Harbinger Publications for demonstrating the distinction of *developmental* editing. Jasmine Star, the skillful editor who helped me see what was missing and then arrange all the pieces into a coherent whole. Rob Roeser and Barbara Burns, who kindly read and refined the chapter on executive function, emotional intelligence, and social development. My coach, Georgina; my sister Suzanne; and my mother, Linda—editors par excellence, who read this book with clear minds and open hearts, kindly suggesting refinements and simplifications.

And most importantly, the Still Quiet Place itself, and each and every person who has chosen to dwell in this exquisite, expansive space.

introduction

This book offers a detailed, step-by-step guide to the proven, eight-week, mindfulness-based Still Quiet Place curriculum. This book is intended to create a heartfelt conversation between colleagues and friends about sharing mindfulness with youth. In our conversation, we will encourage and challenge each other as we explore the many ways to share the Still Quiet Place (also known as awareness) and mindfulness with children and adolescents.

This book is designed to support teachers, school counselors, therapists, physicians, coaches, allied professionals, and parents—anyone who works with, plays with, lives with, enjoys, and cares about youth—in bringing the scientifically proven, beneficial practices of mindfulness to young people. Because a group is the most common format for sharing mindfulness with youth, this book focuses on working with groups. However, the approach you'll find in these pages works well in a variety of settings, from an understated therapy office, to the stark, hard-tiled, run-down spaces of many schools, to the comfort of the living room couch. The book is intended for use by people like you, who have (or who are willing to develop) a consistent daily mindfulness practice and a deep love of young people.

The term "Still Quiet Place" encompasses many dimensions of mindfulness. Physically, it is the actual sensation of stillness and quietness, the brief pauses between the in-breath and the out-breath and between the out-breath and the in-breath. To connect with the Still Quiet Place, take a moment right here, right now, and simply feel the natural rhythm of your breath. Without slowing or holding your breath, see if you can feel the Still Quiet Place between the in-breath and the out-breath, and again between the out-breath and the in-breath.

As children and adolescents practice attending to the breath and resting in the brief pauses between breaths, they experience a natural, reliable stillness and quietness within themselves. Over time, they discover that this stillness and quietness is always alive inside of them—when they are breathing in, when the breath is still; when they are breathing out, when the breath is still; when they are doing homework, singing, arguing.... With practice they can learn to rest in this stillness and quietness, and to bring an attitude of kindness and curiosity to their thoughts, feelings, physical sensations, impulses, and actions, as well as to the cues they receive from those they interact with. Ultimately, these observations of their internal and external worlds equip young people to make healthier, wiser, more compassionate choices, especially when they encounter typical daily challenges—such as a bully on the playground, a difficult math problem, or the temptation to engage in risky behavior.

In adult language, the Still Quiet Place can be translated as mindfulness, or pure and compassionate moment-to-moment awareness. As you continue to read, each chapter will expand upon the terms—and more importantly, the experiences and relevant applications—of the Still Quiet Place and mindfulness in the everyday lives of young people.

The book provides age-adapted variations for children as young as four and as old as eighteen, as well as suggestions for therapists and parents to tailor the program for individual children. The practices in this book have been proven to decrease students' anxiety (Saltzman & Goldin, 2008). In written narratives, children who have participated in this course share that they are calmer, more focused, and less stressed about homework and tests. More importantly, they also report that they are less emotionally reactive, and more compassionate with themselves and others.

A foundation for this book is borrowed with gratitude from the work of Jon Kabat-Zinn, Saki Santorelli, and their colleagues at the Center for Mindfulness in Medicine, Health Care, and Society. However, much of what is offered in this curriculum—on these pages, in my medical office, and in various classrooms—is based on my life experience as a holistic physician, wife, mother, mindfulness teacher, athlete, poet, and longtime student of ontology (the study of being) in the school of Naked Grace coaching and consulting. The invitation is for you to explore and trust your own life experience, and to bring all that you are to those with whom you are privileged to share the Still Quiet Place.

The Story of the Still Quiet Place

My interest in sharing practices for discovering the Still Quiet Place with children and adolescents is both professional and deeply personal. As a doctor, I frequently see children, teens, and adults who are suffering from the physical, mental, and emotional effects of stress. As a mindfulness teacher, I have seen people of all ages, in a wide variety of life circumstances, use the practice of mindfulness to discover the Still Quiet Place within, reduce their stress, and live more enjoyable and fulfilling lives.

Personally, mindfulness practice (paying attention, here and now, with kindness and curiosity, and then choosing my behavior) is a pure source of sanity, grace, and delight in my own life. Even in challenging times—or especially in challenging times—it allows me to be more aware of what is happening within me and around me. Sometimes this awareness is enough to allow me to pause and discover what is actually needed in the moment. This is in no way meant to suggest that I am always mindful or graceful. Despite years of practice, I am sometimes dismayed by how mindless, and heartless, I can be; I have many ungraceful moments.

In spite of—or perhaps because of—my ungraceful moments, when my son, Jason, was almost three he asked if he could meditate (practice mindfulness) with me. At the time, my daughter, Nicole, was six months old, and we were all adjusting to life with a new baby. My sense is that Jason knew he would have my full and calm attention when we practiced together. His sweet request prompted me to begin sharing mindfulness with him. Some of the practices I shared with him, which are also included in this book, are based on basic, well-known mindfulness practices. Examples include mindful eating and the Body Scan. Others, like the Feelings practice below, arose spontaneously when we were together, sitting side by side in the upstairs hallway or lying in bed at night.

Creating a Mindfulness of Feelings Practice in the Moment

One afternoon Jason wanted something, and I said no. He was very sad and upset. Not knowing exactly what I was offering, I asked if he wanted to do "sads meditation." He said yes. So, intuiting my way as I went, I asked him the following sequence of questions, slowly, allowing him time to gently explore his sadness.

- *Where do the sads live in your body?*

- *What do they feel like?*

- *Are they small or big? ... Hard or soft? ... Heavy or light? ... Warm or cool? ...*

- *Do they have a color or colors?*

- *Do they have a sound?*

- *What do they want from you?*

To be honest, I only remember the answer to the last question. He said "love," and then promptly asked, "Can we play?" That was that. He had befriended his feeling and was ready to move on.

Creating the Program

After sharing practices with my children and reading repeatedly about childhood stress in both the professional and lay literature, I began to wonder:

- Will children and teens benefit if they learn the life skills of mindfulness, and remain familiar with the Still Quiet Place within as they grow older?

- If young people learn to observe their thoughts, feelings, and bodily sensations, will they be less vulnerable to the unhealthy effects of stress?

- If children and teens are able to access their natural sense of peace and trust their own inner wisdom, will they be less susceptible to harmful peer influences and less likely to look for relief in potentially risky behaviors?

- When young people practice mindfulness, does it enhance their natural emotional intelligence? Can it increase their capacity for respectful communication and compassionate action? Will it support them in developing healthy relationships, and in contributing their gifts to the world?

Initially, I explored these questions in an informal way by sharing mindfulness practices with children in elementary school and community settings. Children ages four and older enjoyed and seemed to benefit from the practices. In general, teachers commented that their students were calmer and more focused when they began their day by visiting the Still Quiet Place. Teachers of adolescents reported that their students were more aware of, and thus better able to deal with, the increasingly complex thoughts and emotions of teenage life.

This informal exploration led to formal scientific research, carried out in the Clinically Applied Affective Neuroscience lab in the Department of Psychology at Stanford University and supported by Amishi Jha, PhD, currently at the University of Miami. We conducted studies teaching the practices in this book to third- through sixth-graders and their parents in the Department of Psychology and in two predominantly low-income public elementary schools. (The preliminary results of the child-parent study, and other research on the benefits of mindfulness for youth, are reviewed in the last chapter.)

why offer mindfulness to young people?

First, a brief disclaimer: As mentioned in the introduction, I began sharing mindfulness with my son following a sweet request of his. Over time, I have come to a greater understanding of the challenges, stresses, and suffering many children and adolescents frequently experience. Their deep need for essential life skills to support them in navigating their complex worlds with wisdom and compassion is palpable. Together, my personal practice, my experiences teaching mindfulness to adults and subsequently witnessing them living with less angst and greater ease, and the joy of sharing the practices with my son all inspired me to offer the practices to other children. Initially, sharing mindfulness with children was an intuitive choice based on faith in the practice and in young people's all too frequently unnurtured capacities for reflection, kindness, and skillful action.

Now, more than twelve years later, both historical and cutting-edge research on executive function, emotional intelligence, and social development support the leap of faith that I, and other pioneers in this field, took in bringing these practices to children. Chapter 17 presents an academic framework of these interdependent developmental competencies, and a review of the evidence to date demonstrating that mindfulness enhances these competencies.

Childhood Stress

Colleagues throughout the world and I are offering mindfulness to children and adolescents because almost all of us wish we had learned mindfulness when we were younger. Those of us engaged in this endeavor believe it is possible for young people to benefit from the practice in much the same way adults do: by learning to focus their attention, becoming less reactive, being more compassionate with themselves and others, and ultimately living more engaged, fulfilling lives. Ideally, we would offer these skills to children well before they begin suffering from the ordinary daily stresses of modern life, much less the more challenging issues of extreme academic pressure, domestic conflict, financial hardship, family illness, and neighborhood violence.

Unfortunately, many children are already suffering, in large part because our society values doing over being, and product over process. Our culture tends to put test scores, wealth, and status before joy, connection, and well-being. Scientific research and the media tell us that young people's lives are increasingly stressful. For some, the stress is simply living in our fast-paced, media-saturated Western world. For others, the stress comes from being pushed to perform, "succeed," and get into a "good" college. For still others, the stress involves surviving in extremely challenging, even traumatic, home environments and life circumstances.

Regardless of race, education, or socioeconomic status, an alarming number of children and adolescents are being diagnosed with ADHD, depression, anxiety, obesity, eating disorders, and addictions, and engaging in cutting and other self-destructive behaviors, including suicide. Research from Suniya Luthar, PhD, a professor of psychology and education at the Teachers College at Columbia University, has documented epidemic rates of many of these diagnoses in adolescents living in both affluent and low socioeconomic settings (Luthar, 2003; Luthar & Barkin, 2012). Cruelty, bullying, and violence are on the rise. No one is immune.

Let's do what we can now to immunize our youth against the stresses of modern life and the related conditions and give them skills that will benefit them throughout their lives. There is absolutely no reason they should wait until they are forty-five, and have lost a job or had a heart attack, to learn practices that will support and sustain them. In terms of the discussion below, it is important to note that there is data to suggest that long-term stress negatively impacts the development of executive function—specifically working memory (Evans & Schamberg, 2009)—and thus is likely to negatively affect emotional intelligence, social development, and moral behavior. An ounce of prevention....

History of Mindfulness-Based Stress Reduction

Before moving on to a discussion of the foundational elements of mindfulness and mindfulness-based stress reduction (MBSR), let's briefly review the history of MBSR and a few of the many compelling research studies on the benefits of mindfulness for adults. All MBSR is based on the program created by Jon Kabat-Zinn, PhD, who established the Stress Reduction Clinic under the auspices of the University of

Massachusetts Medical Center in 1979. In 1995, the Stress Reduction Clinic became the Center for Mindfulness in Medicine, Health Care, and Society, and affiliated with the University of Massachusetts Medical School.

Initially, MBSR was offered to adult patients with chronic pain and illness. Over the last thirty-five years, MBSR has become a standard clinical intervention and community offering. It is currently offered in a variety of settings worldwide. MBSR has been scientifically proven to benefit adults in diverse circumstances—patients, doctors, nurses, therapists, teachers, lawyers, professional athletes, military personnel, pregnant women and new mothers, those living in the inner city, artists, prison inmates, and corporate executives.

Course Format

The standard adult program consists of eight weekly sessions, each two to three hours in duration, and an all-day session of six to eight hours in length. Between sessions, participants engage in forty-five to sixty minutes of daily home practice. The home practice includes both formal, guided audio practices and informal practice (the application of mindfulness to daily life). The course includes discussions about the physiology of stress, the fight-or-flight response, and the beneficial effects of mindfulness. Most often, these discussions are not didactic in nature; rather, they are interwoven into the class and tied directly to the experience of the participants. Both the formal and the informal practices support participants in exploring and becoming familiar with their repetitive habits of thinking, feeling, and acting, and then choosing more skillful and compassionate ways to respond to life's circumstances.

Research and Results

Initial research studies of patients with chronic pain and illness showed that participating in an MBSR course significantly decreased stress, anxiety, pain, depression, anger, physical symptoms, and use of medication. Participants in MBSR courses also showed an increased ability to cope with pain and felt that their lives were more meaningful and fulfilling (Kabat-Zinn, 1982; Kabat-Zinn, Lipworth, & Burney, 1985; Kabat-Zinn, Lipworth, Burney, & Sellers, 1986; Kabat-Zinn & Chapman-Waldrop, 1988). Continuing research over the past thirty years has replicated and expanded upon these findings.

Recent, groundbreaking studies using sophisticated brain imaging techniques have shown that adults who participate in an eight-week MBSR course have documented changes in brain structure and activity. Specifically, Britta Hölzel, Sara Lazar, and others from the Psychiatric Neuroimaging Research Program at Massachusetts

General Hospital showed that course participants had decreased gray matter density in the amygdala, which is known to play an important role in anxiety and stress. Course participants also had increased gray matter density in the hippocampus, known to be important for learning and memory, and in the temporal-parietal junction, associated with self-awareness, compassion, and introspection (Hölzel et al., 2011). In a study with biotech employees, Richard Davidson, from the University of Wisconsin–Madison Lab for Affective Neuroscience, showed that participants who practiced mindfulness had increased activation in the left prefrontal cortex, the area in the brain associated with happiness, positive thoughts, and emotions (Davidson et al., 2003). Numerous research studies have demonstrated that people with a wide variety of medical conditions—from depression, anxiety, and eating disorders to chronic pain, psoriasis, heart disease, and cancer—benefit from practicing mindfulness. The research on the benefits of mindfulness for adults is extensive. For more information, the Resources section contains links to online bibliographies of published studies on mindfulness and MBSR.

Still Quiet Place: Distilling Mindfulness and MBSR to Its Essence

In many ways, teaching mindfulness or MBSR to children and teens requires that we distill it to its essence. Below is a brief discussion of how the Still Quiet Place curriculum offers young people most of the *foundational elements* (noted in italics) of the standard adult MBSR course, detailed in *Full Catastrophe Living*, by Jon Kabat-Zinn (1990). The intention of this section is to allow those who are already familiar with MBSR to see how the foundational elements are incorporated into the Still Quiet Place curriculum, and to allow those not yet familiar with MBSR to begin to acquaint themselves with the essential principles. Additionally, the presentation of each element demonstrates the layered nuance contained within the simple, age-adapted language used to introduce these elements to our young friends. As you read, do your best to allow these principles to blossom in your heart, rather than become additional intellectual concepts in your mind.

Student reactions. At the end of each course, I ask participants to write a "letter to a friend" who knows nothing about mindfulness, describing how it feels to rest in the Still Quiet Place, and how they use mindfulness in daily life. These heartfelt quotes— taken verbatim from fourth and fifth graders as well as sophomores in remedial English, with all of their incorrect grammar, misspellings, and sincerity—appear in block quotes throughout this chapter.

Here and Now

As mentioned above, the initial definition of mindfulness I offer young people is "Mindfulness is paying attention here and now, with kindness and curiosity, and then choosing your behavior." The simple phrase "here and now" supports people of all ages in coming into their *present-moment* experience, not thinking about the past, or fantasizing or worrying about the future. "Here and now" simultaneously alludes to the principle of *impermanence*. If we are paying attention here and now, we soon discover that things change, moment to moment.

> *Mindfulness is a class I am taking at school. It is a time when we breathe and think about our thoughts, about NOW, not the past or the future. When we settle in breathing we go to our "Still Quiet Place." It feels calming in the "Still Quiet Place." I use mindfulness when I am nervous about something.*
>
> —*Fourth grader*

Kindness

For children, the phrase "kind attention" represents the element of *nonjudgment*, fostered in adult MBSR. "Nonjudgment" is a term that doesn't mean anything to most children and adolescents, and even some adults. However, kindness is intuitively understood by almost everyone. I encourage you to pause here and now, and allow yourself to consider the qualities of kindness. If you ask children to describe someone who is kind, they will probably tell you that a kind person is patient and friendly, and doesn't yell or rush. They may add that a kind person is there when you need her.

The nonjudging aspect of kindness incorporates the neutral adult principle of *acknowledging* and the more "friendly" adult principle of *acceptance*. Acknowledging is simply recognizing that things are the way they are, even if we don't like, or aren't happy about, how they are. Often, the simple act of acknowledging that things are not the way we want them to be makes way for compassion and new possibilities. For example, once a child acknowledges that she is upset because her backpack with her homework, soccer cleats, and favorite key chain is gone, she can begin to address the issues at hand. She can speak with teachers about completing missing work; she can arrange to do chores to pay for new cleats; and she can lament the loss of the key chain.

When my children were very young, I conveyed this concept with an out-of-tune rendition of the Rolling Stones song "You Can't Always Get What You Want." This song simultaneously acknowledges that things are the way they are, and the way they are is *not* the way the child wants them to be. For teens, once they have acknowledged how things are, they can inquire with kindness and curiosity about whether they are judging themselves or circumstances. Often (but not always), acknowledging judgment and preferences allows these patterns to dissipate, yielding acceptance.

> *I find that mindfulness allows me to experience the present moment, something that I am trying to do for longer periods in everyday life. It helps me to find space to just allow things to be as they are. Mindfulness brings peace & acceptance and joy. I do find a place within where I can relax and just "be."*
>
> —*Tenth grader*

Acceptance implies a degree of peace with things as they are. Again, it is important to recognize that sometimes acceptance can be too much to ask of ourselves. In these moments we can begin with simply acknowledging things as they are. The beautiful thing about the interrelated processes of acknowledging and accepting is that with practice they can encompass everything, even judging and wanting things to be different (resistance). If we are judging and resisting, then we can *practice* bringing kindness and curiosity to this judgment and resistance. The practice of acknowledging (and accepting) ourselves and our circumstances as they are is a prerequisite to choosing how to respond in any given situation. The practices presented in chapter 10 ("Session 7: Communication and Love")—the ABCs and STAR practices, for young children, and the PEACE practice, for teens—provide easy-to-remember mnemonics encapsulating the essence of these principles.

The quality of kindness also represents a deep *trust*, both in each young person's essential goodness and in the practice of mindfulness itself. When teaching youth, it is not always necessary for us to discuss this element of trust explicitly. However, it is imperative that our words and actions convey this trusting aspect of kindness. Within this principle of trust is the recognition that every individual is whole, capable, wise, the world's expert on his personal experience, and responsible for how he responds to life. Mindfulness reverses the typical institutional orientation in which a presumed expert instructs or does something to or for the student, client, or patient. Trust is also the foundation for another essential component of MBSR: *self-care*. Ultimately, mindfulness is a gift every participant offers to himself. The principles of trust and self-care evoke the frequently unrecognized—yet inherently trustworthy—strength, courage, and wisdom of each individual.

Curiosity

Now let's consider the quality of curiosity. The curious aspect of attention represents the principle of *beginner's mind* (or beginner's heart), and invites us to view our internal and external experience freshly, without our usual ideas about people and things (or, in adult terms, our preconceived constructs and historical baggage). Often, when we are able to view ourselves, others, and events with curiosity, our experience and our possibilities are changed (transformed).

> *Resting in the Still Quiet Place is very relaxing. It helps you get in touch with your inner self. And find out how you are actually feeling.*
>
> —*Fourth grader*

Some examples of "nonbeginner's" mind, or a fixed mind-set, that are relevant to the themes of this book are when someone has been told and subsequently comes to believe that she isn't good at math; that she is her diagnosis; that being smart isn't cool; that life is over if she doesn't get into a "good" college; that school is a waste of time; or that fighting is the only way to gain respect. Interestingly, research by Carol Dweck, PhD, at Stanford indicates that even a "positive" fixed mind-set can be detrimental to learning. In short, her research showed that when students faced an academic challenge, those who believed that intelligence was a fixed attribute (even if they believed they possessed that attribute) did not fare as well as those who believed their academic results were based on effort. Two studies she conducted explored the role of fixed versus growth mind-sets in adolescents' mathematic achievement. In one study of seventh graders, the belief that intelligence is malleable—what Dr. Dweck calls growth mind-set—predicted an upward trajectory in grades over the two years of junior high school, while a belief that intelligence is fixed predicted a flat trajectory. In a second study, *teaching* growth mind-set to seventh graders promoted positive change in classroom motivation, and an upward trajectory in grades, compared with a control group (Blackwell, Trzesniewski, & Dweck, 2007).

If beginner's mind and heart are not cultivated, and fixed thoughts are not seen with kindness and curiosity as just thoughts, then these fixed thoughts have the potential to severely limit a life. Perhaps you can pause here, and for a moment consider with kindness and curiosity any fixed thoughts that have defined your life. Once we become curious about the constraints of our habitual thinking (especially what I call "Unkind Mind"), we can begin to see beyond them to new possibilities.

Nonstriving and Letting Go

The principles of *nonstriving* and *letting go* are not explicitly contained in the simple definition of mindfulness I offer to children: "paying attention here and now, with kindness and curiosity, and then choosing your behavior." However, being here and now minimizes future-oriented striving. Additionally, if upon kind and curious reflection we become aware that we are caught in judgments, preferences, striving, wanting, or resisting, often (but not always) we can choose to let go. And even when we can't choose to let go, we can choose to acknowledge that and let it be.

It feels good to rest in the Still Quiet Place because you can get all your burdens away from your mind and you won't have to worry about anything that's happening around you. Sometimes when you know you have a lot to do in your life and you can't stand the fact you are always stressing about something that has to be done on time, just take a few deep breaths and relax yourself....

—*Tenth grader*

Universal

Another foundational principle is that mindfulness is *universal*. After a simple practice most children and adolescents understand this intuitively. However, when first bringing mindfulness into school, clinical, and community settings—particularly public schools—it is important to emphasize this aspect of mindfulness. Occasionally I am asked, "Is mindfulness Buddhist?" I usually respond along these lines: "Mindfulness and compassion are innate human qualities that can be cultivated over time. One does not need to be Buddhist to practice them any more than one needs to be Italian to enjoy pizza." If the person asking the question is willing, I guide him through a simple eating or breath awareness practice to allow him to have a personal experience of mindfulness, and to realize that he is capable of practicing mindfulness just as he is—with his current beliefs, and without relying on any particular philosophy or religion.

Occasionally, if the questions continue, I add, "Buddhists have been exploring the universal human qualities of mindfulness and compassion for 2,500 years, and have a great deal to offer regarding these skills. However, as you have just experienced, you don't need to be Buddhist, or anything else, other than human, to practice mindfulness." When considering whether or not to make this addition, I proceed *very carefully*, and include it only after a person or group has had an experience of mindfulness. Because my intention has always been to make these skills accessible to as many people as possible, I usually just stop with the pizza analogy.

I used to say, "I want my offerings to be inviting and accessible to a housewife in Ohio." Now, thanks to Ohio Congressman Tim Ryan, who authored the book *A Mindful Nation* (which details the benefits of mindfulness in education, medicine, business, politics, and the military), I have to choose a different state.

Still Quiet Place has given me a lot of stress relief. I use mindfulness when I'm upset or stressed out. Mindfulness Rocks! Thank you Dr. Saltzman for introducing this wonderful program to me.

—*Fifth grader*

Differences and Similarities Between Still Quiet Place and MBSR

Before moving forward, it is important to note a few primary differences between the standard nine-session adult course and the eight-week Still Quiet Place (SQP) curriculum. In deference to young people's attention spans and standard therapy and school schedules, the guided in-class and at home practices, and the weekly SQP sessions, are shorter than their adult MBSR counterparts. The guided practices usually last only five to twelve minutes, versus thirty to forty-five minutes in adult MBSR, and the weekly sessions are typically only forty-five to sixty minutes long, versus two and a half hours for adult MBSR. Additionally, in the SQP curriculum, the practices of observing thoughts and feelings are initially introduced as separate, distinct practices, whereas in adult MBSR, they are typically incorporated in sitting practice. Some themes in adult MBSR are not covered in the SQP curriculum unless prompted by a participant's comments. (Several of these topics are addressed in the summary at the end of this section.)

The many practices and principles that are shared by the adult MBSR and the SQP curriculum will be covered briefly below, and again in greater detail in the session chapters in the second part of the book. For those of you who do not yet have an established mindfulness practice or experience with MBSR, it's *essential* that you establish an ongoing personal practice before you begin sharing the practices with children. In the meantime, as you continue reading, *feel*, rather than think, your way through the practices, exercises, and discussions.

Introductions

The first sessions of both the MBSR and SQP courses are devoted to introductions. The course instructor introduces himself and provides a brief overview of the course, the level of commitment and participation that is encouraged, and the course guidelines and agreements. The participants introduce themselves to each other, saying their names, why they chose to participate in the course or what they find stressful, and one thing they like about themselves. Then participants are introduced to the practice of mindfulness through mindful eating, breath awareness, and, in the adult course, the body scan. A theme here is tasting: tasting the food, tasting the breath, tasting life. So pause here and savor your breath. Close your eyes, and *feel* ten slow, deep breaths. Feel the sweet rhythm of the breathing cycle: the inhalation, a brief stillness, the exhalation, and another brief stillness.

***

Did you do it? Whether you chose to attend to your breath or not, bring some kind curiosity to your choice. If you did choose to attend to your breath, what did you discover?

What I felt was that I was just closing my eyes and the whole room was silent. I felt peace.

—Tenth grader

Establishing a Practice

In both courses, a major emphasis of the second session is exploring what supports and what gets in the way of participants doing daily home practice. Like adults, most children and adolescents are extremely busy and overscheduled. Thus, the primary themes are helping participants discover what time of day works best for them and encouraging them to experiment with giving themselves the gift of kind attention for five minutes every day, and then seeing what happens. Because the guided home practices for the SQP program are very brief (just five to twelve minutes, versus the thirty to forty-five minutes suggested in MBSR), establishing a routine is often a bit easer for children and adolescents. Most young people find that it is helpful to do mindfulness practice before or between homework subjects, or before bed.

It feels relaxing and makes me clam & chill for those few moments. I have used it by going and doing it at home by chilling myself down if I want to get mad at someone ill just go and think and ill take a deep breath and it relaxes me.

—Tenth grader

Thought Watching

The breath-based practices Jewel (ages four to ten) and Rest (ages eleven to eighteen) introduced in session 1 of the SQP course mirror the *basic* sitting practice introduced in the second session of adult MBSR. Each of these practices uses the breath as the focus of attention, encouraging participants to notice when the mind wanders, and then to gently return their attention to the breath. During sitting practice adults are encouraged to become aware of when they become lost in thought and to briefly notice patterns and themes in their thinking. Given these basic instructions, most adults soon notice their mental habits and self-critical dialogue. In the SQP curriculum for children, the practice of becoming aware of thoughts, and particularly negative internal chatter—what I fondly call "Unkind Mind"—is taught explicitly as a separate practice.

The Bubbles and Thought Watching practices are introduced during session 3. These practices support our young friends in developing the capacity to be aware of both the process and content of thinking. Once young people learn that they can observe their thoughts without believing them or taking them personally, they naturally begin to apply this skill in daily life. The well-known "nine dots" exercise used in MBSR and SQP, and described in chapter 6 of this book ("Session 3: Thought Watching and Unkind Mind"), offers an ideal format to experiment with this principle. This exercise usually evokes the habitual thoughts that accompany attempting to complete a challenging task, and it also provides an experience of how limited perception inhibits our ability to respond creatively.

> *I use mindfulness when I am worried about school things like test and grades I worry about how I did and what grade I have and then when I do mindfulness it makes me relax my thoughts.*
>
> *—Tenth grader*

Feelings

Most adults become aware of their emotional patterns while engaging in basic sitting practice. As with observing thoughts, bringing kind and curious attention to emotions (which children and adolescents usually refer to as feelings) is offered as an explicit separate practice in session 4 of the SQP curriculum. In learning to befriend their feelings, young people can become aware of habits of suppressing or indulging feelings. Ultimately, Mindfulness of Feelings practice supports our young friends in "having their feelings without their feelings having them"—being aware of what they are feeling so that they don't react and say or do something they might regret.

In the SQP curriculum, combining the practices of bringing awareness to the breath, thoughts, feelings, and physical sensations establishes a foundation from which individuals can expand their awareness to their actions and interactions with other people and the world around them. It is helpful to have these elements in place as participants begin to investigate the dynamics of pleasant and unpleasant events.

> *I am doing this thing called mindfulness. It is a way of understanding and being aware of feelings. One thing you do is go to the Still Quiet Place. It feels relaxing to be there. Mindfulness has helped me before homework because it relaxes me so I do a good job with my homework.*
>
> *—Fifth grader*

Pleasant Events

In the SQP course, many of the exercises that adults do as written homework in MBSR have been modified and are facilitated within a given SQP session. To make these exercises appealing to children, I have created simple cartoons that feature child-friendly graphics. The first of these exercises appears in session 2, and involves bringing awareness to the thoughts, feelings, and physical sensations associated with a pleasant event. The exploration of a pleasant event allows children to realize that, without mindfulness, we miss many of the pleasant moments in our lives. As a result, our young friends recognize that pleasant moments are often surprisingly simple moments of connection, and have to do with enjoying things as they are, rather than wanting things to be different. This theme of wanting things to be different, or resistance, is explored in greater depth in session 4 of the SQP curriculum.

Unpleasant Events: Suffering = Pain x Resistance

Similarly, in session 4 of the SQP course, bringing kind and curious attention to the investigation of an unpleasant event is also facilitated during class, with a cartoon. In adult MBSR, the discussion of unpleasant events and stress involves an in-depth exploration of these topics, replete with scientific definitions of stress and coping. In the SQP curriculum, the essence of this discussion is initially offered in a playful way using a mathematical equation: Suffering (upset) = Pain (unpleasantness) x Resistance (wanting things to be different).

Again, for your own practice, perhaps you can pause here and consider a recent unpleasant event—maybe something very ordinary, such as paying your bills. On a 1-to-10 scale of unpleasantness, paying bills might be a 2 or a 3. Now, consider how much you resist this task, also using a scale of 1 to 10, where 10 is maximal resistance. Then multiply the two scores to calculate your suffering score. Now consider how you might decrease your resistance slightly, perhaps by making yourself a cup of tea and putting on your favorite music, and then recalculate your suffering score. Children as young as third grade can use this equation to understand that much of our upset is due to resistance, wanting to have things our way—wanting what we want, when we want it. Slightly younger children may come to the same realization using addition. Again this simplification supports children in considering whether their thoughts and feelings are magnifying the very real pains—whether small, medium, or even almost unbearable—that life brings. When working with this equation, it is crucial that we do not diminish the intense pain of illness, divorce, loss, and trauma.

When I am sad or kind of in a bad mood I take about 10 breaths and I get relaxed. I also forget about my worries. I learned this from mindfulness. I enjoy coming here because I forget about my troubles and I forget about all the things in my life that is sad. My sadness just fades.

—Fourth grader

Body-Based Practices

Both the SQP curriculum and MBSR include the following body-based practices: mindful movement or yoga, mindful walking, and the body scan. These practices support participants in being embodied, meaning being aware of and feeling physical sensations in the body. Listening to and honoring the messages our bodies give us helps us care for ourselves, physically, mentally, and emotionally. With the gentle stretching of yoga, moving the body in new and unusual ways provides another opportunity to investigate how we work with challenges, whether our self-talk is kind or unkind, and our tendencies to judge and compare. Mindful walking allows us to bring awareness to our bodies while doing something very ordinary that we usually devote very little attention to. The body scan supports us in observing the sensations in our bodies, scanning slowly and systematically from feet to head, while we are still. By engaging in these practices, children learn that the sensations in their bodies often provide the first hint that "something is up," and that it might be helpful to check in with themselves, their thoughts, and their feelings.

A significant difference between the two curricula is the timing of when the body scan is introduced. In the Still Quiet Place curriculum, the body scan is introduced in class 6. This shift is motivated by the following observations: Even a simplified and abbreviated body scan usually lasts ten to twelve minutes. For many children and adolescents, this is a *very* long practice. If, as in adult MBSR, the body scan is the first mindfulness practice children are introduced to, participants may struggle unnecessarily and become discouraged. In the SQP curriculum, the practices slowly build in duration, so that by the time the body scan is introduced, participants are more likely to have experienced mindfulness as doable. Also, as mentioned above, young people tend to be more embodied and less aware of their thinking and feeling than their adult counterparts. Thus, it can be helpful to provide thought-watching and feelings practices before the body-based practices.

Reacting and Responding

The essential distinction between reacting and responding is emphasized in both courses. In the SQP curriculum, this distinction is introduced in session 5 using Portia Nelson's poem "Autobiography in Five Short Chapters," which describes a person walking down a street and repeatedly falling into a hole (reacting habitually), and then eventually choosing a different street (responding). Young children love this analogy and can readily tell you about their common holes at school and in relationships with family and friends. These real-life examples provide a natural transition into the theme of reacting and responding in stressful situations and difficult communications.

The practice of responding relies on all the previous practices—awareness of the breath, of thoughts, of feelings and physical sensations, and of preferences—and adds the essential element of choice. The children's practices of ABCs and STAR and the teen practice PEACE, described in chapter 10 ("Session 7: Communication and Love"), represent the distinction of responding through easily remembered mnemonics. To give you a feel for these practices, the next time you face a difficult situation, give PEACE a chance: Pause, Exhale (breathe), Acknowledge (things as they are), Choose (your behavior or how to respond), and Engage.

For youth age twelve and up, the aikido exercise from MBSR, also covered in session 7, offers a physical way of demonstrating various types of responding—submissive, avoidant, aggressive, and moderate (assertive)—during difficult communications and challenging situations.

I think mindfulness is important to use in your daily life in many ways one reason I think it is important is if you think before you speak. A second reason I think it is important is if you seem to be mad, depressed or something like that you can just think to yourself and do what is best.

—Tenth grader

It feels sort of strange but peaceful. I can't really tell how I use mindfulness at home, but I do know it helps me when I am mad at my brother.

—Fourth grader

I have taken some classes this pass Fridays, and they have really helped me not just in school but in my personal life. With this class I have been able to control my anger and found technics to rest and be in peace with myself.

—Tenth grader

Loving-Kindness

Both the SQP curriculum and MBSR incorporate loving-kindness practice. Traditionally loving-kindness is taught by remembering the sense of feeling loved by someone, returning that feeling of love to the person you remembered, and then—in sequence—sending love to someone it is easy for you to love, to yourself, to someone who is in between (neutral), and then to someone who is difficult for you to love.

Pause here and take a moment to remember a time when you felt loved. Remember (as in let it penetrate your membranes) and really *feel* the sensations of being loved.

Then, either out loud or silently to yourself, offer a wish of happiness to the person who loved you: "May you be happy." Then offer the same sweet, heartfelt wish to yourself: "May I be happy." Very young children enjoy blowing kisses to send love. For teens, who are often incredibly hard on themselves, the loving-kindness practice taught in session 7 of this course focuses on sending loving-kindness to themselves, particularly aspects of themselves that they tend to dislike, judge, or hate.

Flashlight Practice

In adult MBSR, the practice of choiceless awareness begins with anchoring the attention on the breath. Once a person's attention is stable, she may allow it to rest on whatever is most obvious: breath, sound, physical sensation, thought, or emotion. When the person's attention wanders (which it will) she may gently return it to the breath as needed. In time, attention is allowed to rest in awareness itself. With the support of the Flashlight practice, taught in session 8, even young children can begin to lay the foundation for choiceless awareness practice. In Flashlight practice, participants are guided to shine the flashlight of their attention on the breath, sounds, physical sensations, thoughts, feelings, and ultimately the stillness and quietness of pure awareness.

Last Class

The last class of both courses involves reflecting on the course and discussing thoughts and feelings related to the course ending. In the SQP course, this reflection, in session 8, is facilitated in two ways. First, participants are invited to write a letter to a friend who knows nothing about mindfulness, describing the Still Quiet Place and their experience with mindfulness. Second, there is a closing circle in which the participants share something that symbolizes the course to them: an object, a photo, a poem, a song, a story, a tangerine…. This last session also includes an exploration of whether and how participants intend to continue to practice on their own. Before the final listening practice, the instructor offers supportive resources to maintain and sustain ongoing practice.

> *I stop fighting and relax. Relaxing makes me feel calm and relieves the anxiety I carry with me everyday. Now when I have bad or uncomfortable feelings I can stop myself, notice and examine my feelings so that my feelings don't make my choices for me.*
>
> —Tenth grader

Summing Up the Distinctions

To reiterate, while the foundations of the SQP course and MBSR are the same, there are some important differences. In the SQP course, the term Still Quiet Place is used to convey an experience of pure awareness. The guided practices in the SQP course for both children and adolescents are short—just five to ten minutes. The brevity minimizes resistance to practicing and allows participants to experience mindfulness as doable. Because the guided practices are shorter, the sessions are also shorter—just forty-five to sixty minutes. There is no all-day session or the equivalent in the SQP course. The practices of bringing awareness to thoughts and feelings and physical sensations are introduced as separate, distinct practices. The participant's personal explorations of pleasant and unpleasant events, and difficult communications, are facilitated in an individual or class session. After session 1, ample opportunity for movement and play are incorporated into each session. Additionally, rather than allowing participants to choose a daily activity for home practice, all course participants are encouraged to do the same mindful activity—such as tooth brushing, showering, or communicating—each week.

Several topics covered in MBSR aren't explicitly explored in the sessions as described in this book (unless a participant's comment invites such an exploration). Because MBSR was initially used with patients with chronic pain and illness, who often identify as their diagnosis, one theme for the first session of the adult course is that "there is more right with you than there is wrong" (Kabat-Zinn, 1990, p. 2). While this statement is true for everyone who is alive and breathing, it is not a theme covered explicitly in the Still Quiet Place course unless prompted by a participant's comment.

The adult concept of automatic pilot may come up in the discussion of holes and different streets. However, it is not necessarily emphasized in the SQP course. In MBSR, stress physiology, the effects of stress on health, and the physical consequences of particular habits of reacting are covered in detail. Some groups of tweens and teens will appreciate a basic discussion of these topics. The topics of diet and nutrition, addressed in adult MBSR, are not usually emphasized in the SQP course. However, the topic of what we take in from family or friends as well as via media is frequently explored with teens.

Responsive Improv: Apple Greed

A general familiarity with the topics above; with other wisdom practices, such as compassion, forgiveness, and gratitude; and, most importantly, an established mindfulness practice will support you in responding skillfully to topics not explicitly included in the curriculum. As an example, during one session with fourth graders I brought apple slices for mindful eating. Some of the kids in the first half of the circle took large handfuls, leaving kids in the second half of the circle without any apple slices. Greed, sharing, and generosity are not standard topics in either MBSR or the SQP course. However, in response to the present-moment circumstances of that session, they became a topic that day. Perhaps you can pause here and consider how you might respond in this situation.

In that session, I asked the students to look around and see how many apple slices each person had, and then to notice their thoughts and feelings. The children without apples felt sad and jealous, and the students with many apple slices felt bad and guilty. Interestingly, without any request or suggestion from me, some students with more apple slices spontaneously chose to share with those who didn't have any. This event led to a discussion about greed, that we all (children, adults, even countries) sometimes feel greedy, and that we can notice our greed, notice the effects of our greed on people around us, and then choose our behavior.

Hopefully, this description of the "apple greed" moment demonstrates the simple truths covered in the following chapters. The "curriculum" discussed above and presented in detail in chapters 4 through 11 is not static. Teaching mindfulness to children and adolescents is a practice all its own, and it requires that we be mindful of and responsive to what is arising within ourselves and our clients, students, and participants—our children—moment by moment.

Mindfulness is a great class because you can chill out, and relax. It will cool you down and make you less stressed. You should try it if you are mad or sad or just want to feel better. That's what I do. Try it!

—Fourth grader

finding your way: paths to teaching and facilitating

When you read, you begin with A, B, C. When you sing, you begin with do, re, mi. When you teach mindfulness, you begin with breathe, breathe, breathe. So let's start at the very beginning. Although you may initially find this chapter daunting, please know that it is intended to provide both clarity and inspiration. No matter what your prior experience, if you are committed to offering mindfulness skills to young people, you can only start where you are and, as my wise mentor Georgina Lindsey says, "take the next sane step." The first part of this chapter is designed to assist you in clarifying where you are and determining the next sane step. Perhaps you can even choose to take the next step with *joy!*

As the saying "The map is not the territory" suggests, reading the first few chapters of this book, this entire book, or any of the ever-growing library of mindfulness books is *not* practicing mindfulness, just as reading about hiking in the Rockies is not hiking in the Rockies. A corollary saying is "There are many paths up the mountain." Ultimately, each of us must make our own way and find the form that feels true to us. There are also other mountains and other paths. So it helps to be as clear and as honest as possible both about where you are now and the journey you intend to take. At the same time, it is also helpful to follow in the footsteps of those who have made the trek before us.

As with other aspects of this manual, the path described below is in no way put forth as "The Path"; it simply indicates major landmarks for you to set your compass by. If you have an established daily practice in a mindfulness lineage other than MBSR, please be aware that in the vast majority of settings in which we offer mindfulness to youth (at least in the United States), it is absolutely crucial that you present the practices in ways that are *secular, accessible, inviting, and jargon-free.* Perhaps the most essential and brilliant aspect of MBSR, as a form, is its ordinary everydayness. Below are some of the landmarks.

Establishing a Practice

The first and most crucial step in preparing to offer mindfulness to youth is to establish your own devoted *daily* practice. The simplest way to begin is to commit to sitting for fifteen to thirty minutes each day, resting your attention on the breath, noticing when your mind wanders, and gently returning your attention to the breath. By repeating this process you will discover the tendencies, preferences, and habits of your mind and heart—or more accurately, the human mind and heart. The easiest way to begin is to download the Brief Sit practice created to accompany this book, available at http://www.newharbinger.com/27572. (See the back of the book for more information.) Perhaps this is your next sane step?

While the rare individual may be able to develop a personal mindfulness (or heartfulness) practice on his own, most of us need much more support. Some support can come from books such as *Full Catastrophe Living; Wherever You Go, There You Are;* and *Mindfulness for Beginners,* by Jon Kabat-Zinn, and *A Mindfulness-Based Stress Reduction Workbook*, by Bob Stahl and Elisha Goldstein. However, given that your intention is not just to practice yourself, but rather to share these practices with young people, wholehearted participation in an eight-week MBSR course or eleven-week Mindfulness-Based Emotional Balance (MBEB) course is strongly encouraged. MBEB is an exquisite curriculum created by my dear friend and colleague Margaret Cullen that combines mindfulness, emotion theory, compassion, and forgiveness.

Participating in an MBSR or MBEB course has multiple benefits. You will be supported by a skillful facilitator in establishing your own practice. You will learn from your own experience and the experiences of your classmates. You will be able to observe how the facilitator shares the practices with different individuals and the group as a whole. For those of you who have a longtime practice in another lineage, participation in a secular MBSR or MBEB course will support you in developing a jargon-free perspective and vocabulary.

To find a course near you, search the database of programs offered worldwide through the Center for Mindfulness in Medicine, Health Care, and Society website: http://www.umassmed.edu/cfm/index.aspx.

If there is no program in your local area, you can participate in a high-quality online course through the following websites:

Mindful Living Programs: http://www.mindfullivingprograms.com/aboutcourse.php

Mindfulness-Based Emotional Balance: http://www.margaretcullen.com/programs

eMindful: http://www.emindful.com

Additional trainings geared toward professionals offering MBSR to adults, which can greatly enhance your facilitation skills, include the MBSR Mind-Body Medicine seven-day training retreat, and the Practicum in MBSR. These opportunities are offered through the Center for Mindfulness in various locations throughout the world. An additional accredited practicum is offered through the Awareness and Relaxation Program in Northern California (http://www.mindfulnessprograms.com). Books geared to teaching mindfulness to adults that will refine your teaching are *Heal Thy Self,* by Saki Santorelli (1999), and *Teaching Mindfulness,* by Donald McCown, Diane Reibel, and Marc Micozzi (2010).

Lastly, for those who are committed to doing this work with authenticity and excellence, I strongly recommend that you participate in at least one silent mindfulness retreat of seven days or longer. This idea may seem daunting. It's certainly challenging to find seven full days, away from all of life's other demands, to devote to anything. And a silent retreat might not be your initial first choice of destinations. However, as you deepen your personal practice and take one "next sane step" after another toward sharing mindfulness with children, you will come to see the value of a focused and dedicated retreat. Truly, it is the best gift you can give yourself, and your students.

Sharing the Practice with Children and Adolescents

Once you have established your own devoted daily practice, there are several additional recommended steps to develop the skills necessary to share mindfulness with young people. If you don't already have experience in working and playing with children or adolescents, devote six months to a year to engaging mindfully with the age group you wish to serve. Use this time to become aware of your thoughts, feelings, triggers, habitual tendencies, and, most importantly, the possibilities in your interactions with youth.

There are several high quality in-person and online trainings for professionals committed to sharing mindfulness with youth. Three times a year, I offer a ten-week, in-depth Still Quiet Place training online. To receive announcements about this training and the wide variety of trainings and conferences being offered internationally, as well as to participate in the ongoing collegial dialogue regarding the joys and challenges of this work and play, join the Association for Mindfulness in Education (http://www.mindfuleducation.org) and Mindfulness in Education Network (http://www.mindfuled.org) e-mail groups.

The number of excellent books about sharing mindfulness with youth is growing rapidly. I've listed many of them in the Resources section, and I do my best to keep an updated list on my website (http://www.stillquietplace.com). To begin, I recommend *The Mindful Child*, by Susan Kaiser Greenland, and *The Stress Reduction Workbook for Teens*, by Gina Biegel.

Walking the Talk, or Practice Makes Practice

The necessity of having a practice will continue to be addressed in subtle and not so subtle ways throughout the book. If you haven't explored your own internal territory, your own humanness, it is difficult, if not impossible, to guide others in exploring theirs. If you haven't cultivated an intimate understanding of your human capacities for anger, love, fear, joy, sadness, jealousy, contentment, greed, and compassion; and if you haven't discovered how these universal experiences arise, persist, manifest in action and fade away, how they work, and what increases or diminishes them—how can you discuss these phenomena in simple, accessible language with children? Kids intuitively know when someone is being real—speaking from the heart, and from personal experience. Conversely, they also know when someone is speaking theoretically (or, in teen-speak, "bullshitting" them). Ultimately, it is your ongoing embodiment of the value of your own personal mindfulness practice that engages and inspires the young people you are privileged to serve.

Progression

Once you have established a personal practice and learned the language of secular mindfulness, there is a natural developmental progression for sharing mindfulness with children and adolescents:

- Listening to, doing, and *experiencing* practices designed for youth

- Guiding practices for the age group you wish to work with out loud for yourself, your cat, or your ficus plant

- Guiding practices for your own children, nieces, nephews, neighbors, individual clients, or small groups

- Guiding practices for larger groups

- Practicing the art of mindful conversation and inquiry about the essential elements of the practices

Examples of such discussions for various ages are included in chapters 4 through 11. Simple questions can allow participants to discover when and how the practices might be useful: "How was that for you?" "What did you notice?" "Did you have any difficulties with the practice?" "When might it be helpful to do this practice?" "How do you feel the practice might help you?" The importance of your responses to various comments should not be underestimated, because it is during such discussions that the principles of mindfulness can be clarified or distorted.

For example, in my trainings when professionals lead practices for each other, a trainee will occasionally say something like "Mindfulness can help control difficult thoughts or emotions." This is a distortion. Although mindfulness often allows intense thoughts and feelings to dissipate more quickly, *mindfulness is not about controlling* thoughts and emotions. Mindfulness *is* meeting our thoughts and feelings with kindness and compassion; there is no need to control them. More importantly, when we meet them with kindness and compassion they don't control us. This distinction is crucial, because if young people get the mistaken impression that the practice is about controlling their internal experience, then, when they can't control their thoughts and feelings, they will feel either that they have failed or that the practice has failed them. It is essential that you emphasize and clarify that mindfulness offers a powerful way of *relating* to experience, rather than controlling it.

A related phenomenon during recent in-person and online courses is that, in their heartfelt enthusiasm for bringing these practices to youth, some trainees who have very limited experience in sharing mindfulness with children are zealously instructing their colleagues (most of whom do not have *any* foundation in mindfulness practice) in sharing the practices with children. As with teaching mindfulness directly to youth, teaching other adults to teach mindfulness to youth *must* be grounded in your personal experience of *actually* teaching mindfulness to youth, or else it runs the risk of becoming formulaic and empty. As with other topics in the course itself, we will revisit this topic in greater depth again after the chapters that cover the individual sessions.

sharing the still quiet place

When sharing mindfulness with children and adolescents we must speak to them in language they will understand, and gradually build an increasingly meaningful and nuanced appreciation through experience. As an example, the definition of mindfulness that I share with young people is as follows: "Mindfulness is paying attention here and now, with kindness and curiosity, and then choosing your behavior." The simplified definition provides a starting point, a way to begin. As children and adolescents begin to apply the practice in daily life they will come to realize, just as adults do, that "mindfulness is simple, but it isn't easy."

A fun way to explore this definition further (especially if you're an English teacher) is to consider mindfulness in the context of the interrogative pronouns "who," "what," "where," "when," "why," and "how." Let's begin.

Where and when: Mindfulness means paying attention here and now, right here where we are, in the present moment, not ruminating about the past or worrying or fantasizing about the future.

What: In the present moment we can attend to the breath, sensations in our bodies, our five senses, thoughts, feelings, people and events in our lives, and our impulses and actions.

How: This particular type of attention is kind and curious, and thus different from our frequent, self-critical, internal chatter. Mindfulness asks that we practice being compassionate with ourselves and others as we move through life doing the best we can. In Asian languages, the character for mind and heart is the same. Thus, mindfulness might more accurately be called heartfulness.

Why: We pay attention in this way so that we have the necessary information to respond wisely and kindly to ourselves, to others, and to what is happening in our lives—at least sometimes (smile).

Who: Who is paying attention? While one obvious answer is "I am; I am paying attention," it is perhaps equally or more accurate to say the stillness and quietness (that is, awareness itself) is paying attention.

Pause here and receive this possibility in your heart. What might it mean for you (and the young people you serve) that the stillness and quietness is paying attention?... There's no need to answer this question now. Just keep the question alive. We will revisit it throughout the book.

The course described in chapters 4 through 11 is an eight-week curriculum for children from about eight to twelve years old, corresponding to third through seventh grade. Each session is a combination of some or all of the following elements: guided practices, discussions, written exercises, and movement games. Some readers may wonder whether the described practices, discussions, and exercises are too simple or, conversely, too sophisticated for children this age. In my experience, participants' engagement in the discussions, and the experiences they share, demonstrate that they find the practices and teachings accessible and helpful in their daily lives. Additionally, most of the practices, dialogues, and explorations in this book can be adapted for both younger and older students, offered independently, and expanded upon in any way you feel will be useful to the young people you serve. While the dialogues are accurate to the best of my recollection, the names of the participants have been change to protect their anonymity.

In this chapter, I will discuss some overarching issues in presenting this curriculum, such as age-appropriate adaptations, and practical nuts and bolts instructions for conducting the sessions. In chapter 13, I'll cover considerations specific to classroom teachers and therapists offering the curriculum to individuals, as well as some additional cautions.

The structured course has a flow: the experiences, skills, and concepts build upon, interweave with, and reinforce each other. While this book provides a detailed description of the curriculum, each individual, each group, each session, and each moment is unique. Therefore, each course is unique. The suggestions and descriptions offered in this book should be viewed as a sketch—one that you will enhance and refine, with the young people you serve. Ultimately, every individual or group creates an original masterpiece—moving lines, creating distinctive forms, and adding shading and color to reveal depth and perspective.

Age-Appropriate Adaptations

Mindfulness and awareness are concepts most young children and many adults have a hard time grasping. However, anyone can experience resting in the Still Quiet

Place. Below is an example of how I introduce the Still Quiet Place to very young children, between the ages of three and six.

> *Hello, my name is Amy, and I would like to share one of my favorite places with you. It is called the Still Quiet Place. It's not a place you travel to in a car or a train or a plane. It is a place inside you that you can find just by breathing.*
>
> *Let's find it now. If you feel safe, close your eyes. Whether your eyes are open or closed, take some slow, deep breaths. See if you can feel a kind of warm smile in your body. Do you feel it? This is your Still Quiet Place. Take some more deep breaths and really snuggle in.*
>
> *The best thing about your Still Quiet Place is that it's always inside you. And you can visit it whenever you like, just by paying attention to your breath. It is nice to visit your Still Quiet Place and feel the love that is there. It is especially helpful to visit your Still Quiet Place if you're feeling angry or sad or afraid. The Still Quiet Place is a good place to talk with these feelings and make friends with them. When you rest in your Still Quiet Place and talk to your feelings, you may find that the feelings are not as big or as powerful they seem. Remember, you can come here whenever you want, and stay as long as you like.*

With minimal adaptation, the concept of Still Quiet Place can be used with students ages three to ninety-three. The language above is for children ages three to six, who can simply experience the Still Quiet Place and feel it in their body-minds. With slightly older children, the language can be more body-focused, with less emphasis on the Still Quiet Place as a location. Children ages seven to nine can recognize that the Still Quiet Place is a reliable place to go for comfort when they feel upset, and some may be able to rest in the Still Quiet Place and then respond to upsetting circumstances. Most children ages ten and up can practice applying mindfulness in daily life much the same way adults do. They can rest in the Still Quiet Place, become aware of their thoughts, feelings, and physical sensations, and then choose to respond rather than react to life circumstances.

The optimal age range for each course element is noted in parentheses when the element is first introduced. Elements that work well with younger children are marked with an asterisk in the outlines that appear at the beginning of each session. Each outline also includes a suggested children's story related to the theme of the session; these stories can be read aloud to young children and even teens. Discussions can easily be simplified for younger children by offering just the first few questions and comments. They can also be expanded upon for teens by exploring the topic in greater detail. These adaptations are presented in the session chapters, with the simplified prompts for younger students presented at the beginning of the conversations for the eight- to twelve-year-olds, and the enhancements for teens following. Of course, attuning to the individual or group you are working with will allow you to choose the level of discussion that will be most beneficial.

For a single guided practice, my general rule of thumb is that initially children can usually practice a *maximum* of one minute per their age in years; five-year-old children can generally do guided practice for about five minutes. With young children, a simple twenty- to thirty-minute weekly session will help them become familiar with the Still Quiet Place. Whether you are working with an individual or a group of children, a typical session for young children includes two practices, each followed by a brief discussion, and a closing with a suggestion for home practice.

With a group of ten or more preschoolers or kindergartners, if every child speaks after each practice, the children may get restless, and the experience of the practice may be long gone before it is the last child's turn to speak. Thus, you may want to hear from some of the children after the first practice, and others after the second. When your students become restless, you may want to offer a brief movement practice. If you are a classroom teacher and have the privilege—and challenge—of being with your students all day, every day, a short practice to begin class and one after recess, lunch, or another transition can be extremely helpful. Ideally, when offering the course to children younger than eight it is best for them to have additional adult support for home practice. Formats that work well include offering a course to child-parent pairs or sending reminders about home practice to parents and caregivers.

For adolescents in individual or group sessions, let their comments and behavior guide you; a typical session is forty-five to sixty minutes and includes two practices, each followed by a discussion about the application of the practices to daily life.

Essentials of Teaching

As discussed in chapter 3, when sharing the Still Quiet Place with children, it is essential that our offerings come from the depths of our own practice, that we use age-adapted language, and that the practices are accessible and engaging. To highlight these elements, I offer the following story.

At some point my son began teaching his kindergarten teacher mindfulness. The teacher then asked me to share some practices with her class. So one morning several years ago, I found myself lying on the floor with nineteen five-year-olds. After the first practice, I asked the children to describe how they felt. As we went around the circle, the children reported feeling "calm," "relaxed," and "happy." I felt pleased.

Then one child said "dead." I watched a look of panic move across the teacher's face. I felt a momentary tightening within myself. The teacher had no mindfulness practice to provide her with either an understanding of the child's experience, or a way of working with her fear.

We continued around the circle, and as often happens in kindergarten, several children repeated some version of the previous answers, including "dead." After everyone had spoken, I asked the children who said dead, "What does dead feel like?" They answered, "like a swan," "like an angel," or "like floating."

Children in our culture don't have words for being awake, still, and at peace. "Dead" was as close as they could come to describing the *experience* of being in the Still Quiet Place.

This vignette illustrates several important points related to teaching mindfulness to children (and adults):

Teaching mindfulness must come from the depth of our own practice. My practice let me be aware of what was arising within me, understand the children's and the teacher's experience, and then respond. This is the essence of mindfulness. Mindfulness is paying attention in the present moment, with kindness and curiosity, and responding, rather than reacting, to the circumstances. In this example, I was aware of my brief attachment to the children having a relaxing experience, and of the sensations of concern and doubt that arose when the boy said "dead." Simply noting these internal experiences and the reaction of the teacher, without getting caught up in them, enabled me to attend to the children, be curious about what they really meant by "dead," and respond accordingly.

Our interpretations of words and experiences can be quite different from the interpretations of our young friends. In this example the teacher—and to some extent, I—initially interpreted "dead" as scary. It is important to be aware of our interpretations and to ask, rather than assume, what particular words mean.

Mindfulness is opening to whatever is occurring in the present moment. If "dead" had been scary or difficult for the children, I would have congratulated them for being aware of and willing to share their experience, and then we would have explored the experience together.

It is essential to facilitate an experience. The beauty of teaching to children is that even if we are tempted to, we cannot rely on words and intellectual concepts to convey the practice. In the example above, the children experienced feeling "like a swan," "like an angel," "like floating." Ideally, whether we are teaching to children or adults, we facilitate an experience of both the stillness and quietness within, and how this stillness and quietness can benefit them in their daily lives.

The specific mindfulness practices provided throughout this book build on this foundation of stillness and quietness. In combination, the exercises offer young children skills for comforting themselves, and older children the ability to observe their thoughts and feelings, and—most importantly—to choose their behavior.

Introductory Evening

In elementary, junior high, and high school, and in community, research, and health care settings, I usually offer an introductory evening for parents. The most important part of this evening is to provide parents with an *experience* of mindfulness, specifically mindful eating. This gives parents an immediate, personal, embodied understanding of mindfulness, paying attention in the present moment with kindness and curiosity. Typically, when parents do this brief practice they intuitively recognize the potential benefits of mindfulness. Additionally, they realize that they and their children can practice mindfulness just as they are, and that mindfulness won't interfere with, and perhaps may enhance, their existing way of living (including their religious practices). Thus, this simple guided practice minimizes confusion about what mindfulness is and isn't.

The introductory evening also includes a summary of the current research regarding the benefits of mindfulness for children and adolescents; highlights some of the most interesting studies with adults; reviews the structure of the course, including a discussion of home practice; explains any research protocols; and, most importantly, provides ample opportunity for the parents to ask questions. Note that in many low-income schools, attendance at such introductory sessions may be sparse, so it can be helpful to send home a one-page flier to parents, in their native language, using the school's usual distribution system.

Arranging the Room

Almost any room is workable. While it is preferable to have a relatively simple, quiet space, I have taught in many noisy, cramped, and cluttered spaces. Arrange the seating to support the students in experiencing stillness and quietness. Depending on the setting, some groups will do fine sitting in a circle on a rug on the floor; others may be able to sit in a circle in chairs; and still others may need the clear boundaries of rows of chairs. Do your best to create a safe and comfortable environment. The sense of safety must be comprehensive and encompass physical, mental, emotional, and social domains. The class agreements, described in session 1, are essential in establishing the foundation for the participants' experience of safety.

Beginning

Do your best to find a balance between allowing the students a little while to arrive and settle in and establishing a precedent for starting on time. Greet everyone individually, being sensitive to how much attention and physical contact each person may be ready for. Whether you are working with an individual or a group, as a therapist, a classroom teacher, or someone who brings mindfulness into another teacher's classroom or into a community setting, it is helpful to establish a few simple routines to indicate that session time is a special time devoted to practicing mindfulness. In this program, beginning and ending each session with mindful listening serves that purpose.

Listening

Typically, each session begins and ends with listening practice, by sounding a vibra-tone or tone chime. Both of these instruments have rich, resonant, lasting tones and can be ordered through Amazon (http://www.amazon.com). I recommend using these instruments rather than singing bowls or chimes. This recommendation is particularly important if you are teaching in a mainstream setting, such as a public school, where it is essential that the secular, accessible, universal nature of the practice be made explicit. Establishing this routine for opening and closing each session emphasizes that the session is a special time for mindfulness. Hopefully, as the course progresses, the participants' use of mindfulness will become more generalized. With time, mindfulness may increasingly permeate more of their daily lives, enhancing the quality of their experiences, influencing how they respond to various circumstances, and informing their interactions with others.

Practices

There were many options for how to share the core elements of the curriculum with you. In chapters 4 through 11, I present the elements in several different ways. Some are simply described so that you can discover the variations that live inside of you. Others are offered as examples of what I might say. These examples aren't meant to be used as scripts, and if you are using them as such, please devote as much time as you need to deepening your own practice before sharing *your* version of the practices with young people.

As mentioned previously, some of the practices described in this book are well-known mindfulness practices, whereas others are practices I made up for students, patients, and my own children. Audio downloads of sample practices accessible to young people between four and eighteen years old are available at http://www.newhar binger.com/27572. (See the back of the book for more information.) Specific age-adapted practices for young children and teens are available on the CDs *Still Quiet Place: Mindfulness for Young Children* and *Still Quiet Place: Mindfulness for Teens.*

Practicing While Leading

Ideally, having a well-established practice of your own will allow you to *do* the practices as you lead them for others. This means being connected to your own experience and *feeling* your way through a given practice, while articulating the practice in age-appropriate language. Conveying the essence of the practice through your tone, pace, and connection is much more important than saying a specific set of words. That said, it is essential that your words make a given experience accessible. You are encouraged to practice until you are fluent and can lead with your eyes open some or all of the time, staying connected to the practice *and* to what is happening in the room.

Conversations

Every session chapter has suggested questions to prompt participants' self-discovery, and vignettes that demonstrate the responsive nature of these interactions. Any of the conversations can begin in pairs, in small groups, or with an entire group. Of course, similar explorations can be done with an individual in a therapeutic setting. Whether you are working with an individual or a group, the process is the same: listening for what is said and what is unsaid, breathing, and responding with a clarifying comment, a question, or an invitation for the child or the entire group to investigate if and how a particular theme plays out in daily life. As with the practices, these examples aren't meant to be used as scripts, but rather to demonstrate the responsive, interactive, fluid process of mindful inquiry. At its best, this process is both compassionately rigorous (really inviting our young friends to examine their habits of thinking, feeling, and behaving) and rigorously compassionate (bringing kindness and a sense of humor to these human habits.) You may notice that many themes, particularly responding versus reacting, are repeated frequently. Over time, the repetition and real-life applications of these themes allow our young friends to realize the benefits of the practice for themselves.

As you will see in the class agreements in session 1, participants have the right to pass, or not speak, during the conversations. Early in the course, having this choice is particularly important for children who are depressed, angry, or shy, or who suffer from social anxiety. As the course progresses and participants become more comfortable with being uncomfortable, you can encourage quieter children to speak more and more vocal children to speak less. For children with severe social anxiety, you can support them in gradually participating more over the duration of the entire course. An example of an incremental sequence is allowing the child to just sit and listen as the group engages in a discussion, encouraging the child to sit and listen in a triad, supporting the child in offering one or two questions or comments in a triad, having the child participate in a nonthreatening dyad, and finally having the child share one or two comments with the entire group.

Notes About Language and Languaging

In keeping with the conversational style of both the book and the teaching, many sentences in the sample dialogues read more like speech than grammatically correct text.

As in the language of teaching, and ordinary speech, I purposely vary the pronouns, moving between "I," "you," and "we." "I" allows me to share my humanity, struggles, and how I use the practices in my daily life. "You" encourages participants to engage, and "we" demonstrates we are all in this together.

Within mindfulness circles, instructors emphasize "languaging"—using the present participle to invite a way of being or an action, rather than directing, instructing, or commanding. For example, we often say, "Now breathing in," rather than "Now breathe in."

Words such as "invite" or "being" are intended to speak to the body and the heart, as well as to the mind. They are meant to encourage you to access your natural human wholeness so that you can then encourage others to do the same. Please keep these distinctions in mind and heart as you read and teach.

The term *mindfulness* is used to describe both practices that encourage the discovery of the Still Quiet Place and the universal human capacity for paying attention with kindness and curiosity.

Lastly, many sentences are written in passive rather than active voice to convey the sense that *perhaps* it is not that you or I are teaching, but rather that the teaching is coming through us.

Transitions

It is helpful to encourage the group to continue being mindful as they transition between practices, exercises, and discussions and into their daily lives. These transitions can be facilitated with simple cues, such as the following:

> As we begin talking, let's see if we can listen to each other with our whole, kind attention, like we just listened to the chime.
>
> Do your best to continue your mindfulness as we move into discussion.
>
> See if you can stay connected to the breath and the stillness and quietness as we begin this exercise.

As you leave, see if you can continue to be mindful of your breath and your body, as you walk out of the room and into your life.

Movement

It is essential that each session and the course overall be responsive to the individuals and the experiences in the room. It is particularly important to attend to young people's natural desire for movement. Sometimes it is wise to let them dance, drum, giggle, wiggle, walk, do energetic yoga, or sway like seaweed in the ocean. Other times it is skillful to let them sit with their restlessness and notice the associated thoughts, feelings, and physical sensations. Remember, we are suggesting that our young friends do something quite unusual: in the midst of their fast-paced, media-saturated lives, we are inviting them to slow down and turn their attention inward. It is important that we meet them as they are and simultaneously support them in easing into stillness.

Signals

While watching videos of myself teaching, I noticed that I said "hang on" more often than I would like. For me, this phrase is not really a clear invitation to resume mindfulness. More skillful methods include simply being silent or using the chime or a simple signal. So now I explain early on in the course, "When I notice that as a group we have lost our mindfulness, I will stop talking, ring the chime, or use a special signal; I will raise one hand, place my other hand on my belly, and take slow, deep breaths. When you hear my silence or the chime, please stop talking. When you notice the signal, please stop talking, raise one hand, put your other hand on your belly, and take slow deep breaths." These actions support everyone in returning their attention to the present moment.

Home Practice

At the end of each session, every participant receives a handout outlining the home practice for the upcoming week. The handout details the guided audio and daily life practice, and includes a graphic illustrating one of the main themes for the week and any relevant poems or readings. Before closing the session with listening practice, I review the home practice by reading the handout out loud, offering clarifying comments and answering any questions. In addition to detailing the home practice, the handouts serve as a review and reinforcement of the themes for the week. The handout for the last session also includes a local resources list. As an alternative to offering weekly handouts, you may provide a workbook with all the handouts at the first session.

Guided Audio

The most important element of the home practice is listening to the guided audio practices. The following practices are available for download at http://www.newhar binger.com/27572. (See the back of the book for more information.)

- Brief Sit: practicing mindful awareness of breathing, for adults

- Still Quiet Place Breath-Based Practice: bringing awareness to the breath

- Thought Watching Practice: bringing awareness to thoughts

- Feelings Practice: bringing awareness to feelings or emotion

- Body Scan: bringing awareness to physical sensations

- Very Basic Yoga Practice: bringing awareness to moving

- Loving-Kindness: practicing giving and receiving love

Mindfulness in Daily Life

Each week the home practice includes a suggestion for mindfulness in daily life. These suggestions support participants in bringing their full attention into their daily lives, starting with basic daily activities such as brushing their teeth and putting on their shoes, and extending to more complex events like participating in difficult communications or facing personal challenges. When you present these activities during your explanation of the home practice, it is helpful to emphasize the five physical senses, as well as the "sixth, seventh, and eighth senses" of thinking, feeling, and "awarenessing." A description of mindful showering might go something like this:

When you step into the shower, see if you can bring your whole attention to being in the shower. Feeling the cool tile. Feeling yourself gripping and turning the shower handle. Hearing the sound of the water. Feeling the wetness and the temperature of the water. Noting the change in the temperature of the water. Feeling yourself reaching for and squeezing the shampoo. Noting the smell of the shampoo and the soap. Sensing your movements while you wash your body. Listening to the sound of the water, and noting how the sound and the sensations change as you put your head under the spray to rinse your hair and your face. And, of course, noticing any thoughts and feelings that appear while you are showering.

Practice Log

In research settings it is important to track the amount of practice participants do. In other settings it may also be helpful to get anonymous estimates of if and how often participants are practicing. Please bring the kindness and curiosity that is mindfulness to any discussion regarding home practice. Otherwise mindfulness practice can turn into just one more "should," something else the kids "have to" do. Ways of mindfully engaging in such an exploration and a sample pencil and paper practice log are included in chapter 4. For technically connected teens, there are now some great apps for tracking practice time.

Supporting Home Practice: Mindful Reminders

I initially offered the first version of this entire course to child-parent pairs in the context of a formal research protocol at Stanford. In that setting the children were supported by their parents to engage in the home practice activities. In low-income settings, students frequently do not have the same type of support. Therefore I have moved all of the pencil-and-paper home practice activities into their respective sessions. This particular adaptation ensures that a given activity is done at least once, and minimizes participant forgetfulness and chagrin, as well as instructor frustration. Most importantly, because of this adaptation, the primary emphasis of home practice is listening to the guided audio practices. Please continue to modify the activities and curriculum in ways that best serve the young people you work and play with.

Generally, if I'm teaching to children without their parents present, I call the parents after the first class to respond to any questions and encourage them to support their child's home practice. Whether children are attending with or without their parents, I always send a midweek e-mail to the children—to their personal e-mail addresses, for those who have them, or via their parents or caregivers, for those who don't. This "mindful reminder" helps keep them engaged in their practice. The communication could be a poem, a comic, or a delayed response to something that came up in class. Often it suffices to send an e-mail with the subject line "mindful reminder" and one or two simple sentences, such as "It is 7:00 p.m. Do you know where your attention is?" "Can you let your attention rest on your breathing for five breaths?" or "How do you feel now?" E-mail also provides a forum for children or parents to bring up any concerns or questions confidentially and receive a response via e-mail, in a private conversation before or after class, or in class, as appropriate. In some low socioeconomic settings where a household may not have access to the Internet or even a working phone, it is helpful to create another way to offer a midweek mindful reminder, such as a note in students' weekly school folders, or a reminder from their teacher. With teens, I often text reminders, and I'm currently playing with using Twitter for this.

As with any other routine, such as toothbrushing or doing homework, many children and even teens will need adult support to remember to do the home practice. In child-parent courses such support is a given. If you are a classroom teacher, you can include mindfulness in your usual homework routine. If you are a facilitator who visits a classroom, you can ask the classroom teacher to include reminders in her usual communications. If you are offering the course in after-school or community settings, particularly low-income ones, some children may not receive adult support. If you can find creative ways to offer them additional support between sessions, do so. If not, trust that what they receive during the sessions is enough. If you are a therapist, review the home practice with individual clients and, if appropriate, with their parents, at the end of the session.

Do-Overs

If after a session you realize you forgot to cover something important or that you were unclear, ungraceful, or even unkind, you can address it in the next session. Alternatively, if you feel it would be beneficial to the child or group you're working with, you can also address it in a phone call, e-mail, or text. Of course, it is best, if you are aware and are able, to skillfully attend to it during a session. However, sometimes we need some time to process before we try again.

Home Practice Review

As in many other spiral curricula, in which students revisit material repeatedly, each subsequent session includes a facilitated review of the participants' experiences with the preceding week's practices, discussions, exercises, and home practice. These reviews allow opportunities for clarification and expansion of various themes. Most importantly, they use participants' real life experiences, and thus support participants in recognizing how mindfulness can benefit them. In group settings, participants also have the opportunity to see that they are not alone in their struggles, and to learn from the wisdom of their peers.

The Practice of Facilitating

Especially for those who wish to teach or facilitate and those who are already teaching or facilitating, *having a practice* means engaging not only in formal daily mindfulness practice, but also in an ongoing inquiry into those places and times where we are mindless or heartless. Although I still occasionally suffer from the delusion that with practice I will somehow become immune to the human tendencies of judgment, arrogance, separation, comparison, and insecurity, the truth is that I have not. And each time I become aware of these contracted, self-centered modes of interacting, the door to compassion and connection swings open again.

The moments of mindlessness or heartlessness can be so small and subtle that only you may notice, or they may be glaringly obvious to everyone in the room. Sometimes awareness comes in the moment; other times it arrives while driving home, exercising, or falling asleep. Occasionally a class participant or a trusted colleague helps me to see these moments, and, unfortunately, sometimes they go completely unnoticed. As with all other aspects of the practice, it helps to investigate these moments with kindness and curiosity, and *then* consider what is needed. In certain situations it is enough to simply acknowledge the behavior internally. Other times it is beneficial to name our behavior. I call this naming "mindfulness out loud"; it can be especially helpful in class, allowing us to demonstrate to our young friends how we work with our own experience. Only by being fully with our humanity can we support others in being fully with theirs.

When I err, I tend to do so in two distinct ways. Sometimes I display a combination of judgment and arrogance, which doesn't honor the wisdom of the participant. Other times I indulge in people-pleasing and wanting to be liked, and therefore fail to offer a clear comment or ask an incisive question that might lead a participant to deeper understanding. While your patterns may not be the same as mine, it is important that you be aware of them and how they manifest. Do you get a headache? Do you talk too loud or too fast? Do you sugarcoat? Do you resort to a formulaic practice, story, or answer? Do you go numb?

Below is an example of an ordinary contracted moment that arose in my second after-school class. Allow me to set the stage. My first after-school class, at Henry Ford Elementary School (an underserved school where the majority of the parents speak Spanish and 80 percent of the students are eligible for free lunch), had six boys and two girls, nine to ten years old. The principal kindly informed me that all eight children had been referred because they had issues with impulse control. It wasn't until the second or third session that I understood the depth of these issues.

Throughout this course I struggled. So often children with impulse control and other issues are told, implicitly or explicitly, that they are "wrong" or "bad" for being wiggly, distracted, or disruptive. The paradox is that the behaviors that follow the impulses usually result in a punishment; unfortunately, punishment rarely supports the children in exploring the initial impulses that led to the behaviors in the first place, much less possible new behaviors. Mindfulness offers an alternative. Mindfulness can help a child recognize the clues that let her know she is becoming distracted or angry and then consider her choices. Over time, mindfulness has the potential to interrupt the pattern of impulse, action, and purposeless punishment, and thus provides a foundation for self-awareness and conscious action.

In this first after-school class, my desire to be liked by the students and to make the class fun for them initially led me to be too permissive, and their problematic behaviors escalated. In retrospect, with this group, it would have been more skillful to set clearer limits on behavior while simultaneously being compassionate about the thoughts, feelings, and developmental deficits underneath their behaviors. My clarified, evolving behavioral guidelines and class agreements are presented in chapter 4, session 1.

In the next course, offered to similar students at the same school, I brought the past into the present. I overcorrected and made the behavioral constraints too tight. Although fifteen of the twenty-four students in this class were referred by their parents or teachers because they had difficulty paying attention, the group as a whole did not have the dramatic issues with impulse control evident in the first class. In both groups I let the children know that it was their choice whether or not they participated in the course. I explained that they needed to demonstrate their desire to participate by behaving in a manner that supported their own learning as well as that of their classmates.

One day, a young girl continued to choose disruptive behavior, and I calmly asked her to step out of the classroom twice. In retrospect, in this circumstance, my response simply intensified her default emotion: anger. If I had it to do over again, I would have used this opportunity to gently explore the thoughts and feelings that led to the behavior. Now, having had such conversations, I can share that the revised dialogue might go something like this:

Me:	Maria, do you know what you were feeling right before you chose to slam your book down and make that comment?
Maria:	No.
Me:	Are you willing to take a guess?
Maria:	(Silence.)
Me:	(To the class.) Based on what you observed, and what you know about your own feelings and behavior, does anyone else want to take a guess?
Class:	(Silence.)

Me:	Well, I know that, for me, when I behave like that I usually feel angry. As human beings we all feel angry sometimes. Can anyone describe how we can recognize anger in our bodies?
Alex:	It feels tight and hot, like I'm going to explode.
Me:	Yes. It often feels like that for me too. How about for the rest of you? Raise your hand if you have ever had anger feel this way. (*Many, including me, raise their hands.*) Have any of you ever had anger feel other ways in your body?
Steven:	Sometimes it feels cold and hard.
Me:	Yup. I've had that too. How about the rest of you? Again, raise your hand if you've felt anger this way. (*Many, including me, raise their hands once again.*) Why might it be helpful to be able to recognize when we are angry or, better yet, starting to get angry?
Tony:	Because then I could stop and I wouldn't get in trouble so much.
Me:	Has anyone besides Tony ever "gotten in trouble" because you felt angry and acted quickly? Raise your hand if this has ever happened to you. (*I smile and raise my hand.*) When we practice mindfulness, we can notice our feelings. We can notice how they feel in our bodies: hot and tight like we're going to explode, or cold and hard. And then, at least sometimes, we can choose what we do next. Maybe this week all of us can see if we can notice how anger feels in our bodies. Maybe you can even try to notice the very first signs of anger as they appear in your body.

Even if she just sat and rolled her eyes, odds are that Maria—and her classmates—would have realized that we all feel anger, and that feeling anger is part of being human. More importantly, they would have gotten a glimpse of how mindfulness might help them engage with intense emotions. As mentioned previously, facilitating such a discussion requires that we be honest about our own anger.

To be clear, this doesn't mean that, if Maria continued to be disruptive, I wouldn't again ask her to step out. However, ideally, I would offer the above inquiry first.

Identifying ourselves as mindfulness teachers requires that we apply the practice—*especially when teaching and facilitating*—and that we inquire into the moments when we are unskillful. Our work obliges us to find some middle path between being in denial versus second-guessing and overanalyzing these moments. If we are willing to be honest about these moments, they help us grow, cultivating rigorous compassion and compassionate rigor toward ourselves, our teachers (the class participants), and all human beings.

It is not so much that we are teaching mindfulness as that mindfulness is teaching us. If we are courageous and open, mindfulness teaches us what it is to be fully human. And as far as I know, practice makes practice; practice does not make perfect. Let your practice permeate your life: your teaching, your professional and personal relationships, your daily interactions, your e-mails, your phone calls, and as many of your moments as possible.

***

Much like session 1 of the curriculum that follows, the first three chapters of this book have provided an introduction to the Still Quiet Place and the practice of mindfulness, and have given a basic overview of the course. Chapters 4 through 11 describe the eight sessions in detail. Each session includes a combination of mindfulness practices, facilitated inquiry, interactive activities, and movement practices. Most sessions also include additional material, such as vignettes, analogies, stories, and poems. The session chapters are followed by facilitated personal inquiry, detailed guidance, and important cautions to be aware of when preparing to offer the course to children and adolescents. Now let's move on to session 1, which introduces participants to the Still Quiet Place and the practice of mindfulness, and gives them a basic overview of the time you'll spend together.

4

session 1: taking a bite, taking a breath

Intentions

The intentions of this first session are to introduce participants to each other, and to the Still Quiet Place and mindfulness. To indicate that session time is a special time for mindfulness, this session, and every subsequent one, begins with a simple listening practice. Listening practice is followed by a brief introduction to mindfulness, which will be expanded upon throughout this session and the entire course. After listening practice, the group participation agreements and guidelines are created or reviewed. Once the group agreements have been established, participants introduce themselves to the group. The remainder of the session is devoted to providing an *experience* and working definition of the Still Quiet Place and mindfulness by engaging in and discussing Mindful Eating, and an age-adapted, breath-based, Still Quiet Place practice. This session (and all sessions) then closes as it began, with simple listening practice.

Outline: Practices, Exercises, and Discussions

- Mindful Listening practice*

- Introduction to mindfulness*

- Group agreements and guidelines*

- Participant introductions*

- Mindful Eating practice*

- Mindful Eating discussion*

- Breath-based Still Quiet Place practice and discussion*

- Read-aloud option: *Everybody Needs a Rock*, Byrd Baylor*

- Overview of home practice*

- Closing Mindful Listening practice*

Mindful Listening Practice (all ages)

Invite the participants to allow their bodies to be still. Then guide them through this simple practice, speaking slowly and allowing time for their experience. The ellipses (…) in this and the examples, explanations, and dialogues that follow indicate a long pause to allow time for the experience.

> *In a moment I will ring this tone bar, and you will hear a sound. See if you can listen to the sound with all of your attention—with your ears, your mind, your heart, and your body. When the sound fades and you can't hear it anymore, quietly raise your hand. Please keep your eyes closed and your hand raised. Okay, please close your eyes…* (Ring the tone bar, then wait until the sound has faded and everyone's hand is raised.) *Now, before you open your eyes, take a moment to listen to the quiet underneath the sound… And now, notice how your body, mind, and heart feel after listening in this way… When you are ready you may open your eyes and we will continue, doing our best to listen to each other with our full attention, just like we listened to the sound.*

With the above transition, you can move into a conversation about the participants' experience of listening: "How was it to listen in this way?…" "How do your body, mind, and heart feel after listening like this?…" Based on your sense of the experience, you may also add questions such as "Did anyone have difficulty listening to the sound all the way through until the end?" and "What kind of difficulty did you have?" As this is the first session and you will have plenty of time to address common difficulties with various mindfulness practices, there is no need to cover this topic in any depth at this time. A few simple comments are enough: "Yes, even when listening for a short time, it is easy for us to get distracted. With practice over the next eight weeks, the muscle of our attention will get stronger. Let's listen together, one more time."

Introduction to Mindfulness (all ages)

Continuing, you may offer the following explanation:

> The listening practice we just did was mindfulness. Mindfulness is paying attention, here and now, with kindness and curiosity, so that we can choose our behavior. When you focused your attention on just listening, you were listening mindfully. With practice, you can learn to bring this gentle, mindful attention to all the activities in your life—listening, eating, talking, singing, reading, even arguing. As we continue talking, let's see if we can listen to each other with the same curious, focused attention that we just used to listen to the sound of the tone bar.

My preference is to have participants *experience* mindful listening before offering a definition of mindfulness. Then, when the definition is offered it is not just theoretical; it is connected to their experience of *hearing* both sound and quiet. Throughout the course, it is likely that you will repeat variations of this definition of mindfulness frequently, emphasizing a relevant phrase and demonstrating a particular aspect of *how* to practice mindfulness; how to pay attention, here and now, with kindness and curiosity, in order to choose behavior. Here, it is enough to simply let our young friends know that the attentive listening they just did was mindful listening, and to share the definition.

Group Agreements and Guidelines (all ages)

After guiding listening practice and offering a working definition of mindfulness, I introduce myself. I say my name, and often share the ages of my own children, especially if the young people in the group are close to the same age. I explain that I teach mindfulness to youth because I have found it very helpful in my own life—especially when dealing with intense feelings or difficult situations—and that I wish I had learned mindfulness when I was their age. I may also share a few stories about my previous experience of teaching mindfulness at the same school or with youth the same age.

Then, to establish a shared understanding that everyone in the room will treat each other with kindness and respect, we review or create the group agreements and guidelines. Depending on the age of the group, their level of participation, and time constraints, I may invite the group to suggest agreements for working well together (adding and reframing slightly as needed), or I may simply offer the guidelines below. If the room has a whiteboard, I write the agreements on the board; if not, we just review them verbally.

Confidentiality: Ask if one of the students can explain what "confidentiality" means. The simplest definition is "what is said in the room stays in the room." Specifically, this means not sharing what others have shared, on the playground, in the hallway, or via text, Twitter, or Facebook. One boy described confidentiality as feeling confident. It is a wonderful definition because when we know that "what is said in the room will stay in the room," we feel safe and confident about sharing experiences that we might not share otherwise.

Right to pass: A person may choose not to speak at any time for any reason. It is particularly important, early in the course to allow each participant to feel safe and accepted just as he is—especially if he's shy, angry, or depressed. In one course, a young boy named Evan sat with his back to the room and didn't participate in the discussion for the first three sessions. (You'll hear more about Evan in session 4.)

Respectful behavior: Ask participants to suggest agreements and guidelines for respectful behavior that will help them feel safe and allow them and their classmates to learn. When complete, the behavioral agreements should encompass the following:

Mindful Listening
   Listening to whoever is speaking with your full attention—with your ears, your mind, and your heart, "just like we listened to the tone bar." (In this day and age, with tweens and teens, it's important to include a gentle reminder to turn off and put away cell phones and other electronic devices.)

Mindful Speaking
   Reporting your own experience, using "I" statements; not interrupting; allowing time for others to speak; noticing when you feel the urge to show off, hide, give advice, tell someone what to do, argue, or be silly, mean, or disruptive; and then, choosing when and how you speak.

Being Responsible with Your Body
   Staying in your "space bubble" (your own space)—not distracting, bumping, poking, or irritating your neighbors. You might say something along these lines:

"Take a moment and imagine a 'space bubble' around you. Sometimes, when we are sitting together like this, side by side, our space bubbles may feel very small and close to our bodies. Other times, like when we do a movement practice, I may ask you to make your space bubble bigger, and make sure your bubble doesn't bump into your neighbor's bubble." With tweens and teens you can use vocabulary more along the lines of sensing and respecting personal space.

Being a Team Player
Creating an environment that supports everyone in learning together by keeping all of the agreements we just made.

Supporting the group in applying these agreements requires moment-to-moment adjustments. It is often the most disruptive and "difficult" children who are most likely to benefit from discovering the Still Quiet Place. These kids are so often told, either explicitly or implicitly, that they are "bad" or "wrong" that I strive to just let them be. However, as described previously, in my first after-school class I took this acceptance a bit too far. The elementary school principal mentioned with a smile that she had sent me all her kids with ADHD and impulse control problems. At the time, I didn't *really* get it, and initially, I was too permissive. It took several sessions to come up with boundaries more conducive to participation, and to support the group in accepting them. The boundaries I ended up choosing are encapsulated in the agreements above.

Currently, my unspoken internal boundary is that participants can hum, whisper quietly to themselves, doodle, rock, fidget, wiggle, and so on, as long as it doesn't disrupt the class—either by distracting their classmates or by pulling my attention. I tell the children something along these lines:

You don't need to participate, and if you choose not to participate, you may sit quietly (or go to the office). If you want to be here, you need to show that with your behavior. If your behavior is disruptive, I'll remind you about our agreements. Then I will ask you to move away from your friends or to sit by me. If your behavior continues to make it difficult for others to listen and experience stillness and quietness, I will ask you to sit out (or go to the office).

For the most part, the students want to participate. They appreciate the stillness and quietness and the opportunity to really be seen and heard. They value the kind attention that they receive from you (the facilitator), their classmates, and themselves. Remember, if you ask a child to leave the room, he must have a safe, supervised place to go.

Introductions (all ages)

After reviewing the agreements and guidelines, invite participants to introduce themselves by saying their name, one thing they find difficult or stressful, and one thing they like about themselves. You may be surprised by what they will volunteer. In one class, a courageous boy said, "My parents made me come, *and* I want to work on my anger." Then two other boys, one mother, and one father felt free to say they had also come to work on their anger.

With some participants, it is important to acknowledge out loud that they may have been strongly encouraged or even required to come by their mother, father, other caretaker, teacher, counselor, therapist, or probation officer. If this is the case, they will have more than the usual number and intensity of thoughts and feelings about participating. It is important to demonstrate that you truly understand, and that *all* their thoughts and feelings are welcome here. *Then,* you may return to the definition of mindfulness, noting that much of the course is about paying attention to, acknowledging, and accepting our intense thoughts and feelings and then choosing our behavior. This way of being with our thoughts and feelings can be especially helpful in difficult situations, or situations we don't like.

With true compassion for the tweens and teens who have been required to attend, *wisely consider* offering the following possibility:

"Perhaps if you had developed these skills you would not have behaved in the ways that resulted in being required to attend this class. As human beings, all of us have intense feelings. When we don't know how to deal with them we often end up behaving in ways we regret. Other kids like you who have taken this course have discovered after learning mindfulness—that is, learning to pay attention to their intense thoughts and feelings with kindness and curiosity, to choose their behavior, and to communicate clearly and respectfully—that generally their relationships improve, they don't act in ways that get them into trouble, and they feel better about themselves."

Again, the utmost wisdom and compassion is required in offering such an inquiry. Often such reflections arise spontaneously; and this conversation can certainly come later in the course. The purpose of mentioning it during introductions would be to allow our young friends to consider how mindfulness might be useful in their daily lives. Usually, even those who are initially resistant find value in the course. However, if after a few sessions it becomes obvious that an individual truly doesn't want to participate, I may speak with the person who is requiring attendance. (See chapter 14: "Teaching Simultaneously to Children and Parents" for a related dialogue.)

After all of the participants have introduced themselves, introduce yourself again using the same format you requested of them: saying your name (like the participants, I use just my first name), one thing you find stressful, and one thing you like about yourself. Including yourself this way demonstrates your commitment to practicing mindfulness and being a true participant in the group.

Mindful Eating Practice (all ages)

Most children and teens love Mindful Eating, and if the time and setting allow, I begin every session with a few mindful bites. Eating is essential if you are teaching classes that begin after school, when our young friends are especially hungry. I usually provide tangerines, apples, or fig bars. Avoid snacks high in sugar, and make sure you check with the students, the teacher, or parents regarding food allergies. Below is an example of Mindful Eating with apples. The instructions below are for children ages five through eight, with a couple of minor adaptations in the vocabulary for older participants in parentheses. Please remember that, in leading this practice—and all the practices in this book—you will need to draw on your own comprehensive personal practice.

> *Take a moment and just notice how you are feeling right now: curious, tired, wiggly (restless)....*
>
> *I hear lots of thoughts like, 'Yeah, I love apples,' 'Ew, I hate apples.' Just notice your thoughts as the apples are passed.... Let's take a moment and just feel the objects in our hands.... Are they heavy or light?... Warm or cool?... Smooth or rough?...*
>
> *What do you see? An apple? Well, if you take away the idea of apple, what do you see?... Is it just one color?... What do you notice about the shape and texture?...*

To promote the awareness of interconnection, you might ask the following questions. Hopefully the participants will provide the majority of the answers.

> *What did the stem do?... Yes, it connected it to the tree. Do you have a stem?... Yup, your belly button is your stem. What did it connect you to?... How did the apple get from being attached by the stem to the tree to being in our hands?... Yes. It fell off the tree, or someone picked it. Then what?... It was put on a truck and then in a box, or in a box and then on a truck. Someone drove it to the store. Someone unloaded it, put a price tag on it, and put it on the shelf. Someone— me—chose it, paid for it, brought it home, washed it, put it in a bag, and brought it to class. The person next to you passed it to you, and now it is in your hand, just waiting to be eaten (smile).*
>
> *As we eat these objects, let's use them to practice mindfulness. Let's bring our kind and curious attention to smell. What does this object smell like?... What is*

happening in your mouth and your mind as you smell this object?... Now close your eyes and bring your attention inward, to just yourself and your object....

We will be doing the next portion of the exercise in silence, and the instructions will be very slow, like in Simon Says. (You can omit the reference to Simon Says with older participants.) Do your best not to get ahead of me. Lift the object to your mouth, taking just one bite and letting the bite rest in your mouth.

Please note it is important that you *do* the practices with the students while instructing them. Otherwise, you are speaking theoretically rather than sharing the here-and-now experience. Theory doesn't necessarily represent the present-moment experience of a surprisingly unpleasant, mouth-puckering orange. One afternoon, I was sitting in a school library, on a map-of-the-world carpet, with fourteen fourth graders, and we bit into extremely sour, mealy oranges. If I hadn't been doing the practices with the students, I would have had no idea how truly unpleasant these oranges tasted. Needless to say, this experience opened the door to a brief discussion on how we can deal with unpleasant experiences, which was expanded upon later in the course. Note that it is okay to speak with your mouth full. Kids find it funny, and it lets them know that we're all in this together.

Let the bite of the apple rest in your mouth, paying attention to what is happening in your mouth.... Don't rush.... Now take just one chew, noticing the taste.... Continue, taking one single chew at a time, noticing how the taste changes, how your teeth and tongue work.... Do your best to put all of your attention into your mouth, with the apple and chewing and tasting....

See if you can notice the urge to swallow before you actually swallow, and then feel the whole swallow as the food moves down your throat.... Take your time.... Be curious about your experience.... Before you open your eyes, notice how your body, mind, and heart feel now, in this moment.

Eating a single bite mindfully may take one to two minutes. This exercise is a very concrete way for students to practice bringing their attention into the present moment.

Mindful Eating Discussion (all ages)

Remember, when discussing various practices, choose wisely regarding the depth of conversation; let the participation of, and comments from, the individual or group you are working with guide you. With younger children, it's best to limit the discussion to one or two simple questions or comments. This brief discussion will nonetheless be effective, as it lays a foundation for evolving understanding.

Let the students know that, like the listening practice, the eating practice they just did *is* mindfulness—paying attention, here and now, with kindness and curiosity. Before the children begin speaking, remind them that during the discussion, everyone will continue the practice of mindful speaking and listening. Then invite them to share their experience of the exercise. Ask, "What was it like to eat that way? What did you notice?"

You may use participants' comments to note the fast pace of our culture, and how we are often hurrying from home to school, from school to soccer or piano, and then home again. You can explore the possibility of slowing down to taste not only our food, but also our lives. After a bit of discussion, support the participants in eating another mindful bite, with slightly less guidance and more quiet.

Make sure to invite comments from those who had difficulty with or hated the snack, or the exercise itself, and to acknowledge that some experiences in life are unpleasant. Future sessions will explore the thoughts and feelings associated with unpleasant experiences in greater depth. For now, acknowledging the unpleasantness and suggesting that there may be new ways to deal with the unpleasant events in our lives is enough. A few simple questions or comments can provide the foundation for subsequent discussions. For example, you might say something like this:

> *Yes. Sometimes things aren't how we want them to be, or we don't get what we want. How do you deal with things when they don't go your way? Later in the course we will be experimenting with different ways to deal with things that are difficult, upsetting, or unpleasant—little things, like having an apple when you don't like apples; bigger things, like losing your backpack; and even bigger things, like your parents getting divorced.*

Breath-Based Practice and Discussion:
Jewel or Rest (all ages)

After each child has spoken or passed, continue with a Still Quiet Place breath-based practice. With young children, ages four to ten, I usually start with a practice I call Jewel, using a stone. With tweens and teens, I begin with a practice I call Rest. It is important to support the continuity of attention by noting that the group is now transitioning from the practice of mindful conversation to another guided practice.

I outline both practices below, and audio versions are available on my children's and teens CDs, respectively. In addition, a sample Still Quiet Place breath-based practice suitable for all ages can be downloaded from http://www.newharbinger .com/27572. (See the back of the book for more information.)

Jewel (ages four to ten)

For this practice, you'll need a basket or bowl of river stones or colored glass drops. These objects should be big enough that they are unlikely to be swallowed by younger siblings, and small enough to fit comfortably in the children's palms. You can gather stones when you walk, or the stones and glass drops can be purchased in bulk at many craft stores. Plan to devote three to five minutes to this practice once the children have chosen their stones.

Allow each child to choose a stone or glass bead. As the children are waiting to choose a stone, encourage them to notice their thoughts and feelings. For example, you might ask, "Are you waiting to choose your stone? What does waiting feel like in your body?... What thoughts are you having while you are waiting?..." Once the children have their stones, guide them in exploring the details of their stones: "Now take a moment to silently give your kind, curious attention to your stone. What color, or colors, is it?... Is it smooth or rough, or maybe smooth and rough?... Is it heavy, or light, or in between?... Is it warm or cool?... "

When everyone has a stone, and if the setting allows, have the children lie down and place the stones on their belly buttons, either inside or outside their clothing. If space is tight, they can sit in chairs and hold the stones against their bellies. Occasionally it is necessary to make a few simple rearrangements or offer specific instructions, such as "Allow your eyes *and* mouths to close," "Bodies apart," or "Alex, please move over here."

While it may be best for you to get down on the floor and do the practice with them so that the practice is completely connected to the moment, the circumstances and dynamics of some groups require that you lead the practice with your eyes open, attending not only to your breath, but also to the activity in the room. Some mindfulness teachers I know (particularly those who work with populations *known* to have experienced significant trauma) *always* keep their eyes open and say something like "So that you can feel safe here, I promise I will keep my eyes open. If you are willing, you can close your eyes. If not, focus on a spot on the desk, or on the floor in front of you." A middle way that works well in many settings is to lead the practice with your eyes closed for much of the time, opening them frequently to briefly scan the room and offer a smile to participants who have chosen to keep their eyes open.

Once everyone is settled, invite them to feel or sense their breath by feeling the stone rise with the in-breath and fall with the out-breath. If the students are sitting, invite them to feel the stone move out with the expansion of the in-breath, and back with the release of the out-breath. After that, encourage them to feel the natural rhythm of the breath—the entire in-breath from the very beginning, just when the stone begins to move, all the way through to the end of the in-breath, when the stone is still, just for a moment. And encourage them to feel the entire out-breath from the beginning, just when the stone begins to move, all the way through to the end of the out-breath, when the stone is still again. Also invite them to feel the brief still space between the in-breath and the out-breath, and the other short still space between the out-breath and the in-breath. Invite them to *rest* their attention in the natural still quiet spaces between the breaths.

The suggested length for a given practice is a *maximum* of one minute per year of age. Initially, the practices may be even shorter. While the children don't need to be completely still, you want to allow time for them to settle, and to end with *most* of them feeling more still and quiet than when they began. If some individuals—or all of them—become restless or wiggly during the practice, you can kindly say something like "Notice if your body is wiggly. It's okay for your body to be wiggly; just notice this."

As you conclude the practice, encourage participants to note how their bodies, minds, and hearts feel after paying attention to the breath and the movement of the stone for just a few minutes. Then, whenever they are ready, they can gently move their fingers and toes, stretch, open their eyes, and sit up carefully, without bumping their neighbors.

Rest (ages eleven to eighteen)

Here's a parallel introductory practice for teens. Plan to devote four to six minutes to this practice. Again, depending on the setting, they may want to do the practice sitting up or lying down.

Give it a rest. For the next few minutes give it a rest, all of it—homework, parents, the hallway gossip, your inner gossip, the next new thing.... Let everything be exactly the way it is.... And rest.

Let your body rest. If you feel comfortable, allow your eyes to close. If not, focus on a neutral spot in front of you. Feel your body supported by the chair, the couch, or the floor. Allow the muscles in your body and your face to rest. Maybe even let out a long, slow sigh....

And let your attention rest on the breath... the rhythm of the breath in the belly. Feel the belly expand with each in-breath and release with each out-breath. Narrowing your attention to the rhythm of the breath, and allowing everything else to fade into the background.... Breathing, resting.... Nowhere to go, nothing to do, no one to be, nothing to prove.

Feeling the natural rhythm of the breath, from the first sip all the way through to where the breath is still, and the out-breath, from the first whisper all the way through to where the breath is still. Now, without changing the breath, see if you can let your attention rest in the short still quiet space between the in-breath and the out-breath.... And rest again in the small still place between the out-breath and the in-breath....

Breathing, resting, being…it is more than enough.… Just hanging out with the breath and the stillness.…

Feeling the stillness and quietness that is always inside of you.

And when your attention wanders, which it will, gently return it to the experience of breathing—feeling the rhythm of the breath in the belly.…

Choosing to rest. Choosing to focus your attention on the breath. Allowing things to be just as they are… Allowing yourself to be exactly as you are… Nothing to change, or fix, or improve.…

Breathing and resting. Resting and breathing.

As this session comes to a close, you may want to remember that in our fast-paced, media-driven world, resting is a radical act. With practice, you can learn to breathe and rest anytime, anywhere: When you're putting on your shoes… When you're struggling in class… When you're hanging out with friends… Even when you're arguing with someone.… This kind of resting and breathing is especially helpful when you're nervous, depressed, bored, or angry.… So give yourself permission and rest.

Breath-Based Practice Discussion (all ages)

As a transition into discussion of the preceding breath-based practice, let participants know that following the breath and paying attention to the spaces between breaths is often the easiest way to find the Still Quiet Place. When leading the practice and during subsequent discussion, it is necessary to emphasize maintaining the natural rhythm of the breath. It is particularly important that children with respiratory issues not try to lengthen the pause between the breaths or hold their breaths. During the discussion, reiterate that the stillness and quietness is always alive inside of us—when we are breathing in; when the breath is still; when we are breathing out; when the breath is still; when we are feeling happy or sad, angry or excited, confident or afraid, when we are dancing, reading, or struggling.

Then let those who wish to, share their experience of the practice. As they do so, be attentive to your own responses. It can be seductive to hear that participants felt relaxed or calm. And it is important that you do your best to hear *all* experiences without judgment or preference. Be aware of the tendency we have as instructors to say "good" or "great" when participants note that they felt calm. These types of comments can lead to confusion about mindfulness. It's important not to create or support a misconception that mindfulness is about being calm or relaxed. Rather, affirm that it is about being aware of whatever is arising in the moment.

Remember to ask about difficulties—the mind wandering, the body being fidgety. If someone notices anxiety or boredom, this *is* mindfulness. In later sessions you can discuss how to be with (notice without getting caught up in) boredom, anxiety, and other unpleasant states. If someone mentions a distracting neighbor, it provides a good opportunity to remind the group about the class agreements, and to simultaneously encourage the individual to notice when his attention wanders from the suggested focus—in this case, the breath—and to practice returning his attention to the breath.

Overview of Home Practice (all ages)

Following the breath-based practice, provide the handout outlining the home practice for the upcoming week. A sample is provided at the end of this chapter. When introducing the home practice, I don't use the word "homework" because of all of its associations and connotations. Read the home practice aloud, reviewing the themes and practices of the day and offering clarifying comments as needed. Consider including age-appropriate graphics illustrating the theme of the week. Alternatively, you may choose to create a workbook for the entire course, which includes the home practice sheets, copies of the in-class exercises, graphics, and poems.

Home practice for session 1 includes mindful toothbrushing, which can be briefly described and pantomimed as follows:

As you begin to brush your teeth, bring your full, kind, and curious attention to toothbrushing. Feel yourself pick up the toothpaste, unscrew the cap, pick up the toothbrush, squeeze the toothpaste, and put down the toothpaste. Feel the movement of your hand, arm, tongue, and cheeks as you brush. Notice the taste of the toothpaste, and how you spit or swallow. (This comment usually gets a few laughs and looks of disgust.) *When you notice your mind has wandered into the future or the past, gently bring it back to brushing and tasting. Listen to the water as you rinse your toothbrush. Feel your movements as you put the toothbrush and toothpaste away. During the few minutes it takes to brush your teeth, see if you can give your complete attention to brushing your teeth, and not to anything else—homework, a difficulty you had during the day, an exciting event that is coming up, (texting a friend)...*

In the first session, also hand out the home practice log included at the end of this chapter. The practice log provides a simple and effective way to document the amount of guided audio and daily life practice participants are doing. While the practice log is essential in research settings, documenting home practice in therapeutic, school, and community settings can be instructive. You may want to allow for anonymity, so as not to influence participant responses. This can be done by replacing the space for the child's name with an ID number, or telling participants that, if they prefer, they may leave the name space blank.

If time allows, you may include a short, guided breath-based practice.

Closing Mindful Listening Practice (all ages)

Borrowing from my friend and colleague Susan Kaiser Greenland, founder of the Inner Kids childrens' mindfulness program, I like to invite one or two students who have participated wholeheartedly by being honest, attentive, or curious to ring the tone bar for the listening practice that concludes the session. This invitation builds incentive for constructive participation. Ending class as it began, invite everyone to close their eyes and listen to the sound, and raise their hand when the sound fades and they can't hear it. (By the time the course concludes, I've created an opportunity for every participant to ring the opening or closing bell. Students who tend to be more disruptive are eventually thrilled to earn this privilege.)

As mentioned in chapter 3, I recommend that you make contact with participants by e-mail, text, or phone in the middle of the first week. The communication can be quite simple, such as "Hello. I'm just checking in to see how the home practice is going. Do you have any questions? Can I help you in any way?" Most often our young friends forget about the home practice, and this contact serves as a gentle reminder. Occasionally, participants mention a particular difficulty, perhaps finding time to practice or figuring out how to do the practices. Ways of addressing these difficulties will be covered in session 2, in the home practice review.

Practicing at Home—Session 1

Mindfulness is simple.

It means paying attention here and now, with kindness and curiosity, and then choosing your behavior.

Listen to the Still Quiet Place practice at http://www.newharbinger.com/27572 (see the back of the book for more information), or the Jewel or Treasure practice or Rest practice (on the CDs *Still Quiet Place: Mindfulness for Young Children* and *Still Quiet Place: Mindfulness for Teens*), at least once a day.

Practice mindfulness in daily life.

• *Brush your teeth mindfully.*

With kindness and curiosity, and without guilt, fill out the home practice log. You can simply put a check mark in each box, or write the name of the CD practice and activity.

If you have a mindful moment (a moment when you notice something you might not have noticed before), or if you have questions or difficulties that you would like to share, please call or e-mail me. Also, please let me know if you won't be able to attend the next class.

Practice Log

At Home: Week 1   Name _____

	Guided Audio Practice	Mindfulness in Daily Life
Monday		
Tuesday		
Wednesday		
Thursday		
Friday		
Saturday		
Sunday		

Please use the space below to share anything you would like about your experience resting in the Still Quiet Place and practicing mindfulness: something you noticed, difficulties, or questions that you don't want to share in the group.

_____

_____

_____

_____

_____

_____

_____

_____

_____

_____

_____

_____

_____

5

session 2: beginning again

Intentions

The primary intention of this session is to support participants in establishing a daily practice. To begin, you will engage the individual or group in a kind and curious discussion about their experiences with, and obstacles to, doing the guided audio and tooth-brushing practices. Then, you can solicit suggestions from those who did practice, and offer your own tips for making time for doing the practice. The second half of the session is a facilitated exploration of pleasant events. The intention of this exercise is to support participants in bringing their attention to the details of their experiences, and to begin to incrementally develop their capacity for observing their thoughts, feelings, and physical sensations.

Outline: Practices, Exercises, and Discussions

- Mindful Listening practice*

- Mindful Eating practice*

- Home practice review

- Seaweed movement practice*

- Breath-based practice: Jewel* or Rest

- Pleasant Events exercise and discussion*

- Read-aloud option: *The Story of Ferdinand*, Munro Leaf*

- Overview of home practice*

- Closing Mindful Listening practice*

Mindful Listening and Mindful Eating Practice (all ages)

After greeting participants, invite everyone to "begin again"—to bring their attention into the here and now by listening to the sound of the tone bar and the silence that follows. From here, you can move into eating practice. Support participants in slowing down and bringing their full attention to the colors, textures, smells, thoughts, feelings, sounds, and flavors of each bite.

Home Practice Review (ages six to eighteen)

After Mindful Eating practice, move into a discussion of the home practice. As with any other self-care routine or homework, most children below age six will require adult support to establish a daily practice. Thus, the discussion below applies to children ages six and up. (If you are working with younger children, you may simply invite a show of hands from those who did home practice, and then proceed directly to the Seaweed practice.)

Remind the class that they are practicing paying attention to their lives with kindness and curiosity, and that now they will bring these qualities to discussing the home practice. Begin with a discussion of the guided audio practice:

Now we are going to discuss the home practice. Before we continue, just notice any thoughts and feelings that showed up when I said "home practice." Did you maybe think, "What home practice?" [Smile as you say this.] Did you feel panic, pride, or embarrassment? (Did you think, "I don't care about the home practice"? Did you judge yourself, or start comparing yourself to others?)

Did any of you practice with the recording? Did any of you forget completely about the recording? Either way is fine. Whether you practiced or forgot to practice, we are going to bring kindness and curiosity to talking about your experiences.

During this discussion, make sure that participants who didn't do home practice feel comfortable reporting this. Then help them explore the hows and whys of not doing it without judgment:

- *What got in the way?*

- *What did you do instead?*

- *Can you challenge yourself to give yourself the gift of kind attention for five minutes a day?*

- *What time of day do you think would work best for you?*

- *For those of you who did do the practice, what can you share about it? What time of day worked best? What did you notice after doing it?*

Discuss common scheduling barriers to doing the guided audio practice and offer suggestions for removing these barriers. Usually at least a few of the participants will report that they did practice and they found it beneficial. If no one offers such reports you can simply note that many kids find that the easiest times to practice are after school, before homework, between homework subjects, or before going to bed. Kids who practice before or while they do their homework comment that it actually helps them focus and complete their homework more easily, and kids who have trouble sleeping often say they sleep better if they practice before going to bed.

For those who forgot about the home practice, reinforce that each moment is a new moment, and they can begin their practice again, now. It helps to remind participants that they are developing a strength or skill, and just like learning a sport or playing an instrument, mindfulness takes *practice*. You might explain it along these lines:

In fact, using a special machine called an fMRI, which takes pictures of the brain in action, scientists have shown that when people practice mindfulness, areas of the brain associated with learning and memory get thicker, and other areas, associated with worry and fear, get thinner. So when you practice mindfulness, you're building your "brain muscle" and improving how your brain works.

Next, inquire about participants' experience with mindful toothbrushing. Again, emphasize the five senses, as well as thoughts (often considered a sixth sense) and feelings (a seventh sense) that they noticed while brushing their teeth. Here are a few examples of the types of questions you can use to help them explore their experience:

- *Could you feel the weight of the toothpaste as you picked it up?*

- *Did you feel your muscles working as you squeezed the toothpaste tube?*

- *Were you aware of the flavor of your toothpaste?*

- *Did the flavor change while you were brushing your teeth?*

- *Did your mind wander? If your mind wandered, what did it wander to?*

- *Did you notice the motions of spitting and rinsing the brush?*

Seaweed Movement Practice (all ages)

Because our young friends are frequently required to be unnaturally still for much of the day, it is helpful to incorporate *at least* one simple movement exercise into each session. On rainy or snowy days when the kids haven't had any recess or outdoor time, it may be wise to do more than one movement practice. Let the group's behavior and your wisdom guide you. Later in the course, you may play with having participants attend to the thoughts, feelings, and physical sensations associated with restlessness or boredom.

One of my favorite movement practices to use with children is to have them pretend they are seaweed moving in ocean waters. (And yes, this exercise works even with "cool," reluctant teens.) Each student is a strand of seaweed anchored to the floor. Initially the participants are all in a strong current, making big, rapid movements (without clonking their neighbors). Gradually the current decreases and the movements become smaller and smaller until there is very gentle swaying and then stillness. Throughout the practice, gently remind students to bring their attention to their experience and be aware of their physical sensations, thoughts, and feelings. Below is an example of how to guide this practice.

Please stand. Gently stretch out your arms. Make sure you have enough room to swing your arms without bumping anything or anyone. Now we are going to pretend we are seaweed. Our feet are stuck to the ocean floor, and we are in a powerful current. Being responsible for your body, let the current move your body, your arms, your head. Can you feel your body moving in space? Can you feel the stretch and release of different parts of your body as the current moves you?

Now the current is slowing down just a little. Allow your movements to get a bit smaller, as the current slows down. Can you bring kindness and curiosity to what you are thinking and feeling? Are you feeling embarrassed, or excited and energized? Are you thinking "Ah, it feels so good to move my body," or are you thinking "This is dumb"? Do you want to tease or bug your neighbor? Can you notice that want (urge) without actually doing it?

Now the current is slowing down even more. Let your movements get even smaller.... Notice where your attention is. Is it here with your body and the movement, or somewhere else? If you discover that your attention is somewhere else, gently bring it back to your body and the movement.

Now the current is still. Let your body be still, too.... What do you notice as you become still? Can you feel your breath here?... How do your body, mind, and heart feel after moving your body for just a few minutes?

Breath-Based Practice: Jewel or Rest (all ages)

From here you can move seamlessly into a breath-based practice. Simply offer a fresh version of the practice you shared in the first session. While conducting the practice, you might note that the mind will wander from the breath, and that this is natural. Convey that the heart of the practice lies in returning attention to the breath again and again.

Pleasant Events Exercise and Discussion (all ages)

This exercise encourages participants to begin paying attention, in detail, to events in daily life. It's most appropriate for children ages eight to eighteen. With younger children, you may omit this exercise. If you choose to offer it to children ages four to seven, invite them to draw a picture of a pleasant event or a simple happy time from the last few days. Then support them in a very short, spoken reflection, perhaps with a partner, about what they remember about what happened in their minds (thoughts), hearts (feelings), and bodies (physical sensations) during the event.

With older participants, you can use the Pleasant Event Cartoon, available online at http://www.newharbinger.com/27572. Ask participants to recall a pleasant event from the last couple of days. Remind them that although TV and advertising might suggest otherwise, pleasant events are often brief and simple: petting your cat, laughing with a friend, solving a math problem, rockin' out to your favorite song, eating a mindful snack, walking to school on a chilly morning, and so on. After they've remembered a pleasant event, they can fill in the thought bubble with the thoughts associated with the event, the feelings bubble with the feelings (emotions) associated with the event, and the body bubble with the physical sensations associated with the event. Remember to offer participants the option of drawing, rather than writing, the respective bubbles. While they are completing the cartoon, walk around the room and check in with any students who seem confused. Encourage them to recall the five senses, their facial expression (possibly a smile?), and how their body felt, and perhaps to reexperience the pleasantness as they recall the event.

Some students may believe that they haven't had a pleasant event. While honoring their life circumstances, *gently* challenge this perception. If they are in class, in that moment they are clothed, safe, and supported by a caring teacher. Do not forget that in many low-income settings a majority of our young friends may be hungry, neglected, or worse. Work gently to help students discover something in their life that is pleasant, perhaps saying something along these lines:

"Some of you may have difficulty recalling something pleasant. As I mentioned before, TV and advertising can convince us that a pleasant event needs to be a big deal, like getting a special gift, going to an exciting party, or taking an awesome vacation. For this exercise, think small. Did you hear a great new song or a funny joke? As you walked to class could you feel the sunshine or the breeze on your face? Did you see a friend in the hallway? Was the mindful breathing we did a few minutes ago pleasant?"

After the students have completed their cartoons, invite them to share their events and the thoughts, feelings, and physical sensations they recalled and depicted in the cartoon bubbles. As they share, add brief comments to support the principles of mindfulness. Such an exchange with a fourth grader might go something like this:

Student: My pleasant event was being with my cat. I felt happy. My body was relaxed.

Facilitator: What does relaxed feel like?

Student: Warm…soft.

Facilitator: Were there any thoughts with the event?

Student: "This is good."

Facilitator:	Interesting. Often when things are pleasant, we're just hanging out here and now, and our thoughts are often very simple, like "This is good." What did you see, hear, taste, smell, touch?
Student:	I felt soft fur, and I heard purring.
Facilitator:	What was your face doing during the event?
Student:	Smiling.
Facilitator:	And what is your face doing now?
Student:	Smiling!

Over time, mindfulness of pleasant events creates a solid foundation for future gratitude practice. Formal gratitude practice is relatively simple: invite students to reflect on things they are grateful for, quietly to themselves, with a partner, or by drawing or writing them. Again, it can be fun to have them "think small" and consider things that are actually big that we tend to overlook: this breath, clothes, running water, the ability to hear. Covering the practices, exercises, and discussions included in a given session, especially when you're first beginning to teach, may feel overwhelming. Be gentle with yourself as you become familiar with the material. In time, as you feel more comfortable—or if you are working in a setting where you see the children more frequently, or for longer than eight sessions—you may opt to include formal gratitude practice.

Overview of Home Practice (all ages)

Remember to leave time at the end of class to read the home practice for the upcoming week out loud. Encourage participants to *actually* do the recorded practice and remind them about suggested times to practice. Ideally, this gentle nudging is motivating without being guilt-inducing or off-putting.

Explain that part of the home practice for the coming week is to notice pleasant events, both large and small, during the week. Home practice for this session includes the informal practice of mindfully putting on shoes, which you can demonstrate and describe as follows:

When we mindfully put on our shoes, we bring our full attention to the process, just like we did with mindful toothbrushing. Feel yourself bending and reaching for the first shoe; feel your foot sliding into your shoe. If you have slip-ons, feel your toes wiggling into place. If your shoes have Velcro or laces, feel the Velcro or laces in your hands, and the movements your hands make to strap the Velcro or tie the laces. Then, of course, bring the same level of attention to putting on the other shoe.

Answer any questions participants may have about home practice.

Closing Mindful Listening Practice (all ages)

Close by allowing one or two participatory students to ring the bell for a final listening practice.

Practicing at Home—Session 2

Mindfulness is real.

The present moment is where we live our lives.

Listen to the Still Quiet Place practice at http://www.newharbinger.com/27572 (or the Jewel or Rest practice) at least once a day.

Practice mindfulness in daily life.

- *Notice pleasant events, both big and small, during the week. See if you can notice the pleasantness and the associated thoughts, feelings, and body sensations.*

- *Put on your shoes mindfully.*

With kindness and curiosity, and without guilt, fill out the home practice log.

If you have a mindful moment, questions, or difficulties you'd like to share, or if you won't be able to attend the next class, call or e-mail me.

session 3: thought watching and unkind mind

Intentions

One recurring intention for this session is continuing to support participants in developing a daily practice. A new intention is cultivating the capacity to observe thoughts, particularly the thoughts that arise during challenging situations, and our frequently critical internal dialogue—what I fondly call "Unkind Mind." As you will discover, the well-known "nine dots" exercise provides a direct, in-the-moment experience of these topics.

Outline: Practices, Exercises, and Discussions

- Mindful Listening practice*

- Mindful Eating practice*

- Preferences discussion*

- Home practice review

- Action Circle movement practice*

- Mindfulness of thoughts practice: Bubbles* or Thought Watching

- Thought Watching discussion

- Meeting Unkind Mind*

- "Nine dots" exercise and discussion

- Read-aloud option: *You Are Not Your Thoughts*, Brian Despard*

- Overview of home practice*

- Closing Mindful Listening practice*

Mindful Listening and Mindful Eating Practice (all ages)

As participants are typically feeling more comfortable with one another and the class in general, there tends to be a bit more casual conversation before class begins. As usual, open with Mindful Listening practice, asking a participant to sound the tone if you like. Then move into Mindful Eating practice.

Preferences Discussion (all ages)

At this point, students have come to expect snacks and are not shy about expressing their preferences: "Yeah! Apples again!" or "Ew, I don't like Fig Newtons." For younger children a simple statement or question can bring the kindness and curiosity of mindfulness to these moments: "This is a new apple and a new moment." "How do you usually deal with things you don't like?" After briefly responding to the comments, you may suggest eating in silence.

With slightly older children and adolescents, you can use their previous comments to continue to explore the inner experience of expectations, wanting (desire), and not wanting (aversion). Here is an example of such a dialogue.

Me:	So much of our unhappiness and upset comes from wanting things (ourselves, others, circumstances) to be different, wanting more of what we don't have (tangerines), or wanting less of what we do have (apples). What might life be like if we could accept things (ourselves, others, and circumstances) as they are?
Participant 1:	Less stressful?
Participant 2:	Easier.
Me:	What might this (acceptance) sound like?
Participant 3:	Well, Becky just said, "I don't really like apples, but I'll try one."
Participant 4:	Or you could say, "I don't really like apples, so I'll pass."
Me:	How might it feel if you said that?
Participant 1:	I don't know.
Me:	Why don't you all experiment with just letting things be the way they are, the next time things don't go your way. And then you can report back.

With tweens and teens, you may wish to elaborate, clarifying that acceptance does not mean that we like the way things are or that we don't take action. Rather, when we see things as they really are, we are more prepared to act wisely. This possibility will be revisited throughout the remainder of the course.

Home Practice Review (ages six to eighteen)

You may weave in threads from the last session, inviting students to speak about whether they have been doing the home practice and what they have discovered. It is especially important to continue to elicit comments from those who are struggling to find time to do the practice and those who are having difficulty with the practices. You may want to inquire about what gets in the way. Is it forgetting, homework, the Internet, Facebook, TV, extracurricular activities, or something else? Often a child will spontaneously offer the comment that his life is too busy, and this creates an opportunity to explore the pace of our culture. Remember, unlike the thirty to forty-five minutes of practice typically recommended for adults, most of the practices in this program are short: just four to seven minutes. So we are simply inviting students to devote a few minutes a day to giving themselves the gift of kind attention. For those who are having difficulty with the practices themselves, it is sufficient at this point to remind them that noticing distraction, restlessness, and boredom *is* mindfulness. Encourage them to stick with the practice and remember that, as with the apples, they can bring the kind and curious attention of mindfulness to the process of doing or not doing the home practice. This is a sneaky way to get them to practice even when they "aren't practicing."

Motivating Home Practice

To help motivate participants in engaging in home practice, you might share your version of a common adult experience: almost everyone I know who learned mindfulness as an adult wishes she had learned the practice when she was younger. In an early class, I had a wonderful assistant, Megan Cowan, now program director of Mindful Schools. In this class Megan told the children, "You're very lucky. I learned these practices when I was twenty, and at that time all of my teachers, who were in their fifties and sixties, said they wished they had learned mindfulness when they were twenty. When I learned these practices in my twenties, I wished I had learned them when I was ten. So you're very lucky to be learning these practices when you are ten!"

Addressing Complaints That Practice Is Boring

Children may complain that home practice, or practice in general, is boring. It's helpful to have a range of responses to choose from, depending on the situation. Below, I outline several possible approaches. Again, you are balancing allowing participants to have their experience just as it is, and simultaneously investigating their habits and patterns.

One potential response to the complaint that practice is boring is to say something like this:

It is certainly unusual. In our culture almost everything teaches us to focus our attention outward, and to want every experience to be new, fast, and exciting. In this class we are learning to focus our attention inward, to slow down and be at peace in the moment. I completely understand that you think it is boring. And, in time, you may be surprised that you actually come to really enjoy these practices. But don't take my word for it. For the next few weeks, just give it a try. Experiment and then decide for yourself. This week, I challenge all of you who think the practice is boring to see if you can discover one new thing about the pattern of your

breath, or the patterns of your thinking, and report back. You can start now, notic-
ing what you are thinking right now, after I said all that. (Smile.)

Additionally, or alternatively, when participants comment that the practice is boring, you can choose to switch up the practices to reengage their attention. You may opt to tie the breath to blowing bubbles or a pinwheel; to moving pebbles from one pile to another; or to taking turns touching the pinky, ring, middle, and index finger to the thumb on subsequent out-breaths. You may offer a vigorous movement practice, or a movement practice before a breath-based practice. You may challenge them to see if they can attend to the breath for one, two, or three minutes.

Do your best to find a middle path that supports them in simultaneously being engaged and investigating boredom. To support their investigation you can ask questions such as: "When and where do you tend to get bored in the rest of your life?" "What happens when you get bored?" "Does it sometimes create difficulties for you?" and "Can you notice the very beginning of boredom, like the very beginning of the in-breath?"

You can also let the children know that (at least in the beginning) many adults also find practicing mindfulness boring, difficult, or both. Offer specific examples from your own life, or from your experience of sharing mindfulness with adults. Then, without "overselling," consider sharing one or two tidbits about how you or young people you have worked with have found the practice beneficial. Do your best to encourage them to actually do the "experiment" by doing the practices for the duration of the course, so that they can discover for themselves whether mindfulness helps them in their daily lives. Be mindful; there's a fine line between encouraging and "should-ing" or "guilt-ing."

Tweens and teens are often intrigued to know that many celebrities use this practice. So far, my most enticing example of this fact comes from when I was sharing mindfulness with the tenth grade remedial English class at Menlo Atherton High School. According to a *Newsweek* article, at the time, MA was the most socioeconomically diverse school in the country. My young friends had been in remedial English in ninth grade. Some of their peers had moved to regular English for tenth grade. The students I was working with had remained in remedial English for tenth grade. Unfortunately and astonishingly, there is no remedial English in eleventh or twelfth grade. Thus, the principal had asked me to work with these students because he felt they were most at risk of falling through the cracks, failing and dropping out. This also happened to be the year the San Francisco Giants won the World Series. When the students came in, in their gray and orange hats and T-shirts, it was great to be able to hand them an article on how Tim Lincecum, the Giants pitcher, uses mindfulness (Kettmann, 2010). Not only did it entice some of the more reluctant students to consider the possibility that mindfulness could be helpful and *cool*, it also got them reading—no small feat!

After exploring boredom and the potential value of mindfulness in students' daily lives, and before shifting into some mindful movement, inquire briefly about their experiences with putting on their shoes mindfully.

Did any of you remember to put your shoes on mindfully?... What did you notice?
If you forgot, what do you think had you forget?... Yes, rushing and habit are powerful forces in our lives, and often they have us act without thinking. Sometimes this can be helpful, like stepping back onto the curb to avoid an oncoming car. Other times habit isn't so helpful, like having the same argument over and over again.

Action Circle Movement Practice (all ages)

Following the discussion about home practice, assess whether the group is ready and able to do a relatively still practice, or whether they would be better served by doing a moving practice first. If their behavior indicates that some movement would be beneficial, invite the group to stand in a circle. Explain that everyone will participate in a "silent" mindful movement exercise as follows: The first student will do a simple, safe, and respectful movement that feels good in her body—such as jumping, stretching, turning, or wiggling. Then the rest of the group will copy the movement. After the group has copied the first person's movement, she will graciously extend her hand in a "right this way" gesture to the person next to her. The second person may then demonstrate his unique, respectful movement. After the group copies his movement he will offer the "right this way" gesture to the person next to him. Select a student to begin. Let each person lead one movement. As the group does the movements, encourage the students to notice their thoughts and feelings—such as pride, embarrassment, judging, or comparing. Noting thoughts provides an excellent transition to introducing the Bubbles (or Thought Watching) practice, and the concept of Unkind Mind.

Mindfulness of Thoughts Practice:
Bubbles or Thought Watching (all ages)

Short of the oft-uttered, frequently annoyed question "What were you thinking?!" most children, adolescents, and even adults have not been exposed to the possibility of—much less methods for—observing the processes of thinking. Without this metacognitive option, many people act automatically on thoughts that they are not even aware of, often to the detriment of themselves and others. Thus, it can be helpful to introduce children and adolescents to the possibility of observing thoughts, and some simple methods for doing so. Below I have provided two practices to introduce mindfulness of thoughts: one for people of all ages, and one for tweens and up. An audio download of Thought Watching practice suitable for all ages is available at http://www.newharbinger.com/27572. (See the back of the book for more information.)

Bubbles Practice (all ages)

For Bubbles practice, bring a mini container of soap bubbles for each person. These are inexpensive and can be purchased online or at a discount store. For our youngest friends it can be helpful if you open the containers in advance and peel off the foil seal. To begin, encourage the participants to simply blow bubbles and observe what happens. Some bubbles pop, some float and then pop, some clump, some are larger, some are smaller, some are faster, some are slower.

Allow them to observe the bubbles for three or four minutes. Then have them put the wands back in their containers, close the containers, and put them aside. Once bubble blowing has ceased and all the containers are closed, invite the children to consider the following questions.

Are the bubbles like anything else we experience? In our minds?... (As a hint, you can ask the question that follows.) *What do we call the shape that appears above a character's head in the comics?* (If need be, supply the answer.) "A thought bubble."

Can you describe some ways that thoughts and bubbles are similar? (Potential answers include the following.) *We can watch both thoughts and bubbles take shape, some thoughts or bubbles are bigger, some are smaller, some move faster, some move more slowly, some thoughts or bubbles clump with other thoughts or bubbles, and eventually all thoughts and all bubbles pop.*

With practice we can learn to observe our thought bubbles. Can anyone tell me one thought bubble you noticed in the last ten minutes? (Some examples.) "When's lunch?" "I hate homework." "I can't wait for the weekend."

With young children, simply introducing the possibility of observing thoughts without acting on them is enough.

Thought Watching Practice (ages ten through eighteen)

Ask participants to sit in chairs or lie on the floor, and guide them to anchor their attention on the breath. Then invite them to begin to watch their thoughts go by as if they are watching a parade. They may notice that some thoughts are loud and brightly dressed, other thoughts are shy and lurking in the background, and still others come back again and again. After they've been practicing for a minute or two, ask them to notice if they are marching with the parade—in other words, getting lost in their thoughts. Explain that when this happens, they can simply return to the sidewalk, by returning their attention to the breath, and then when their attention is stable, begin again to watch the parade of thoughts going by. A version of this practice is available at http://www.newharbinger.com/27572. (See the back of the book for more information.)

Thought Watching Discussion (ages six through eighteen)

The Bubbles and Thought Watching practices introduce the essential practice of observing both the process and the content of thinking. Expanding on the simple questions offered in Bubbles can support participants ages six and older in realizing that thoughts come and go. Doing the Thought Watching practice with older children opens the door to talking about how some thoughts tend to come back again and again, how thoughts tend to be universal rather than personal, how thoughts are very often inaccurate, and how one thought can lead to a whole gang of thoughts and feelings.

> *Who is willing to share at least one thought that you noticed? Did anyone have repetitive thoughts? Are there patterns to your thinking? Are thoughts permanent? Did anyone notice that sometimes one thought leads to other thoughts or feelings? Can you give me an example?*
>
> (Students might say things like "I need to remember my math book. Oh yeah, and I have reading. Ugh, I have so much homework.")
>
> *How many of you had thoughts similar to the thoughts Rebecca just shared? Isn't it interesting that many of us have very similar thoughts? And isn't it nice to know we aren't alone? Did any of you have thoughts that might be inaccurate or untrue, like "I forgot my library book," when in fact you have your library book? How many of your thoughts were kind? How many were unkind?*

This last query can lead into an exploration of Unkind Mind.

Meeting Unkind Mind (all ages)

Unkind Mind is my shorthand for all negative internal dialogue. It is a subset of thinking that can be incessant. Unkind Mind is judgmental, bossy, and crabby. It says things like "I can't do this," "I'm stupid," "Math is stupid," or "I'm going to fail." This voice also tends to make things seem worse than they are by exaggerating, being dramatic, and distorting reality—saying things like "This is impossible," "Everybody hates me," "I'm ugly," or "I hate everybody." Unkind Mind also often judges other people or circumstances with statements like "He's a jerk," or "Spelling is dumb."

The questions "How many of your thoughts were kind?" and "How many were unkind?" from the Thought Watching discussion above provide an easy segue into the topic of Unkind Mind. When introducing Unkind Mind for the first time, or to younger children, it is enough to give a few short examples such as the ones listed above or pulled from comments the students have made. For older youth, the concept of Unkind Mind can be expanded upon throughout the course.

When working with young people, it's essential to relate the discussions to their interests or concerns. In some cases our young friends are very vocal, and it is easy to explore their thoughts directly. However, sometimes our young friends are quite subtle, and express their unconscious thoughts through silence, eye rolling, or other body language. If you are observant, and listening for what is unsaid, you'll have plenty of opportunities to fine-tune your presentation to participants. The two vignettes below illustrate this process.

"Head in the Game"

Below is an example of a discussion about a Thought Watching practice with a group of fifth graders. One morning, while doing Thought Watching practice in a class where the majority of the boys had been rather skeptical of mindfulness, the boys noticed that many of their thoughts were about the basketball game they'd be playing that afternoon. They had lost the previous game, and now they were up against a team they thought was better than they were. Many of them were worried about losing, playing poorly, and letting their teammates down. They wanted to win.

During our previous sessions, one boy in particular had fairly consistently put effort into being "cool," "funny" (disrespectful), and less than participatory, in the way that some fifth-grade boys can. I asked him, "If you're thinking about winning and losing and the outcome of the game, is your head *really* in the game? Is it really in what's happening right here, right now?" His eyes got big. His mouth hung open. He was "in." Mindfulness was now relevant to him. It helped to be able to tell the class that two of the most successful teams ever in the history of professional basketball, the Los Angeles Lakers and the Chicago Bulls, used mindfulness skills to bring their attention to actually *playing the game*—to the ball, the hoop, their teammates, and their opponents. (Note that by the time you read this, these references will be ancient history for most kids. So you will want to have more contemporary examples: like Kobe Bryant, Tim Lincecum, or the Seattle Seahawks.)

Going Beyond "Why the 'F' ?"

When supporting youth—particularly teens—in exploring their thoughts, it is often helpful to go "waayy" beyond what they might be willing to confess to in order to humanize their thinking, which they may mistakenly believe is unique to them.

Remember my friends in the tenth grade remedial English course? One day as I was guiding them through a Thought Watching practice, two young women chose to chat and file their nails. As I led the practice, I meandered down the aisle and eventually stood by their desks. Continuing to lead the practice, I simply said, "Notice your thoughts. For example, you may be thinking about your homework or your plans for the weekend, or you may be thinking 'Why the "F" is she standing by my desk?'" They stopped talking.

After the practice, the more vocal, previously less engaged young woman asked somewhat incredulously, "Can you read minds?" I said, "No I can't read minds. But I *have* a mind, and my mind is very much like your mind. I've spent a lot of time watching my mind, so I have a pretty good idea of what your mind might say." By going *beyond* what the student was willing to voice, my comments normalized her thinking, increased her curiosity about mindfulness, and increased her willingness to practice.

Nine Dots Exercise and Discussion (ages eight to eighteen)

The "nine dots" exercise is a very useful tool to further investigate habits of thinking; it has many compelling facets. Pass out copies of the Nine Dots Puzzle (located at the end of this chapter), and read—or have a participant read—the directions aloud. As the kids try to solve the puzzle, walk around the room and offer occasional comments. "How do you talk to yourself when you are trying something new and challenging?" "Is your self-talk kind or unkind, helpful or discouraging?" "Are you tempted to quit or cheat, or willing to keep trying?" "Is your choice with this exercise similar to or different from how you deal with other difficulties?"

Be mindful when responding to their queries, such as "Is this right?" I generally stick with repeating the instructions: "The instructions say four straight lines." "You are missing the dot in the middle." Please do your best to avoid saying "No, that's not right." Too many of our young friends hear that message far too often as it is. When they have given it their best shot, you can touch on the points below before showing them the multiple solutions to this puzzle.

Encourage them to consider how much of their internal dialogue was kind: "When we are doing something new or challenging, what does kind self-talk sound like? Give me some examples."

Many students will focus on getting the right answer—the fact that they solved the puzzle correctly, and it was easy; or that they didn't get the right answer. Let them know that the exercise isn't about getting the right answer. This usually gets their attention, because, for the most part, their school days are devoted to doing exactly that. Also, remind them that something that is easy for them may not be easy for someone else, and that something that is easy for someone else may not be easy for them.

Have them brainstorm about various options they could consider when faced with typical difficulties in daily life, such as struggles with schoolwork or a disagreement with a friend. Help them recognize that there are a variety of options, and that there is a time and place for most of the options. Wisdom is remembering we have choices, and then choosing the best option we can come up with at the time: give up, take a break and try again, collaborate, ask for help, look for solutions on the Internet, keep trying....

Discuss that the solution requires "thinking outside the box." Expand on this idea by discussing how our thinking (our Unkind Mind) often puts people, both ourselves and others, and events in boxes, with thoughts like "I am not good at sports," "She is mean," "This class is boring." Perhaps you can pause here and consider a student, client, or child you have put in a box, such as "She is hyperactive," or "He is lazy." And I further challenge you to look for moments during the next week, however brief, when this child behaves in a way that is outside your box.

Overview of Home Practice (all ages)

As usual, close with a review of the home practice. In keeping with the week's focus, the guided audio practice is Thought Watching. Encourage participants to actually do the recorded practice, and to notice Unkind Mind throughout the week.

Home practice also includes the daily life practice of mindful eating. Encourage participants to bring mindful awareness to selecting the food and the amount they choose to eat. They may want to experiment with mindfully eating something they think they really enjoy, and something they think they like less.

Closing Mindful Listening Practice (all ages)

Close by allowing one or two attentive students to ring the bell for a final listening practice.

Practicing at Home—Session 3

Mindfulness is curious.

It asks us to explore our inner and outer worlds.

Listen to (Bubbles or) Thought Watching at least once a day.

Practice mindfulness in daily life.

- *Notice when Unkind Mind shows up. What does it usually say?*

- *Eat something mindfully.*

With kindness and curiosity, and without guilt, fill out the home practice log.

If you have a mindful moment, questions, or difficulties you'd like to share, or if you won't be able to attend the next class, call or e-mail me.

Nine Dots Puzzle

Below is an arrangement of nine dots.

Connect all the dots by drawing four straight lines without lifting your pencil from the paper, and without retracing any line. The lines may cross.

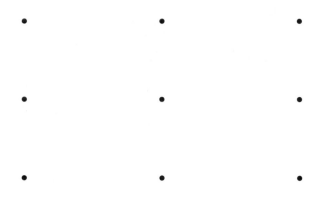

***

The most common solution to the puzzle appears below. This example begins on the top left dot, moves straight down *beyond* the lower left dot, diagonally to the right through the lower middle dot, *beyond* the middle dot on the right aligning to the right of the top dot on the right, back to the top left dot, and diagonally down to the bottom right dot. Expanding the possibilities further, it is useful to note that there are actually four variations of the solution—one beginning in each corner—or more than one "right" answer.

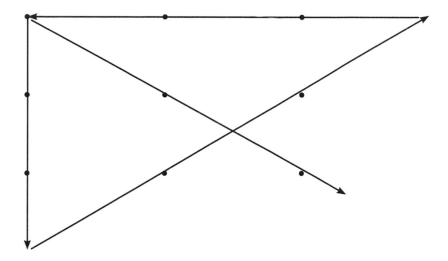

session 4: feelings and unpleasant experiences

Intentions

There are three primary intentions for this session. The first is to review the participants' experiences with Bubbles and Thought Watching. This review leads naturally into the second intention, exploring the thoughts and feelings associated with unpleasant events, and a discussion of how so much of our upset is due to resistance, or wanting things to be different. The equation Suffering = Pain x Resistance offers an engaging way to introduce and play with this concept. The third element of this session is Feelings practice, which develops emotional intelligence—or as I say to our young friends, the ability to "have our feelings without our feelings having us." The session concludes with a brief discussion about being at the halfway point in the course.

Outline: Practices, Exercises, and Discussions

- Mindful Listening practice*

- Mindful Eating practice*

- Home practice review*

- Unpleasant Events exercise and discussion*

- Suffering = Pain x Resistance discussion

- Unkind Mind review and discussion

- Mindful Dance Party*

- Finger Yoga practice* and discussion

- Mindfulness of Feelings practice*

- Feelings drawings and haikus exercise and discussion*

- Read-aloud option: *My Many Colored Days*, Dr. Seuss*

- Halfway point discussion

- Overview of home practice*

- Closing Mindful Listening practice*

Mindful Listening and Mindful Eating Practice (all ages)

Again, begin with mindful listening and eating. Although the snack I bring often depends on what is easily available, sometimes I intentionally choose to bring a different snack or to bring the same snack again. For example, after the mealy oranges mentioned in chapter 4, I intentionally brought oranges again the following week to demonstrate the concept of impermanence, the reality that things change. Fortunately, the second batch of oranges was delicious.

As the students become more familiar with these practices, it is important that you continue to encourage them to pay attention to *this* sound, *this* apple, *this* bite, and *this* experience. Often a simple, brief aside is best. Occasionally, however, you may want to explicitly mention this idea:

As human beings, when we think we are familiar with something—mindful eating, mindful listening, our walk to school, what our best friends or parents are going to say—we sometimes tune out. And then we miss what is actually going on—this apple, this sound, the experience of walking, what our friends or parents are actually saying, our life…

Home Practice Review (all ages)

Following Mindful Eating practice, explore participants' experiences with the home practices of Bubbles or Thought Watching and noticing Unkind Mind. The level of discussion will depend on the age of the individual or group. With younger children you may want to use just the first few prompts below. With older children, while all of the prompts are worthy of exploration, remember that you can return to these themes later, and do not need to offer all the prompts in one go. As always, you will want to tailor the prompts and any clarifying comments to facilitate *this* individual's, *this* group's emerging understanding.

- *What thoughts did you notice?*

- *Could you notice thoughts as they come and go?*

- *Were your thoughts kind?*

- *Do you know that many children (teens) have similar thoughts, wishes, fears?*

- *Were there any patterns in your thinking?*

- *Were your thoughts true?*

- *Did you believe your thoughts?*

- *Did you take your thoughts personally?*

- *Could you notice if and how your thoughts, feelings, and physical sensations were related?*

Even though the class sessions have provided an opportunity to discuss Mindful Eating, it can be fun and instructive to hear about if and how the participants practiced Mindful Eating at home. You may tie the eating and Thought Watching practices together by asking, "Were you aware of any thoughts when you were eating mindfully?"

Unpleasant Events Exercise and Discussion (ages six to eighteen)

To transition to the Unpleasant Events exercise, you might build on a participant's comment during informal chatter at the beginning of class, eating practice, or the home practice review. As with the Pleasant Events exercise in session 2, this exercise is most appropriate for children ages eight to eighteen, and you may wish to omit it with younger children. If you choose to offer it to children ages four to seven, make it brief, simple, and fun. Simply invite them to draw a picture of an unpleasant event from the past few days. Then, support them in a brief spoken reflection about what they remember about what happened in their minds (thoughts), hearts (feelings), and bodies (physical sensations) during the event. Better yet, sing a song with them; a wonderful choice is "I Am Breathing" from *Calm Down Boogie*, by my dear friend and colleague Betsy Rose. This CD is available through iTunes and Amazon.

With older participants, you can guide them in recalling an unpleasant event and completing the cartoon that's available online at http://www.newharbinger.com /27572. Pass out copies of the cartoon and guide them through the following process.

> *Take several slow, deep breaths and allow yourself to settle into stillness and quietness. When you are ready, bring to mind an unpleasant event from the past week. Maybe as I said this, an event immediately came to mind; maybe not. Some common unpleasant events for kids your age are having a difficult time with homework, having a disagreement with a friend or family member, losing your backpack with all your stuff, failing a test, or missing the winning shot in the basketball game. Some of you may have bigger (more intense) unpleasant events. For this exercise you may use the event you remembered or, if you want, choose a smaller (less intense) event.*
>
> *After you have chosen an unpleasant event, take a moment to remember the thoughts you had during the event.... See how many specific thoughts you can remember.... When you are ready, remember the feelings you had during the event.... Maybe there is one feeling; maybe there are many feelings.... Now, see if you can remember what was happening in your body during the event... How was your posture?... What was your facial expression?... How did your body feel inside?...*
>
> *In your own time, open your eyes, and begin to add the thoughts, feelings, and body sensations to the cartoon. If you want, you can draw your thoughts, feelings and body sensations.*

While participants are completing the cartoon, walk around the room and offer a comment or a gentle hand on a shoulder to students who might benefit from such support.

After participants have completed their cartoons, encourage them to share their unpleasant events and the associated thoughts, feelings, and physical sensations. As with any of the discussions presented in the book, the subsequent conversation can begin in pairs, in small groups, or with the entire group. If you are working with an individual, the exchange can be a simple shared conversation. Below is an example of such a conversation with a fourth grade girl in an afterschool course.

Me:	Yes, Angela. What was your unpleasant event?
Angela:	I wanted to go play with my friend, and my mom made me clean my room first.
Me:	Yes, not being able to do what you want to do when you want do it can be unpleasant. What were your thoughts?
Angela:	I hate my mom. My mom is mean. She *never* lets me do what I want to do. She is *so* unfair.
Me:	Excellent mindfulness; you noticed a lot of thoughts. And how about feelings?
Angela:	I felt mad and sad.
Me:	Anything else?
Angela:	Yeah. Actually, I was mad at myself, too, because my mom had told me to clean my room before, and I forgot.
Me:	Again, very mindful. Sometimes it is much easier to be mad at someone else than to be responsible for our choices. And what was happening in your body when all these thoughts and feelings were swirling around?
Angela:	Um… My arms and hands were kind of tight, and my face was a little squinched and grumpy.
Me:	Thank you, Angela, for your brave sharing. Anyone else want to share an unpleasant event?

After people share, you may note that there is the event, the bare experience (the having to clean your room, the long car drive, the difficult math problem, the argument, and so on); and then there are the thoughts and feelings we add to the experience: "I hate this drive," "I can't do this problem; I'm stupid," "She never listens to me," or even "This crazy teacher doesn't know what she is talking about" (smile). The discussion below offers a playful way to further explore the distinction between bare experience and what we add.

Suffering = Pain x Resistance Discussion (ages eight to eighteen)

As alluded to above, often much of the upset of an unpleasant experience has to do with the thinking and feeling we add to the event. Much of that thinking and feeling has to do with the past or more often the future. "My mom won't let me play with my friend today" becomes "My mom *never* lets me play with my friends." "I am bored now" expands into "I am going to be bored *forever*." And "I can't get this problem" turns into "I'm stupid, and I won't get *any* of the problems, *ever*." A great deal of the upsetting thinking and feeling is resistance to how things are—which, in its simplest terms, is wanting things to be different.

My friend and colleague, Gina Biegel (2009), who has done rigorous scientific research documenting the benefits of teaching mindfulness to teens, shares the following mathematical equation from Shinzen Young.

Suffering = Pain x Resistance

A child friendly translation is

Upset = Unpleasantness x Wanting Things to be Different

For this discussion suffering can be translated as upset, pain as unpleasantness, and resistance as wanting things to be different. Almost all youth old enough to multiply (age eight and older) can relate to this equation. If the children are struggling with multiplication, and finding it unpleasant (smile), you can use this as a real time example, or you can use addition to convey the same idea.

The equation allows the students to understand in a very concrete way how resistance (wanting things to be different) frequently increases suffering (or upset). Using a scale of 1 to 10, where 10 is maximum pain, invite participants to give estimates of the pain or unpleasantness of a particular event. Again using a 1 to 10 scale, have them estimate their resistance to the event—how much they wanted things to be different. Then have them calculate their level of suffering or upset. I often do this on a whiteboard, and work through two or three examples offered by the participants. I often interchange and combine the words in the above equations, saying, "In the situation you just described, how painful or unpleasant was the event, on a scale of 1 to 10?"

Explain that often, but not always, the level of pain or unpleasantness is fixed and cannot be changed, and that the part of the equation we can adjust is how much we want things to be different. For example, not making the soccer team might be a 6 in pain or unpleasantness. Resisting the outcome with thoughts like "The selection process was unfair" might be a 6 in resistance. In this scenario, the suffering is 36.

Ask if anyone can offer an example of a way of thinking that might cause less suffering. "I'll train and try again next year" might represent a resistance score of 2, decreasing the suffering score to 12.

Because it is so common, below is an actual example regarding homework unpleasantness.

Me:	Yes, Tommy, what was your unpleasant experience?
Tommy:	Doing my math homework.
Group:	*(Groan.)* Yeah, me too.
Facilitator:	And on a scale of 1 to 10, how unpleasant was it?
Tommy:	11.
Group:	Yeah, at least 11.
Me:	Okay, it may be an 11, and I'll take your word for it. And I am a going to invite you to consider if it is really an 11. For me an 11 would be my child getting in a serious accident, or my house burning down, or someone I love dying.
Tommy:	Okay, probably not an 11. Maybe a 7.
Me:	Okay, 7. Now, what were your thoughts about your homework and your ability to do it?
Tommy:	I hate this stupid homework.
Group:	Yeah!
Tommy:	And I can't do it. I'm stupid. I give up.
Me:	And what were your feelings?
Tommy:	Mad, stupid, hopeless.
Me:	Thank you for being so honest and mindful about your feelings. And what was happening in your body?
Tommy:	I had a headache, and I felt stressed.
Me:	And how does stress feel in your body?
Tommy:	Like tightness.

Me:	And taken all together—your thoughts, your feelings, your head-ache—on a scale of 1 to 10, how much resistance or upset did you have?
Tommy:	8.
Me:	So what was your suffering score?
Tommy:	7 times 8, that's … 56?
Me:	Now, assuming that you can't change your homework and make it magically disappear or do itself, how might you decrease your suffering?
Tommy:	By decreasing my upset?
Me:	And how might you do that?
Tommy:	By not calling it stupid, and looking back at my notes?
Me:	That sounds like a great start! When you say that, how does it feel in your body?
Tommy:	Less tight, better, relaxed.
Me:	So how about if all of you who had homework as an unpleasant event experiment with decreasing your upset (resistance) this week, and report back.

I have found that, for many kids, this equation is a doorway into the relationship between pain (circumstances and life events) and suffering (what we add to those experiences). Again, it is crucial to recognize that many participants are working with profoundly painful situations—illness, financial hardship, incarceration, or death in the family. In these cases, to honor their experiences you may increase the pain scale. "That is really tough. For me, having my brother go to jail would be a 20. Let's just take a moment in stillness and quietness and acknowledge that pain…."

Additionally, it is important not to imply that wanting things to be different is bad or wrong. Rather, simply help participants realize that wanting things to be different than they actually are often increases suffering or upset. It is also important to be clear that acknowledging things the way they are doesn't necessarily mean giving up or not doing anything to change the situation. In fact, often, acknowledging things as they are allows us to make a "good" (wise) choice about what to do next—clean up the room so I can go play; talk to the soccer coach to get feedback; go over my math notes.

Unkind Mind Review and Discussion (ages eight to eighteen)

This discussion of the thoughts associated with unpleasant experiences can transition into a brief review of Unkind Mind. Often the thoughts associated with unpleasant experiences are untrue, and projected into the future: "This will go on forever;" "I am a loser;" "No one will ever play with me at recess." We suffer because we believe the thoughts and take them personally. A sixth grader named Rachel described Unkind Mind as "gossip inside my head."

Interestingly, once tweens and teens discover that they do not need to believe all of their thoughts, they can play with the possibility that perhaps they do not need to believe the judgmental and unkind (sometimes incredibly cruel) thoughts of their peers, coaches, teachers, and parents, as well as the incessant media stream that tells them who they should be, how they should look and behave, and what they should wear and buy. With teens, you can use the following questions to explore this topic in more depth.

- *Who do you think you should be?*

- *Who do your parents think you should be?*

- *Who do your friends think you should be?*

- *Who do your teachers think you should be?*

- *Who does the culture or media tell you you should be?*

- *How do all of these "shoulds" compare with who you are?*

- *Can you occasionally remember that all these "shoulds" are just thinking, and that you don't need to believe them or take them personally?*

Together, the topics of Unkind Mind and unpleasant events support participants in learning to observe their patterns of thinking and feeling, and beginning to understand how these patterns affect their experience.

Mindful Dance Party (all ages)

If the group is becoming restless you may have a two- to five-minute mindful dance party. It is helpful to have some simple rhythmic music stored on your phone.

It seems that many of you are feeling wiggly (restless). Who is feeling wiggly (restless)? Thank you for being mindful and answering honestly. Let's stand up. Please find a space where you can move your body safely without bumping something or someone. If you are willing, please close your eyes. If not, please focus your eyes on the floor. In a moment you will hear some sounds. Let your body move to the sounds. (Turn on the music.) *See if you can notice your thoughts and feelings as you listen and move. As you move, notice whether you like the music or hate it. Notice whether you feel embarrassed, cool, or in between. Tune in to whether you enjoy or resist moving. Listening, moving, breathing, noticing. As the sound fades, allow your body to become still.... Rest in the stillness.... Notice how your body, mind, and heart feel now.... When you're ready, quietly sit down* (return to your seat).

Finger Yoga Practice and Discussion (all ages)

Once the group is seated you can move seamlessly into finger yoga. Have students place their left hand on their left thigh. Ask them to gently use their right hand to pull the fourth finger on their left hand backward. Have them notice their limit—the place where they need to stop pulling to avoid causing pain or injury.

If time allows, you can add some additional simple stretches or yoga postures. For example, have them stand and stretch both arms up overhead and then lean from the waist in an arc to the left, feeling the sensations of the stretch.... Then have them repeat the stretch, leaning to the right.... Another example would be clasping their hands together behind their backs and gently raising their arms up behind them as high as they can while keeping their chests up, feeling the sensations in their chests, shoulders, and arms.

You may also briefly expand the idea of stretching toward their limits and introduce the possibility of stretching toward limits not just physically, but also mentally and emotionally:

You can play with stretching a bit beyond what is comfortable (your comfort zone), not just with your physical body, but also with your mind and your heart. For example, if you have a challenging school assignment or an emotional upset, you can experiment with stretching and relaxing into your frustration or sadness. Maybe you can just be with your frustration or sadness for three breaths? Like with physical stretching, it is important to know when to stop stretching, to release, to ask for help. We may discuss this more later. For now, it may be helpful to know that with kindness and curiosity we can carefully stretch into things that are a bit uncomfortable. Just like when we stretch our bodies, when we stretch our minds and hearts, they become stronger, more flexible, and more balanced.

This topic will be covered again, in greater depth, in the next session. One way of stretching into uncomfortable feelings is Feelings practice.

Mindfulness of Feelings Practice (all ages)

Feelings practice is intended to cultivate emotional intelligence, and involves becoming more completely aware of the current feeling state, or emotion. A sample Feelings practice suitable for all ages is available at http://www.newharbinger.com/27572. (See the back of the book for more information.) Invite the participants to sit or lie in a comfortable position, find their breath in their bellies, rest in the stillness and quietness, and then simply note the feeling or feelings that are present. Encourage them to acknowledge that some feelings may have ordinary names—like angry, happy, sad, or excited—and others may have more unusual names—like stormy, bubbly, fiery, or empty. (One boy playfully named a particular feeling Herb.) It is helpful to tell them that there may be layers of feelings or that the feelings may be small (subtle) and kind of shy, or big and powerful (intense).

After noting the feelings, suggest that they notice where the feelings "live" in their bodies: sitting in the chest, stirring in the belly, resting in the big toe. Then encourage them to notice the felt sense of the feeling, *how* the feeling *feels* in the body. Is the feeling small or big, heavy or light, soft or hard, warm or cool, wiggly or still? Be sure to offer the descriptors in a way that does not imply one state is preferred over another.

Let students know that if any instruction shifts them into thinking about rather than *experiencing* the feeling, they may simply breathe and return to being with the feelings. (This instruction is often more important when teaching to adults, because we tend to bounce into thinking about rather than *experiencing* our feelings.)

In time, prompt students to notice whether, or imagine that, the feeling has a color, or colors—perhaps dark red, pale blue, or bright green—and to listen to discover whether the feeling has a sound, such as giggling, groaning, or whining…. Then suggest that they ask the feeling what it wants from them, noting that usually feelings want something simple, like attention, time, or space. Finally, ask them if they are willing and able to give the feeling what it asked for. Close with briefly resting again in the stillness and quietness.

Feelings Drawings and Haikus:
Exercise and Discussion (all ages)

After the practice, invite the participants to draw their feeling or to write a haiku about their feeling. True haikus are poems with seventeen syllables in three lines as follows: five syllables in the first line, seven syllables in the next line, and five syllables in the last line. However, unless I'm working with an English class, I often use the following simpler instructions: "Write what can be said in one breath." Here is a sweet example of a one-breath Feelings haiku, from a fourth grader named Stephen: "Excited, golden, ticklish."

After the participants have completed their haikus or drawings, invite them to share what they noticed about their feelings. Ensure that what you say, your tone of voice, and your body language convey acceptance of their experience *exactly as it is*. If they have no feeling, or multiple feelings, that's fine. If the feelings don't have a color or a sound, that's fine, too. If they are angry or heartbroken, that is part of being alive. In general, this process allows kids and teens to really *feel* their feelings. Unlike many adults, our young friends rarely struggle with the guidance or overthink the practice. For example, young children and even teens will very matter-of-factly report that the feeling was sadness; it was dark purple, and it groaned and needed space.

Shy Yoga Discussion

While participants always have the right to pass in any discussion, including this exploration of feelings, any nervousness about sharing is simply another opportunity for Feelings practice. As alluded to above, engaging in Feelings practice can be tied to stretching in physical yoga. For example, with children who tend to be shy, suggest that they *stretch* toward speaking up and sharing their experience, while simultaneously honoring their limits. Remind them that, as with physical stretching, their ability to be friendly with (befriend) their feelings and to share their feelings changes from day to day and from moment to moment. Explain that they are learning to be with feelings without ignoring or hiding (suppressing) them or magnifying (indulging) them.

Earlier in the book I mentioned Evan, a shy boy who sat with his back to the room for the first three sessions. After Feelings practice, I asked him if he was willing to do "talk yoga" and gently stretch to share his experience. He agreed and then answered three simple questions. This was a small miracle for him!

Me:	What are you feeling now?
Evan:	Nervous?
Me:	How does nervous feel in your body?
Evan:	Jittery.
Me:	Does your jittery nervousness have a color?
Evan:	Orange.
Me.	Thank you for being so brave and stretching to share your feeling!

Dialogue with Emotions

Occasionally the feeling will want something a child is unwilling, or unable, to give. Or the feeling may want something that it would be unwise for the child to give. In such instances it may be helpful to facilitate a dialogue with the feeling. If you are working with a group, this individual facilitation can be done in front of and with the support of the group or, if wisdom suggests, privately after the session. Sometimes anger will want a child to "punch John's face in," or sadness will want a teen to cut herself; or, as in the example below, fear will want to be in charge.

My daughter, Nicole, has kindly given me permission to share her dialogue with fear as an example of such a discussion. To set the stage, it was the evening before her fourth-grade talent show. The afternoon rehearsal had not gone well; she had "messed up." She felt afraid that she would mess up again, in the actual talent show, in front of the *whole* school. During the Feelings practice, when Nicole asked the fear what it wanted from her, fear said it wanted to be in charge.

As an aside, I noticed my initial thought was, "Wait, it can't want that; that is not how the practice goes. A feeling is supposed to want time, space, and attention." However, I took fear at its word and asked Nicole, "How do you feel about that?" She said, "I don't want it to be in charge." I said, "Okay, so tell it that." She told it, and it said, "Well, I still want to be in charge." A few moments later, Nicole told her fear, "You can come, but you can't be in charge." Fear agreed to this compromise. Nicole chose to symbolize the agreement by putting a little Guatemalan worry doll that my mother had given her in the pocket of her dress. So fear got to go, and joy was in charge.

Befriending Overwhelming Emotions

Here it can be helpful to note:

Each of us, children and adults, tends to have (habitual) ways of interacting with our feelings. Without mindfulness (inquiry and insight), most of us tend to live within a fairly narrow range [use hand gestures] *along the continuum of ignoring (suppressing) feelings and being controlled (overwhelmed) by them. Take a moment and consider what you tend to do with big (intense) feelings.*

For those of us who usually ignore (suppress) our feelings, the Feelings practice we just did can support us in bringing kindness and curiosity to our emotions (becoming more emotionally fluent). For those of us who tend to be controlled (overwhelmed) by our feelings, it may be helpful for us to take some time to really settle into the Still Quiet Place before we do Feelings practice. With practice we can "have our feelings without our feelings having us." "Having our feelings without our feeling having us" means being aware of our feelings, without our feelings controlling our behavior. As we all know, when feelings control our behavior, we often do things we may not feel good about, or regret later.

Emotions Beneath Boredom

If a child repeatedly reports that he is bored, invite him to look underneath the boredom; often he will discover sadness, anger, or fear. For example, Lee, a boy in one of the first groups in the Stanford child-parent pairs study, repeatedly reported that he was bored. Because this course was part of a research protocol, the children and parents filled out reams of paperwork. But the paperwork went to the research team. In the first class, I let the participants know that I was not privy to any of the information they shared in the assessments, and that if they had any circumstances they wanted me to be aware of, they should let me know directly. Since Lee had mentioned a couple of times that he was bored, I chose to check in with him (and his mom) after class. To make a long story short, it turned out that Lee's mother had opted not to disclose that Lee's father had recently had an affair and abruptly moved out of the country. Obviously, this new information gave me a fresh view of Lee's circumstances, and prompted me to suggest that Lee look underneath his boredom to see if perhaps there were other feelings present. Not surprisingly, Lee discovered anger, sadness, and confusion. Over time, with continued Feelings practice, Lee was able to acknowledge and express his complex, multilayered feelings regarding his father's betrayal and departure.

When working with participants' feelings, be discerning and consider what you are truly capable of handling. Depending on your skill set, such disclosures may warrant connecting the child with additional support. This process involves supporting the child mentally and emotionally during the time when he is establishing a connection with another skilled professional. Your ability to support an individual in this way depends on both your practice and your ability to observe your own thoughts, feelings, judgment, and concern and respond, rather than react. If you are not trained as a therapist, you may judge and panic; if you are trained as a therapist, you may retreat into "professional" mode. Do your best to *be with* the individual and his experience and *respond* with care and wisdom.

Halfway Point Discussion (all ages)

Remind participants that this class marks the halfway point in the course, and briefly review the primary themes of the course. Ask for volunteers to share briefly what they remember about various key topics covered in sessions up to this point: the group agreements, the Still Quiet Place, the definition of mindfulness, awareness of breath, pleasant events, thoughts, the "nine dots" exercise, Unkind Mind, unpleasant events, Suffering = Pain x Resistance, and feelings.

Within this context you can inquire again about how the home practice is going, and whether anyone is having difficulty finding time to practice or with the practices themselves. Again, invite participants who have found a rhythm with the practice to share what has worked for them. Remind them that in our culture it is unusual to slow down and turn our attention inward, and that they are learning a very special way of being that most people never learn. Support them in creating a specific time for their practice, and encourage those who have not been doing the home practices to simply begin again in this new moment.

It is also helpful to revisit the mindful activities the children have done at home over the past three weeks, exploring what they noticed when they brushed their teeth, put on their shoes, or ate mindfully. Again, if they have forgotten this aspect of the home practice, they can simply *begin again* this week.

An important aspect of mindfulness is noticing when we have wandered, coming back, and beginning again:

Noticing we have wandered from the breath, coming back, and beginning again to pay attention to the breath.

Noticing when we have been carried away by our thoughts and feelings, coming back, and beginning again to pay attention to the here and now.

Noticing that we have stopped practicing at home, coming back, and beginning again to practice.

After this it is time to review the home practice, and close with the listening practice.

Overview of Home Practice (all ages)

To close, review the home practice. In keeping with this week's focus on mindfulness of feelings, the guided audio practice changes to Feelings. Encourage participants to actually do the recorded practice, and to create at least two artistic expressions of their feeling—two drawings, two haikus, or one drawing and one haiku—and bring them to the next class.

Invite them to notice how wanting things to be different increases suffering, or upset, throughout the next week.

Home practice for this session includes the daily life practice of mindful bathing or showering. This practice is described in chapter 3.

Closing Mindful Listening Practice (all ages)

Close by allowing one or two attentive students to ring the bell for a final listening practice.

***

At the halfway point it is also a good time to check in with your own practice.

- *How is your practice?*

- *Are you practicing? Formally? During the process of teaching?*

- *Are you mindful of your pleasant events?*

- *Are you mindful of your thoughts, particularly putting yourself and others in boxes? Unkind Mind? Resistance?*

- *Are you bringing kindness and curiosity to your Feelings?*

- *If your practice has waned, are you willing to begin again in this moment?*

Practicing at Home—Session 4

Mindfulness is kind.

It encourages us to treat ourselves and others with kindness and compassion.

Listen to the guided Feelings practice every day.

Create at least two haikus, poems, or pictures showing the feelings you had during Feelings practice, and bring them to class next week.

Practice mindfulness in daily life.

- *Observe how wanting things to be different increases upset.*

- *Shower mindfully.*

With kindness and curiosity, and without guilt, fill out the home practice log.

If you have a mindful moment, questions, or difficulties you'd like to share, or if you won't be able to attend the next class, call or e-mail me.

8

session 5: responding and reacting: holes and different streets

Intentions

The intentions of this session are to review and expand upon the Feelings practice (incorporating emotion theory and improv if time allows) and the real-life experiences of unpleasant events and Suffering = Pain x Resistance. Gentle stretching or yoga is used to explore the themes of self-care, balance (physical, mental, and emotional), and stretching toward one's limits. The poem "Autobiography in Five Short Chapters," by Portia Nelson, provides an analogy for responding versus reacting. Most of our young friends connect with this analogy immediately, and find it very useful.

Outline: Practices, Exercises, and Discussions

- Mindful Listening practice*

- Mindful Eating practice*

- Brief Go-Round exercise*

- Home practice review*

- Emotion theory discussion

- Emotion Improv exercise*

- Suffering = Pain x Resistance review and discussion

- Yoga practice*

- Holes and Different Streets discussion

- Read-aloud option: *Alexander and the Terrible, Horrible, No Good, Very Bad Day*, Judith Viorst*

- Breath-based practice (time permitting)*

- Overview of home practice*

- Closing Mindful Listening practice*

Mindful Listening and Mindful Eating Practice (all ages)

Again, begin with Mindful Listening. Then transition to Mindful Eating, preferably in silence. It is enough to simply say, "Okay, we're going to eat the first three bites of this snack in mindful silence. Before you begin, please take a moment to look at this pear and notice its weight… temperature… shape… color… texture… smell…. And when you're ready, take three slow mindful bites, putting all your attention in your mouth with chewing and tasting. Please don't rush; take time for tasting."

Brief Go-Round Exercise (all ages)

After the last mindful bite, and before the participants open their eyes, suggest that they note how they are feeling in the moment: tired, relaxed, nervous, happy, angry, energetic.... After they have opened their eyes and expanded their attention to include the room, go around the circle and, one by one, have participants say a word or phrase that captures how they are feeling. This is a quick and simple way of reinforcing mindfulness of emotions and body sensations, bringing everyone into the moment, and getting a sense of how each person is doing. There is no need to comment. Simply allow each individual to share her word or phrase.

After briefly resting in stillness, it can be instructive to go around again. If, as is often the case, one or more participants' feelings have changed during this brief interval, you can simply draw attention to this: "Interesting. Before, you were grumpy, and now you are peaceful. Especially when feelings are intense, it can be helpful to remember that feelings aren't permanent, and that they change."

Home Practice Review (all ages)

Invite participants to share their artistic representations of the feelings that they experienced during the week. If anyone forgot his art or poetry, he can simply share a feeling he noticed during the day. As they share, respond mindfully, perhaps commenting on an individual or a group theme, or simply nodding in acknowledgment; attentive silence can be a powerful response.

Also look for opportunities to underscore various principles of mindfulness. For example, you can highlight impermanence with questions or comments along these lines: "Do you still feel that way?" "If you look back, can you guess how long that feeling lasted?" "Like the breath and thoughts, feelings come and go." Likewise, you can address acceptance with questions such as "Were you able to bring kindness and curiosity to your feeling?", and "Did you ignore (suppress) or act out (indulge) your feeling?" "Were you able, even for a moment, to have your feeling and be aware of it, without the feeling having you and being in charge of your behavior?"

Emotion Theory Discussion (ages eight to eighteen)

If time allows, it can be helpful to include some basic emotion theory. The brief introduction to emotion theory offered below is adapted from the Mindfulness-Based Emotional Balance (MBEB) course mentioned previously. The emotion theory

103

portion is largely based on the work of Paul Ekman, PhD (2003). Since being trained to offer the MBEB curriculum, I have shared a *simplified* version of basic emotion theory with individual patients and groups. The primary concepts of emotion theory are listed below, along with some questions to prompt discussion and key information to cover in the discussion. The wording in these examples is oriented toward children ages eight to ten. To modify the language for older participants, ages eleven through eighteen, use the phrases in parentheses.

Emotions are part of life for all mammals.

> *Can you name some mammals?*
>
> *What do mammals have in common?*
>
> *Mammals feed their young by nursing; they tend to live in groups; and they are social creatures.*

The scientists who study emotions have found seven universal emotions that everyone shares.

> *Can you guess what some of the primary emotions are?*
>
> *The primary emotions are happiness, fear, anger, sadness, surprise, contempt, and disgust.* [Most young people can come up with at least the first four.]
>
> *Emotions help us survive (serve an evolutionary purpose) by helping us detect threats, deal with challenges, and connect with loved ones.*

For the emotions we named, which ones help us detect threats, deal with challenges, and connect with loved ones?

> *Happiness helps us connect with our loved ones.*
>
> *Fear helps us survive by avoiding danger.*
>
> *Anger helps us survive by overcoming obstacles.*
>
> *Sadness lets our loved ones know we are upset, so they can comfort us.*

Each of the primary emotions also has a very specific facial expression and body response.

> *Can you show me a surprised face?* [It may be helpful to demonstrate the face you mean: eyes wide open, eyebrows raised, jaw dropped open.]
>
> *Pull the corners of your mouth up toward your ears (smile). How do you feel? What do you notice in your body?*

Pull the corners of your mouth down toward your shoulders. How do you feel? What do you notice in your body?

These are small (incomplete) examples of the whole (specific) facial expressions of surprise, happiness, and sadness. Often, just doing even one part of the face (facial expression) of an emotion can have us begin to feel the emotion.

When emotions are not made smaller (suppressed) or bigger (magnified) they have a natural timing or rhythm.

From your experience, how might you describe, or graph, an emotion over time? [The typical graph is a simple wave or bell curve, which you can draw on a whiteboard or clipboard.]

In your daily life, can you notice when an emotion begins, when it peaks, and when it ends?

In your experience, what happens at the top (peak) of an emotion?

At the peak of an emotion is something called the "refractory period." During the refractory period we are taken over by the emotion and can't think clearly.

Can you describe a time when you were in the refractory period?

Refractory Period

When we are in the refractory period we are controlled by our lizard (reptilian) brain and subject to the fight-flight-or-freeze response. This means that, like lizards, we want to either fight, run away, or freeze. When the refractory period has passed we have access to our whole wonderful human brain (and heart), including the parts that can look at the big picture, consider what we feel and want, consider what other people feel and want (different perspectives), be creative, solve problems, and so on.

Mindfulness can help us notice the beginning of an emotion, the refractory period, and the end of the emotion.

Is this progression like anything else we have been mindful of (the breath, thoughts, sound)?

When we are aware that we are in the grips of an emotion we can make choices, at least some of the time (smile).

Sometimes the best we can do is choose to, as my son says with a smile, "shut up and sit there." This is a skill he used often with a very difficult carpool companion. [Later, this skill can be tied to the example of taking a different street to avoid one with a large hole.]

After learning about emotion theory, Alex, a ten-year-old boy I worked with individually, described watching the progression of his anger as like watching a lit bomb fuse, which he could *sometimes* put out with the water of mindfulness. Justin, another ten-year-old boy I worked with individually, said when he began to feel angry it was like waiting in line for an explosive ride at a local amusement park. Additionally, he noted that if he was aware, he could get out of line and not go on the ride (usually a big fight with his mom).

An analogy I like to use is watching waves:

Often, strong emotions can take us by surprise, like a tsunami. Mindfulness can be used as an early warning system. If we are paying attention, we can see the first ripples of an emotion, and then watch the emotional waves get bigger and more powerful. Once we see the waves building, we can choose to step back, and move to higher ground so the waves don't come crashing down on us.

To expand on this theme you can draw the following patterns on a whiteboard and explain:

In real life it is often a bit more complicated, because usually our waves are not separate (isolated). Usually, our waves are combining with other people's waves. When two big waves peak at the same time, it creates an extremely large, powerful wave. When a big wave and a small wave, or calm water, combine, it makes the big wave smaller (minimizes or neutralizes the large wave), creating smoother waters. Sometimes—like in a family, a classroom, or a group of friends—there are many different waves.

With teens (as well as with parents and teachers), you can tie this explanation to basic wave theory in physics:

In physics, when two waves combine to create a bigger wave, this is called constructive interference. When a wave combines with a dip or trough, they cancel each other out, and this is called destructive interference. Sometimes things are not so simple, and this is called mixed interference. To further complicate things, a person may have more than one emotion, and there may be multiple people involved. Consider this the next time you have a significant fight or disagreement.

The illustrations below offer visual images for these wave combinations, with each line representing the emotions of one person. These analogies can be particularly useful when discussing challenging moments with friends and family.

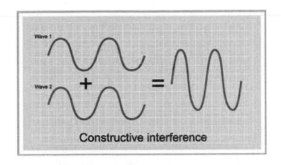

Constructive interference

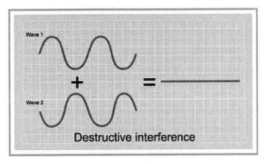

Destructive interference

Mixed interference

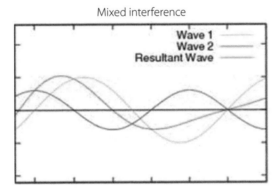

Emotion Improv Exercise (all ages)

In one of my online courses, my friend and course participant Curtis Cramblett shared a wonderful emotion improv exercise that brings emotion theory to life. The basics of the exercise are as follows: A rectangular space is defined. Visual cues are used to designate 25 percent, 50 percent, 75 percent, and 100 percent of the distance from one end of the rectangle to the other. Participants are instructed to move forward, demonstrating an emotion at a given percentage.

Because it is very common and frequently problematic, I usually begin with anger. (For younger children, you can use the language of a small, a medium, and a large amount of anger.)

> *Now we are going to play with expressing different feelings (emotions) with our bodies and faces. Please stand up. We will use the rectangle from the whiteboard to the window; the front end of the bookcase is a small (25 percent), and the back end of the bookcase is a medium (50 percent), and the trash can is a large (75 percent) amount of a feeling (emotion). Take a moment to rest in stillness, and then in silence, please step forward to the back end of the bookcase and show a small amount (25 percent) of anger with your body and your face. Feel what this feels like in your body, mind, and heart.... Now step forward, in line with the back end of the bookcase, and show a medium amount (50 percent) of anger. Feel what this feels like in your body, mind, and heart....*

You can comment on what you observe and ask questions about what participants notice in their bodies, faces, minds, and hearts. Here are some examples:

- *I see lots of tight jaws, and clenched fists.*

- *What happens to your thoughts when you show (embody) anger?*

- *What is happening in your chest?*

- *Do you know (recognize) this feeling? Is this feeling familiar?*

- *Do you feel like this a lot (often)?*

- *Do you feel awkward or uncomfortable being angry?*

Because this is a powerful exercise, it is often wise to limit the emotional expressions to 75 percent of maximum. Conversely, it is unlikely that participants will be able to express 100 percent of an emotion during this exercise.

> *"Now step it back to 5 percent—just a smidge of anger. Is there a benefit to knowing what your body feels like when you are just a little bit angry?... Could this have anything to do with the refractory period?... Exactly! This is like the early warning system we talked about before. Sometimes, when you know you are just starting to get angry, you can make better choices than when you are really angry, and in the refractory period.*
>
> *"Now let's stand in stillness and quietness, and see what happens to the feeling (emotion). Does it grow (intensify)? Disappear (Fade)? Change?"*

If time allows, you may repeat the exercise with other emotions: sadness, fear, jealousy, excitement. Just as I usually begin with anger, I usually end with joy.

Unpleasant Events Discussion (ages eight to eighteen)

Invite participants, particularly those who haven't spoken much in past sessions, to report on the unpleasant events they experienced over the past week. Encourage them to discover that both pleasantness and unpleasantness are temporary and impermanent. Entice them to consider how much of their upset is due to believing the current unpleasantness will last forever (projecting it into the future), and to wanting "things," themselves, others, or the situation to be different than they are (resistance).

Yoga Practice (all ages)

When the discussion of unpleasant events, suffering, pain, and resistance has run its course, you can move into some gentle yoga. This yoga isn't about "doing" any particular posture, or sequence of postures. It's about supporting participants in being fully present in their bodies. As with the other practices, if you don't have an established personal yoga practice, out of respect for the practice and the young people you are serving, please develop a solid personal practice before you share this discipline. Lack of skill in this domain can lead to physical injury.

Below are some basic instructions for a few simple postures. Please note that within even these most basic instructions are comments intended to ensure the safety of the participants, such as the one about the placement of the foot on the calf or thigh (not the knee!) in tree pose. In addition to guiding specific postures, please offer comments and encouragement such as those included below. As with the other practices, it is recommended that you do the postures as you lead them, looking up frequently to see that your guidance is clear enough for the participants to understand the basic form of the intended posture.

> You know how to find the Still Quiet Place in the spaces between the breaths, and maybe you have even found it while you're reading or relaxing. Now we will find it inside some simple gentle movement. This practice is about listening to and respecting our bodies, and being curious about how we do something new and unusual.
>
> Stand with your feet together; feel your feet on the floor; feel your toes touching the floor; feel your heels touching the floor; feel the inside edges of your feet touching the floor, and the outside edges of your feet touching the floor. See if you can feel the energy moving up through your feet and legs. Feel how strong and long your legs are.

Find your breath in your belly. Feel the filling of the in-breath and the empty-ing of the out-breath.... Stretch up tall.

Pull your shoulders up by your ears, and then let them drop and gently relax. Close your eyes, finding your breath again in your belly.... Resting here.

Feel how you balance here. Can you feel that what we call balance is actually a series of wobbles and adjustments?... Do you know that other parts of life are like that too?... We may wobble in school or sports, with friends or family. And just like standing here, we can make adjustments, and find our balance in these parts of our lives, too.

When you are ready, open your eyes.

Look at something in front of you that is still, like a light switch or a door-knob.... Keep your eyes focused on this still point. Stretch your arms so your body looks like a T. Step onto your right foot and feel it touching the floor. Feel your right leg straight and long. Place the bottom (sole) of your left foot on your right calf or thigh. Gently open your left knee out to the side. Find your breath in your belly. Nice [smile].

It is fine to wobble, and put your foot down. And then give it another try. Be gentle and kind with yourself. Have fun inside this challenge! This is called tree pose. Do you feel like a tree? Tall and strong? Maybe with branches waving in the wind? See if you can let your mind and heart be still, even if your body is wobbling. It helps to have a sense of humor about it. Lower you arms and leg. Shake out your body; enjoy the shaking.

Coming to stillness.... Now lift the right corner of your mouth toward your right ear, and the left corner of your mouth toward your left ear (smile). What do you notice when you do this pose?

Again, look at the still point. Stretch your arms out to the side, forming a T. Step onto your left foot; feel it touching the floor. Feel your left leg straight and long. Place the bottom (sole) of your right foot onto your left calf or thigh, and let your right knee move gently to the side. Finding your breath in your belly; let your-self smile. You are doing great [smile].

Notice how you are talking to yourself. Just be curious about what you say to yourself as you attempt this pose. Is what you say kind? Would you speak to a friend the way you are talking to yourself? Can you practice being kind?

That's it; you're doing great! Start over if you need to.

Lower your arms and leg. Shake out your body.

Now bend your knees just a bit and reach your hands down toward the floor. Let your upper body hang from your waist like a rag doll. If it hurts, bend your knees a bit more.

Work up to your limit. As with the finger yoga, listen to and feel the place where your body tells you, "This is enough." There is no need to push beyond your current limit.

Notice how it feels to be sort of upside down. Feel the stretch in the back of your legs. Feel the heaviness of your head. Notice what it feels like to breathe in this position. Do your best to bring your attention into your body, feeling the sensations....

Now gently bend your knees, and then reach your hands out in front of you and put them on the floor so that your body and the floor make a sort of triangle. Feel the stretch in the back of your legs. If it hurts, bend your knees a little more. Feel the strength in your arms, as they hold you up. Remember to breathe.... Notice whether you start comparing what you are doing with what someone else is doing, and then return your attention to your body, and the breath.

Now paying attention to how you move from one position to the other, push yourself back so that you are kneeling, sitting on your feet with your toes pointing behind you, flat on the floor. Gently put your forehead on the floor and circle your arms back so that they are almost touching your feet. Rest here in this oval shape. Can you feel your whole body breathing here? Can you feel the breath in your belly?... Your back?...

Slowly uncurl. Sit back, and cross your legs in front of you, so that you are sitting cross-legged. Close your eyes and rest your hands on your knees. This is called mountain pose. Mountains are still and steady when it is sunny, when the wind is howling, when the snow is swirling. Sometimes our thoughts and feelings are like howling wind and swirling snow. With practice we can learn to be still and steady like the mountain, even when our thoughts and feelings are howling and swirling.

Again, find your breath in your belly. Now see if you can find the Still Quiet Place as you rest and breathe. Could you feel the stillness and quietness inside these gentle movements?... If not, no worries.

To finish, take three more deep breaths. Remember that your Still Quiet Place is always with you—when you are still, when you are moving, when you are happy, when you are sad. And you can find it simply by paying attention to your breath, to your body, or to whatever you are doing in the moment.

Holes and Different Streets Discussion (ages eight to eighteen)

This teaching is based on the poem "Autobiography in Five Short Chapters," by Portia Nelson (1993). Begin by asking the individual or group you are working with to sit quietly and listen as you read the poem.

Chapter One
    I walk down the street.
        There is a deep hole in the sidewalk.
        I fall in.
        I am lost… I am helpless.
            It isn't my fault…
    It takes forever to find a way out.

Chapter Two
    I walk down the same street.
        There is a deep hole in the sidewalk.
        I pretend I don't see it.
        I fall in again.
    I can't believe I am in this same place.
            But, it isn't my fault.
    It still takes a long time to get out.

Chapter Three
    I walk down the same street.
        There is a deep hole in the sidewalk.
        I see it is there.
        I still fall… it's a habit… but,
            my eyes are open.
            I know where I am.
    It is my fault.
    I get out immediately.

Chapter Four
    I walk down the same street.
        There is a deep hole in the sidewalk.
        I walk around it.

Chapter Five
    I walk down another street.

After reading the poem, invite participants to discuss it and complete the Holes and New (Different) Streets Cartoon (available for download at http://www.newhar binger.com/27572). The hole can be any difficulty a participant faces, but the emphasis should be on repetitive difficulties. The new street represents a creative response to the difficulty. Tweens and teens can add a few brief notes to the left of the new street, addressing their thoughts and feelings about the difficulty.

Most children above the age of eight can tell you what their common holes are and can explore new streets (creative, alternative behaviors). Common holes include problems with:

- Homework: procrastination, disorganization, attacks by Unkind Mind

- Siblings: mean teasing, repetitive fights

- Friendship: feeling excluded or jealous, going along with something to be "cool," not saying what you want, being mean

- Parents: not listening, not being listened to, disagreements about responsibilities and privileges, risk taking

When going over these with participants, it is helpful to note that "sometimes it may feel like we have been pushed into a hole; other times we may push or drag someone else into a hole; and sometimes we can fall into a hole all by ourselves. Then ask, "Can you give me some examples?"

Child-parent pairs find the hole analogy particularly useful, and often it becomes a household joke. This poem provides a quick, accessible shorthand for the concepts of reacting (falling into habitual holes) and responding (choosing a different street). With tweens and teens, you may introduce the distinction between *reacting*—acting automatically, out of habit, usually during the refractory period—and *responding*—pausing, breathing, and choosing your behavior.

During a recent office visit, after I read her the poem, a young patient named Rachel described a typical sibling hole. Rachel is a third grader who was brought to see me, in part, because she is very quick to anger, and her anger is very intense. She often plays in the yard with her two younger sisters. She described a hole she knows well. "When I play in the yard with my sisters I like to run and do cartwheels. I fall into an anger hole when my sisters do (slower) somersaults." I asked her "What might a different street be? Rather than falling into the anger hole and fighting with your sisters?" She came up with a few different ideas: "My sisters do somersaults somewhere else. My sisters could run and do cartwheels with me, or we could all take turns." I then shared the following story:

When my daughter was five years old, my son, Jason, was making a very complicated Star Wars Lego spaceship. My daughter was bored, and so she was jumping on her brother's Lego instructions, just to bug him. I asked her, "Nicole, what are you doing? What type of behavior is that?" She looked at me, curious. I said, "It starts with an H." The word I was thinking of was actually "hassling." She looked at me and said, very matter-of-factly, "It's hole behavior."

Referring to the story, Rachel and I discussed the fact that sometimes siblings try to drag each other into holes. Perhaps her sisters enjoy doing somersaults partly because they know she'll get upset, and watching her get upset is entertaining. For Nicole, it was entertaining to watch Jason get upset. We then considered a couple of additional streets she hadn't come up with: perhaps she could also do some somersaults, or maybe she could do something else entirely. In closing, we agreed that it might help to discuss the new streets with her sisters at a calm time, instead of in the yard when she's already frustrated.

Breath-Based Practice (all ages)

After a discussion of holes and different streets, you may have time to move into a short breath-based practice, such as Still Quiet Place, Jewel, or Rest. Most days it is time to review the home practice, and close, as always, with listening practice.

Overview of Home Practice (all ages)

Finally, review the home practice; a brief guided yoga practice may be downloaded from http://www.newharbinger.com/27572. (See the back of the book for more information.) In keeping with this week's focus on responding rather thn reacting, mindfulness in daily life practice shifts to noticing common holes and different streets.

Also answer any questions participants may have about home practice.

Closing Mindful Listening Practice (all ages)

Close by allowing one or two attentive students to ring the bell for a final listening practice.

● Practicing at Home—Session 5

Mindfulness is responsive.

It supports us in choosing our behavior.

Do the guided mindful yoga every day.

Practice mindfulness in daily life.

- *Notice common holes, and experiment with taking different streets.*

- *Continue to notice Unkind Mind.*

With kindness and curiosity, and without guilt, fill out the home practice log.

If you have a mindful moment, questions, or difficulties you'd like to share, or if you won't be able to attend the next class, call or e-mail me.

9

session 6: responding and communicating

Intentions

The intentions of this session are to review our young friends' experiences with falling into holes (reacting) and choosing different streets (responding), to explore the ins and outs of difficult communications, and to introduce Kind Heart as an antidote to Unkind Mind. Additionally, Body Scan and Walking practices are introduced.

Outline: Practices, Exercises, and Discussions

- Mindful Listening practice*
- Mindful Eating practice*
- Home practice review
- Body Scan practice*
- Difficult Communication exercise and discussion
- Mindful Walking practice*
- Kind Heart discussion*
- Read-aloud option: *Because Brian Hugged His Mother*, David L. Rice*
- Overview of home practice*
- Closing Mindful Listening practice*

Mindful Listening and Mindful Eating Practice (all ages)

As usual, begin with Mindful Listening and Mindful Eating. At this point in the course you may offer very simple comments to support participants in bringing their attention into the moment ("Listen with your full attention…." "Breathing, listening, being…." "Chewing, tasting…." "Can you put your kind and curious attention in your mouth?"), or you may simply do these practices in silence.

Home Practice Review (ages six to eighteen)

You may inquire briefly about the participants' experiences with the yoga. However, the main focus of the discussion is their reflections regarding holes and different streets. Here are some brief prompts you might use regarding the yoga:

- *Did you practice the yoga?*
- *Whether you practiced or not, what thoughts and feelings appeared when I asked if you had practiced?*

- *If you did the yoga, how was it for you?*

- *If you did yoga more than once, was it kind of the same, or different each time?*

- *Did any of you lose your balance during yoga? In another part of your life?*

- *How does losing our balance with schoolwork, friends, and family relate to holes and different streets?*

If you opted not to use the last question above, transition into exploring what participants discovered about holes and different streets (responding rather than reacting to life's circumstances), during the past week.

You can begin with open-ended questions: "Did anyone fall into a hole this week?" "Did anyone take a different street?" "Did anyone fall into a hole and then get out?" "Is anyone in a hole right now?" "Remember we all sometimes fall into holes." As participants offer examples you can respond, offering questions and comments as it feels helpful.

The dialogues below are examples of group conversations about holes shared by individual participants. They are offered here to give you a sense of such dialogues.

The Baseball Analogy

In one child-parent class, Jacob, an eleven-year-old only child, described a hole that he and his mother fell into frequently. He wanted attention, while his mother wanted time and space. When he continued to request her attention they usually ended up fighting. Jacob also happened to love baseball. So we used the analogy that his mother threw him a curve ball—meaning that she was not available.

As a group, we explored what "home run" responses might look like. An older boy named Jonathan suggested that Jacob make an agreement with his mom to do his own thing for fifteen minutes, and then she would play with him for fifteen minutes. Jacob and his mother both felt this was preferable to their usual unsatisfactory mode of interacting.

We continued around the room and all of the participants were given the opportunity to describe a potential "curve ball" (hole) scenario in their lives—such as spouses arriving late for dinner, or parents wanting children to go hiking and children not wanting to go. For the most part, the child or parent presenting the difficulty offered his own "home run" response. And, when the person presenting the scenario could not come up with a "home run" response, we had plenty of wise "batting coaches" in the room to offer ideas.

While I may use this specific baseball analogy or some variation of it in the future, I want to emphasize that it arose simply from knowing that Jacob loved baseball, and from the intention to speak to him using language that was meaningful to him. Since Jacob presented the scenario, the discussion was focused on exploring the range of *responses* available to him. Of course, there is a very important, parallel conversation to be had with his mother regarding her role in creating the hole, and different streets she could consider.

Almost Moments

Michael, a fourth grader at a low-income school, described an unpleasant moment: his new cat bit him, it hurt, and he wanted to hit the cat. I asked, "Did you?" He smiled and simply said, "No. But I almost did." As a class we dubbed this an "almost moment."

For the remaining five weeks of the course, we explored other almost moments at home, at school, and in life: not hitting the cat or the bully on the playground; hanging in there with a difficult math problem or after a disagreement with a buddy. There are equivalent almost moments for teens: not cheating to get a better grade, not using drugs, not having unprotected sex, not getting in the car with a drunk friend, not joining a gang, or not standing in front of a high-speed train. Our children's lives literally depend on them developing the ability to choose wisely and take a different street in these "almost moments" when things are difficult.

Tragically, in 2010, in Palo Alto, the university town just south of where I live, over the course of six months, six teenagers took their lives by standing in front of a high-speed train. They were each likely grappling with persistent feelings of depression and suicidal thoughts—Unkind Mind on steroids: "My life is hopeless." "I'd be better off dead." "No one cares." What might have been different if even one of them had learned to investigate those thoughts and feelings with the curiosity, perspective, and kindness that Michael learned? We'll never know. But perhaps, if someone later asked them, "Did you stand in front of the train?" they would still be here to smile and simply say, "No. But I almost did."

I Will Always See

In Michael's course, the discussion of "almost moments" segued into a conversation about getting caught, and often punished, when one is not able to pause and therefore misses the "almost moment," reacts, and falls into a hole. This, in turn, led to a discussion about guilt and the experience of feeling guilty even if one isn't caught. The conversation prompted me to share the following teaching story with the group. (As an aside, children of all ages love to sit back and relax and listen to a story).

Once upon a time, on the outskirts of a big city, there stood an old school. From a young age, girls and boys would come to live in the school and to learn from the teacher. One day the teacher who ran this small school decided to teach his young students a lesson. He gathered them around him and spoke: "My dear students, as you can see, I am growing old and slow. I can no longer provide for the needs of the school as I once did. I know I have not yet taught you to work for money, and so I can only think of one thing that can keep our school from closing." The students drew close with eyes wide.

"Our nearby city is full of wealthy people with more money in their purses than they could ever need. I want you to go into the city and follow those rich people as they walk through the crowded streets, or when they walk down the deserted alleyways. When no one is looking, and only when no one is looking, you must steal their purses from them. That way we will have enough money to keep our school alive." (At this point, Michael and many of his classmates gasped and shook their heads.)

"But Teacher," the girls and boys chorused in disbelief, "you have taught us that it is wrong to take anything that does not belong to us." "Yes, indeed I have," the old teacher replied. "It would be wrong to steal if it were not absolutely necessary. And remember, you must not be seen! If anyone can see you, you must not steal! Do you understand?"

The girls and boys looked nervously from one to the other. Had their beloved teacher gone mad? His eyes shone with intensity such as they had never seen before. "Yes, Teacher," they said quietly. "Good," he said. "Now go, and remember, you must not be seen!" The girls and boys got up and quietly began to file out of the school building. The old teacher rose slowly and watched them go. When he turned to go back inside, he saw that one student was still standing quietly in the corner of the room. "Why did you not go with the others?" he asked the girl. "Do you not want to help save our school?"

"I do, Teacher," said the girl quietly. "But you said that we had to steal without being seen. I know that there is no place on Earth that I would not be seen, for I would always see myself."

"Excellent!" exclaimed the teacher. "That is just the lesson that I hoped you and the others would learn, but you were the only one to see it. Run and tell your friends to return to the school before they get us into trouble." The girl ran and got her friends who were nervously gathered just out of sight of the school, trying to decide what to do. When they returned, the teacher told them the words the girl had spoken and they all understood the lesson.

This story usually stimulates much discussion, so typically there is no need for prompts. However, you may ask, "What does it have to do with our discussion about holes and 'almost moments' and choosing our behavior? No matter what we do, we always have a mindful part of ourselves that is quietly watching, and that can guide us if we can pause and listen."

When the conversation about holes and different streets, almost moments, and always seeing has run its course, you may transition to Body Scan practice.

Body Scan Practice (all ages)

Many elements of the course are intended to support participants in becoming more embodied and developing an increased awareness of their physical sensations. This enhanced awareness of "inner" sensation provides participants with vital information about the state of their physical bodies (health and illness, functionality and injury, energy and fatigue, fullness (satiety) and hunger, and so on). Additionally, because thoughts and feelings manifest in the body as physical sensation, increasing body awareness also enhances awareness of complex interrelated mental-emotional states. Body Scan practice supports participants in becoming more fully embodied.

As mentioned previously, I have found it beneficial to introduce the Body Scan in session 6 (as opposed to session 1 in adult MBSR). Even a very brief body scan takes about twelve minutes. So it is helpful for the kids to have some experience with stillness and quietness, and some way of working with distraction, boredom, and restlessness before they engage in this "longer" practice. A guided body scan for all ages can be downloaded from http://www.newharbinger.com/27572. (See the back of the book for more information.)

Participants may lie on the floor or sit in chairs for this practice. Begin by having them feel the breath in the belly and rest in the Still Quiet Place. Then invite them to notice the sensations in their toes, playing with feeling the sensation in each individual toe, and the spaces between the toes, or the feel of their socks and shoes, or the air making contact with their toes. Allow the attention to move along the bottom of the feet, feeling the curved arches of the feet, and up through the feet into the ankles. On the out-breath let the toes, feet, and ankles soften (just be). On the in-breath, breathe the attention into the lower legs.... Continue moving slowly up through the body, offering enough specific sensations in each region to anchor their attention, using the out-breath to release a region, and the in-breath to shift the attention to the next area.

As you will hear on the audio track, I use the word "pelvis," and describe it as the place where the legs connect with the rest of the body or the torso. Occasionally, mention of the pelvis will bring embarrassed giggling, or comments from tweens and teens. If this occurs, you can simply say, "Bring your kind and curious attention to the thoughts and feelings that appear as you pay attention to this part of your body. Do you feel embarrassed or uncomfortable? Do you want to joke, to be cool, to prove you're okay with it? It is all fine; just notice."

Conclude with breathing and attending to, being aware of, and sensing the whole body, letting the whole body just be as it is, and then resting in stillness and quietness. Please do the exercise often enough that you can draw on your own experience in leading the practice. Encourage the group participants to maintain their mindful awareness and their silence as you explain the Difficult Communication Cartoon.

Difficult Communication Exercise and Discussion (ages eight to eighteen)

Whether we are young children or "grown-ups," much of our stress, unhappiness, and difficulty arises from our less-than-skillful communication with others. To complicate matters, our less-than-skillful communication with others often contributes to their stress, unhappiness, and difficulty. Many of the basic skills presented in this section support children and adolescents (and adults) in listening deeply to themselves and others, and then communicating more clearly and compassionately.

This exercise is designed to support our young friends during difficult communications by helping them learn to pause to consider what they feel and want, what another person feels and wants, and how they might work things out. In combination, these steps nurture empathy and compassion for oneself and others and lay a foundation for creative problem solving and true cooperation (literally, operating together). When conflicts are resolved in this way, children are less likely to carry distracting mental and emotional baggage into the classroom and relationships with peers and family members. Subsequently, they are better prepared to engage in the important processes of learning and connecting inside and outside the classroom.

Difficult Communication Exercise

As you pass out the cartoon (available for download at http://www.newharbinger.com/27572), you may introduce the exercise by saying something along these lines:

When we are upset, in the heat of the moment, and at the peak of the refractory period, we often react and just blurt out thoughts and feelings as they appear. If the person we are interacting with does the same thing, soon we find ourselves being tossed about on big waves of reactivity, and drowning in a shared tsunami of thoughts and feelings.

So let's use the cartoon to practice. Close your eyes; take several slow deep breaths; settle into stillness and quietness; and remember a difficult discussion you had this week—a disagreement with a classmate, friend, family member.... Now let's work our way through the cartoon. The first step in the process of communicating skillfully is asking yourself, "What do I feel?" "What do I want?" When you have remembered what you wanted and how you felt, write it down. Just a few brief words are fine.

Sometimes the answers to these questions are quick and clear. At other times, it may be helpful to slow down and really listen to what is true for you. This takes practice, and it is important to understand how you feel (your emotions) and what you want (your desires) before moving on to the next steps.

121

The second step in the process is considering what the other person feels and wants. Without this step it is very difficult to communicate and move toward a solution. So take some time, let go of what you felt and wanted, and really consider what the other person felt and wanted. When you feel you understand the other person, write down a few brief words or phrases.

Now that you have a better understanding of what you wanted and felt, and what the other person wanted and felt, how might you get out of this hole? What are some different streets? Creative solutions? If you have some ideas, write them down. If you feel stuck, you will have a chance to talk with a partner about possible solutions in a minute.

In moments of difficulty, the combination of paying attention to our own feelings and wants and then considering the feelings and wants of others helps us be kinder to ourselves and kinder to other people.

With tweens and teens it is helpful if you invite them to *slow down* and really explore each question, saying something along these lines:

Do your best not to rush this process. Really take your time to understand what is true for you and for the other person. For example, if you have been left out (rejected) by a "friend," you might try to pretend that you don't care. The truth may actually be "I feel hurt, sad, confused, and angry. And even though my 'friend' continues to be unkind to me, I still want to be her friend." It can be scary and feel vulnerable to admit, even just to yourself, how you really feel and what you really want.

When you take the time to discover what is really true you might realize that you really don't want to be friends with the other person, or that the person you want to be friends with feels insecure and doesn't want or know how to be your friend, or that as much as you truly want to be friends with the other person, the other person doesn't want to be friends with you. Even if you don't like what you discover, acknowledging what you feel and want and then considering what the other person feels and wants provides you with important information as you consider your choices. In the example above, if you understand that you want friendship, and the other person is at best unsure about being friends, you may choose to reach out to the other person, to be a friend to yourself by treating yourself with kindness and respect, or to seek out other friends. Or if you realize that the other person is actually being cruel, you may seek the support of a trusted adult.

Difficult Communication Discussion (ages eight to eighteen)

Once participants have completed their cartoons, have them form pairs—preferably not with a close friend—to share the difficult communication they just outlined in the cartoon. If the circumstances they chose for the cartoon feel too private (embarrassing, tender, intense), they may choose a slightly "easier" difficult communication instead. (If you are working with an individual, obviously the discussion about the exercise is just a simple conversation.)

Once everyone has a partner, either have each pair choose who will be partner A and who will be partner B, or designate who will be partner A and who will be partner B. There are many simple ways of designating partners. For example, the person with the shortest hair is partner A, the younger person is partner A, or the person whose name comes first alphabetically is partner A.

Explain that partner A will begin by sharing a difficult communication, while partner B practices mindful listening—listening with her heart and her attention, as well as her ears. To support the process, it is helpful if you read the following prompts, allowing partner A about a minute to respond to each question. All pairs will work simultaneously as you offer the prompts to the group.

- *What was the difficulty? Describe it to your partner briefly.*

- *How did you feel during the difficulty?*

- *What did you want?*

- *How do you think the other person felt?*

- *What do you think the other person wanted?*

- *What ended up happening?*

- *Looking back on it now, what were other possible streets, solutions, ways of resolving the difficulty?*

When partner A is done sharing, partner B may practice mindful speaking—speaking with kindness and curiosity, asking questions, or offering observations based on what she heard. Then the partners switch roles.

Once the participants have shared with their partners, you can facilitate a discussion with the entire group: "Raise your hand if you are willing to share your difficulty and what you wrote down with the group, or if you struggled to find a creative solution and would like some help from the group."

During this process it can be helpful to emphasize the exploration of how the other person felt and what he wanted. Encourage the recognition that often, at the most basic level what the other persons wants is usually very similar to what we want, even in the midst of difficulty and disagreements.

It sounds like he just wanted to be happy, to have things go his way.... Did you want to be happy, have things go your way?... Don't we all usually just want to be happy and have things go our way?… Isn't it interesting, even when we have difficulty with someone, we still share this simple desire for happiness with them. For me, when I am really angry, it helps me if I remember that the other person just wants to be happy too.

Notes on Facilitation

It is important to support children and adolescents in discovering and speaking their truths, even if they are not "politically correct": "I was so angry I just wanted to hit him." (Or for some teens, "kill him.") For your own practice, please pause here and notice your thoughts, feelings, and physical reactions in response to the previous sentence….

Did fear arise? Did you begin to judge? Did you find yourself wanting to correct, or fix? If so, are you now judging your fear and judging, and attempting to fix your desire to fix? Remember that, ideally, as facilitators and as human beings doing the best we can, our role is to first *make space for ourselves and others to be exactly as we are.* Are you willing to admit that at times you have been so angry you have thought about harming another?

Inevitably you'll encounter young people like Michael who, in talking about their "almost moments," will honestly tell you "I wanted to hit him." ("Him" may be a cat, a sibling, a friend, the schoolyard bully, or a member of a rival gang.) When a young person speaks so honestly, rather than making him wrong, thank him. Meet him where he is in the moment and say something along these lines:

Thank you for being so honest. I understand. Like you, I have sometimes been so angry I wanted to harm someone. Being honest about these feelings and wants can help us choose our behavior. Sometimes when we pretend we aren't angry, then the anger sneaks out and we do something we wish we hadn't. So it is very brave and helpful to be honest with ourselves.

Paradoxically, this type of comment acknowledging the intensity of anger, and the impulse to attack or defend when we feel threatened, normalizes this very common human experience, and demonstrates that it is possible to feel intensely angry, to want to cause harm, and then to *choose* otherwise.

That said, it is equally important not to leave participants stuck in their feelings and desires, and to support them in moving through the subsequent steps of considering the other person's perspective and then choosing their behavior. It is essential to remind our young friends that engaging in the investigation of difficult communications doesn't mean that they will get what they want (or, more accurately, what they *think* they want—usually a specific outcome in the material world).

Sometimes they may move through the process and discover that they want something other than what they thought they wanted. This can be a good time to remind them that Suffering = Pain x Resistance, and that when they are busy wanting things to be different than they actually are, they are contributing to their own upset. Simultaneously, it is important not to imply that they shouldn't want what they want; or that they shouldn't take steps to create the outcome they desire, as long as it will not cause harm to another. Ultimately this process is about understanding how we really feel and what we really want, and what others really feel and want, so that we have the best chance at coming up with choices that allow us, and others, to be as happy as possible.

With tweens and teens you can introduce the idea of "one finger pointing out; three fingers pointing back." This short saying invites us to explore that often what we find most difficult in another person is a reflection of our own behavior. "He was so busy arguing, he didn't even listen to me." "Can you see where you were so busy arguing—even if it was just in your head, rather than out loud—that you didn't listen to him?..."

The benefits of repeatedly engaging in this process of working with difficult communications are increased self-awareness (teens may even be able to recognize patterns of behavior); increased perspective taking, empathy, compassion, and resilience; more effective communication; enhanced conflict resolution and cooperation; and, ultimately, greater energy for engaging in learning and living.

Mindful Walking Practice (all ages)

Most likely, after this discussion students will be squirmy (restless) and ready to move. If the energy of the group is very high, you may begin with hasty walking, described below, and then shift to slower walking. If the weather permits, you may want to take the group outside.

Outside or inside, Mindful Walking goes like this: Have participants stand with their feet together and close their eyes. Invite them to rest in stillness and then bring their attention to what is happening in their feet. Encourage them to feel the small adjustments their feet make to maintain balance. Then have them open their eyes and take one very slow, mindful step with their right foot, feeling the sensations as they lift the foot, swing it forward, and place it on the ground, putting their full attention into the foot. Then invite them to take ten *slow*, mindful steps and stop. If people are walking quickly or clumsily, you may want to have a contest to see who can walk most slowly and attentively *without* stumbling. As with the breath, encourage them to notice when the mind wanders, and then return their attention to the sensations of walking. Once they have the basic idea, you can vary the practice. For example, you might instruct them to walk in individual lanes or as a group in a circle.

Mindful Hasty Walking Practice (ages eight to eighteen)

For a group of fifteen to twenty participants, using natural boundaries, designate a specific walking area measuring about 15 feet by 15 feet. Instruct the participants to walk at a natural pace within the space, and to turn and change directions *before* bumping into someone or reaching the edge of the space. You may need to offer reminders about kindness, safety, and being mindful of and responsible with their bodies. Challenge them to maintain their attention and to walk a bit more quickly.

Gradually have them increase their speed and change their direction every seven steps, or sooner if needed to avoid collisions. Suggest being aware of their bodies, their classmates, *and* the spaces between their classmates (which are like the spaces between the breaths, or between thoughts). Then have them walk very quickly, changing direction every five steps. Then have them walk very quickly with their fists clenched, shoulders up, and jaws clamped, changing direction every three steps. Invite them to notice how this feels. Some participants may find this type of tense, hurried walking familiar.

Finally, invite them to come to stillness and simply notice how they feel after having walked in this way. "What's happening in your body?" "How is your breath?" "How is your heartbeat?" What is happening in your mind?" As they transition from standing stillness to sitting, encourage them to maintain their attention, noting their thoughts, feelings, and physical sensations as they return to their seats.

Kind Heart Discussion (all ages)

Next, invite participants to settle into seated stillness and quietness. As a very brief introduction—or "appetizer"—for loving-kindness practice, simply invite them to offer themselves a brief kindness, in the form of the simple wish "May I be happy."

> *Now we are going to do a very short new practice. In a moment I am going to invite you to say something silently to yourself. Do your best to notice your thoughts, feelings, and what happens in your body. Okay, in your own time please offer yourself a simple wish of kindness by saying, "May I be happy." … After you have offered this simple kindness to yourself, and noticed your response, open your eyes.*

Facilitate a brief discussion, encouraging them to notice their willingness to offer themselves kindness and their response to their own kindness with questions such as these:

- *Were you willing to offer yourself kindness?*

- *If not, what got in the way of offering yourself kindness?*

- *Did you enjoy or ignore your kindness?*

- *What did you feel when you offered yourself kindness?*

Often participants notice softening, relief, indifference, or resistance. In conclusion, simply mention that offering ourselves kindness is a helpful response or antidote to Unkind Mind, and that the group will do more loving-kindness practice in the next session.

Overview of Home Practice (all ages)

Remember to leave time at the end of class to read the home practice for the upcoming week out loud. The guided audio practice is the body scan—which may be downloaded at http://www.newharbinger.com/27572—and participants may alternate listening to the body scan with independent mindful walking. They may do slow walking like they did during the session, or they may take a nature walk, paying attention to their *eight* senses as they walk. The mindfulness in daily life practice is being aware of difficult communications, and pausing to consider their feelings and wants, and the other person's feelings and wants, and then choosing their behavior. This process is one way to stay out of—or get out of—holes, and discover different streets.

Answer any questions participants may have about home practice.

Closing Mindful Listening Practice (all ages)

Close by allowing one or two participatory students to ring the bell for a final listening practice.

Practicing at Home—Session 6

Mindfulness is honest.

It asks us to be true to our own experiences, and to honor the experience of others.

Alternate the Body Scan and Mindful Walking practice.

Practice mindfulness in daily life.

*   *Take a nature walk and notice the sights, the sounds, the smells, the feel of the air, and your thoughts and feelings.*

*   *Investigate difficult communications.*

Practice responding (rather than reacting) to Unkind Mind and holes, and during difficult communications.

With kindness and curiosity, and without guilt, fill out the home practice log.

If you have a mindful moment, questions, or difficulties you'd like to share, or if you won't be able to attend the next class, call or e-mail me.

10

session 7: communication and love

Intentions

The intentions of this session are to engage the participants in a discussion in which they reflect on and demonstrate the application of mindfulness in difficult communications, and to continue to develop the capacity to respond rather than react. Impulses are explored. Easy to remember mnemonics put it all together; and, to close, loving-kindness practice is formally introduced.

Outline: Practices, Exercises, and Discussions

- Mindful Listening practice*

- Mindful Eating practice*

- Impulses exercise and discussion*

- Home practice review*

- Hook Report

- Responding versus reacting discussion

- Read-aloud option: the chapter titled "Paul," from *Sideways Stories from Wayside School*, Louis Sachar*

- Making Rain movement practice*

- Mindful Aikido exercise and discussion

- Putting it all together: ABCs, STAR, and PEACE practices*

- Loving-Kindness practice* and discussion

- Overview of home practice*

- Closing Mindful Listening practice*

Mindful Listening and Mindful Eating Practice (all ages)

As usual, begin with Mindful Listening, and then perhaps a short breath-based practice. At this point in the course, if you ask for volunteers, a child or teen may be brave enough to lead a simple practice. It can be both instructive and heartening to hear their interpretations. If no one volunteers, you can lead an additional brief practice, or move into Mindful Eating.

Impulses Exercise and Discussion (all ages)

With younger children, and occasionally even with teens, I often transition to the topic of impulses by reading the chapter titled "Paul," from the book *Sideways Stories from Wayside School*, by Louis Sachar, while they continue eating. This story is a conversation between Paul and temptation. It's about noticing urges and choosing whether to act on them. It offers a humorous take on "almost moments" and holes and different streets (in other words, responding versus reacting).

Briefly, temptation encourages Paul to pull Leslie's pigtails. Initially he resists. Then he pulls first the left, and subsequently the right pigtail. After each pull, Leslie yells, and explains that Paul pulled her pigtail, and Paul gets a check mark by his name on the blackboard. Then Leslie yells again (it is unclear whether Paul actually pulled her pigtail), and he gets a third check mark by his name and is sent home early on the kindergarten bus. This story provides a wonderful springboard for discussing impulses and choice, using questions such as these:

- *Have you had times when you have noticed the impulse to do something unkind or sneaky, like pull pigtails, take candy, gossip, or cheat on a test?*

- *Have you heard a voice in your head that says, "No! What am I doing? I'll only get into trouble"?*

- *Have you heard another voice that says, "Just a little tug?"*

- *How can noticing these impulses and voices help us?*

- *Why is it sometimes so hard to listen to our wise, kind voice, and take a different street?*

Itch

The following example offers a short, simple, fun, tactile way to explore impulses. Observe your own experience as you read through the paragraphs to familiarize yourself with the exercise. Then, in session, use your experience to guide your young friends in exploring this ordinary, powerful impulse:

Please close your eyes. In a moment I am going to say a word, and I want you to notice what happens in your body and your mind. Do your best to just notice without doing anything or making any movements. Okay, here's the word: "itch."...

What did you notice?...

Raise your hand if you were suddenly aware of an itch that you weren't aware of before. Raise your hand if you were able to notice the itch without scratching it. If you did scratch the itch, were you able to notice the thoughts before you scratched? What were they? Did you maybe think, "Oh, just one scratch," "She won't notice," "I don't care what she said," or "She didn't mean it"? Again, this isn't about feeling good or bad or right or wrong; it's about noticing our bodies, our thoughts, and our feelings and then choosing our actions. Isn't it interesting that one simple word can produce sensations in our bodies, and those sensations can lead to thoughts and urges, and those urges can lead to actions?

If time allows, you can try a similar exercise with other words, such as "cookies" or "homework." With older kids, you can also add a discussion in terms of media images and advertising, with questions and comments such as these:

What might this exercise have to do with advertising?... Exactly, advertising uses words and images to create thoughts and impulses.

Are there types of thoughts that advertising tries to trigger?... Yup. Desire or wanting, and Unkind Mind or insecurity.

Why might it be helpful to remember this? So that you can observe your thoughts and impulses and then choose if you want to spend your money on a particular brand of jeans.

Home Practice Review (all ages)

After reading the story you can move into the usual home practice review.

Being in the Body

Inquire about participants' experience with the Body Scan and Mindful Walking. As usual, offer simple clarifying comments or questions:

- *Did anyone do the body scan?*

- *What was it like for you?*

- *Did anyone have difficulty with the body scan?*

- *No worries; when you realize you are drifting off, just return your attention to the area of your body that the recording is describing.*

- *If you feel the impulse to move, see if you can notice it and stay with it for three breaths before you move. And when you move, see if you can move mindfully.*

- *Did anyone play with Mindful Walking?*

- *If you forgot, are you willing to try it this week?*

- *How about the nature walk?*

- *What was it like to walk outside and pay attention to the sights, the sounds, the sensations of your body moving through space?*

Difficult Communication: "Get Off the Computer" (ages eight through eighteen)

With older participants, continue by reviewing the experience of difficult communications during the previous week. I encourage you to share a difficult communication of your own from the preceding week and to receive any observations and suggestions participants would like to offer. Sharing in this way lets your young friends know that adults often struggle with similar issues. It also allows them to witness the process in relation to a real yet impersonal situation, and provides them with the opportunity to share their hard-won wisdom. Equally importantly, it allows you to benefit from their wisdom and fresh perspective.

The difficult communication described below was brought up by Henry, a sixth grader, in a child-parent course at Stanford. (Working with child-parents pairs creates unique opportunities and challenges, which will be explored more thoroughly in chapter 15.) While the example below was shared in a child-parent course, it could just as easily have been shared in a tween-only course. It is presented as it occurred to give you a feel for how I chose to explore a particular difficult communication with a particular group on a particular fall afternoon; it is just one of endless possible responses to a given moment. The basic process for facilitating such an inquiry is the same whether you are working with an individual, a group of children or teens, or a group of children and parents.

In this particular class, a hot topic for both the children and parents was negotiating the use of the home computer. Often, the children wanted to continue playing, and their parents wanted them to stop and do their chores or homework, or perhaps the parents wanted to use the computer themselves. After the scenario was presented by Henry, the most vocal, computer-engaged boy in the group, I invited him to role-play the parent. Another boy volunteered to take his natural role as the computer-using child. As you will see, Henry was quite skillful in his role as the parent.

Parent: Please get off the computer.

Child: But Mom, I am right in the middle of level 37 of this game!

Parent: I understand, honey, but I need to use the computer now.

Child: But Mom, I have never gotten to level 37 before. Just let me finish.

Parent: How long do you think it will take?

Child:	Five minutes.
Parent:	Okay, I'm willing to wait five minutes. I'll set the timer. When the timer goes off it will be my turn.
Child:	Okay.

The subsequent discussion acknowledged that children do not always accurately estimate the time needed to complete the level, and do not always stop playing when the timer rings. However, both the children and the adults felt that this role-play was more skillful than their usual fraught communications on this subject, and that it contained the essential ingredient of mutual respect and trust. The children wanted the parents to understand that the game was important to them. The parents wanted to avoid long, drawn-out negotiations.

We also noted the benefits of discussing the situation and making family agreements in a neutral moment, *before* anyone wanted to use, or was already using, the computer. The following week the families reported that, for the most part, the exchanges about the computer were much less stressful and much more pleasant.

The process is similar when used with participant-participant pairs, or working with an individual in your office. For example, if a teen came into group or your office and shared that her parents were always hassling her about getting off her cell phone or computer, you could have her role-play her parent while you or a peer role-played her. After the role-play, you may weave in threads from the course: breathing, noticing thoughts and feelings, applying emotion theory, mindful listening to oneself and others involved, choosing different streets, and so on.

Hook Report (ages eight to eighteen)

"Hook Report" is a play on words that offers a useful analogy for exploring responding versus reacting. Children between the ages of eight and eighteen routinely write book reports. A Hook Report simply involves observing and reporting on a time when the child was "hooked." Who were the main characters? What was the hook? What happened? What thoughts and feelings were underneath the action? What are other possible endings? What wiser choices could have been made? (Note: You'll need a cartoon to complete this activity. A copy is available for download at http://www.newharbinger.com/27572.) With a smile, say something like this:

> *Now I am going to have you write a brief book report.* (Invariably there will be a few groans.) *Notice thoughts and feelings that appeared when I said this. Did you think, "Ugh, why is the mindfulness teacher making us write a book report?" If I were you, I probably would have thought the same thing* (smile). *Anyway this short "book" report is really a "hook" report, about a time when you got "hooked"*

by someone or something. Can anyone offer me an example of when you got hooked in the last couple of days?… Yes, when you lost your real book report because your computer crashed. Okay, how about another one?… When your friend teased you about your outfit. Great. Can everyone think of an example? If you can't think of an example, raise your hand. (Briefly chat individually with participants who can't think of an example, and help them find a simple time when they were "hooked.")

Now that everyone has an example, fill in the Hook Report cartoon, with just a few brief phrases describing the "hook"—the event that hooked you—the main characters involved, your thoughts and feelings, your actions, other possible endings or different streets, what your wisest self might have done, and so on…

Responding Versus Reacting Discussion (ages eight to eighteen)

At this point, it is helpful to review the entire course in the context of responding rather than reacting to difficulties. Ask the group, or the individual child you are working with, to list the steps involved in responding rather than reacting. Of course, if they forget a step, you can prompt them to help them remember.

- Noticing that there is difficulty

- Using the breath to settle into the Still Quiet Place

- Paying attention to your thoughts, feelings, and physical sensations

- If there are other people involved, considering their thoughts and feelings and what they want

- Choosing a street rather than falling into a hole

Making Rain Movement Practice (all ages)

Making Rain is an experiential exercise in which participants play the role of a small orchestra and together, with you as the conductor, create the sound of a rainstorm building and receding. If you haven't ever seen or done this, google the phrase "orchestra making rain" to view a professional example; this is definitely a case in which a video is worth ten thousand words.

Have participants stand in two rows, in a semicircle facing you. Ask them to close their eyes, feel the stillness, and listen to the quiet and sounds in the room. Then invite them to open their eyes and copy your movements as you spread each movement from left to right. I usually offer the instruction "When I point to your section, please copy my movement and keep doing the same movement until I give your section a new movement." Begin by facing the section of the orchestra to your left, pointing to that section, and making the first movement: rubbing your palms together. *Slowly* swivel to the right, spreading the movement from left to right. Then, with a conductor's raised eyebrows and smile, turn back to the leftmost section, point to that section, and make the second movement: snapping your fingers. Proceed in the same way through the entire sequence outlined below, spreading each movement from left to right and indicating when each section of the orchestra is to begin that movement:

- Stillness

- Rubbing palms together

- Snapping fingers

- Slapping thighs

- Jumping and landing

- Slapping thighs

- Snapping fingers

- Rubbing hands together

- Stillness

As you conclude, encourage participants to close their eyes again, feel the stillness, listen to the quiet and the sounds in the room, and notice their thoughts and feelings. This exercise may be offered as is, as a brief, simple, fun movement practice, or you may use it to remind participants that like natural storms, mental and emotional storms may appear on the horizon, last as long as they last, and eventually pass.

Mindful Aikido Exercise and Discussion (ages ten to eighteen)

Aikido is a martial art in which the practitioner enters and blends with an attacker's energy to redirect it. This exercise, which explores various responses to being "attacked," is drawn from MBSR. It's mostly likely to benefit children ages ten and older. If time allows, you may include this exercise to help a group or an individual further explore ways of dealing with difficult communications and interpersonal conflicts.

This session is rich and full. While it is not necessary to include this exercise in it, mindful aikido is worth having in your repertoire. The purpose of this exercise is to guide participants through a facilitated experience of four distinct ways of responding to conflict: submissive, avoidant, aggressive, and assertive. The guided experience and subsequent discussion are intended to support our young friends in exploring the thoughts, feelings, and physical sensations that accompany each type of response, and to help them discover patterns in how they tend to react in various situations. For many young people, simply understanding that there are four primary ways of responding to conflict is powerful new learning, and being able to recognize these behaviors in themselves and others is invaluable. Ultimately, this exercise provides yet another way to support young people in developing their capacity to choose skillful responses, rather than reacting in habitual or problematic ways.

Choose wisely, depending on group dynamics and space, whether you wish to demonstrate this with one individual or a series of individuals, or if you wish to have the group pair off and do the exercise with partners. Trust your instincts, and be willing to stretch toward your learning edge. Often, it is the individuals and groups that we are most reluctant to take risks with—because we are afraid they will get out of hand, or because they are habitually reactive—who have the greatest insights. Again, use your wisdom, meet your fear, and choose wisely. Although I am a petite woman (five feet, one inch on a good day), I often (but not always) choose the "alpha" male, or female, to demonstrate one or all of the responses with me. Descriptions of how to present this exercise as a demonstration and as a partner practice are provided below.

Demonstration

Ask the group to watch in silence and notice their physical sensations, feelings, and thoughts as you act out the four responses to conflict. Choose one participant to assist you with all four responses, or choose a different participant for each response. Then have the person you have chosen walk toward you with angry energy, and with her arms straight out in front of her.

Submissive: As the person approaches, cower to the floor, with a fearful expression on your face.

Avoidant: As the person approaches, step out of the way with a nonchalant expression.

Aggressive: As the person approaches, push back forcefully with an angry expression on your face.

Assertive: As the person approaches, take her outstretched arm and, moving and dancing with her, turn her 180 degrees with a calm expression on your face.

After each demonstration, invite mindful reflection.

- *What were your thoughts, feelings, and physical sensations as you watched this?*

- *Did you feel more like me, the person being approached, or more like Anna, the person approaching?*

- *What might the person approaching be thinking and feeling?*

- *What might the person being approached be thinking and feeling?*

- *When have you felt like the person approaching? The person begin approached?*

- *What situations cause you to react or respond as I did in this scenario?*

Participation

If you choose to have the group do the exercise in pairs, have participants pair off and line up in two lines about ten feet apart, facing each other. Let them know that they will be doing the practice in silence. (Note that participants are seldom completely silent.) Encourage them to pay attention to their thoughts, feelings, physical sensations, and actions as they do the exercise. Before beginning, it is wise to have them take a few slow, deep breaths and notice their thoughts and feelings. In addition, it's essential to remind participants that they are responsible for doing this practice in a way that's safe for everyone in the group. Then whisper "secret" instructions to each group as follows:

For the submissive response, instruct individuals in group A to walk angrily, with arms outstretched, toward their partners in group B. Instruct the partners in group B to cower and look fearful when they are approached.

For the avoidant response, instruct individuals in group B to walk angrily toward their partners in group A with arms outstretched. Instruct group A to sidestep their group B partners with a nonchalant expression as they approach.

For the aggressive response, again instruct individuals in group A to walk toward their partners in group B angrily, with arms outstretched. Instruct group B to push back against their group A partners, with arms outstretched and an angry expression.

For the asssertive response, again have individuals in group B walk angrily toward their partners in group A with arms outstretched. Show group A how to gently take their group B partner's left hand with their left hand, place their right hand on their partner's back, and slowly turn their partner 180 degrees.

After each version, invite mindful reflection:

- *How was the experience for those approaching with anger?*

- *How was the experience for those being approached?*

- *Does any of this feel familiar?*

- *What situations typically cause you to react or respond in this way?*

Aikido Discussion

After going through all four scenarios, elicit a group discussion on how these four ways of responding to conflict relate to the class's exploration of difficult communications and holes and different streets. In guiding this discussion, please be sensitive to the following considerations.

Unless we are careful, we can imply that the assertive way is generally the preferred, "right," or "better" way to respond. However, in my experience, it's helpful to look at these behaviors along a continuum, from submissive to avoidant to assertive to aggressive. For me, true mindfulness is skillfully choosing what is called for moment by moment. Sometimes it is wise to be submissive. Sometimes a certain amount of clear, forceful energy is called for. If we are not mindful, we react out of habit, doing what we always do, trying to please or dominate others. The invitation is to recognize our usual ways of behaving and practice choosing our responses wisely, based on the circumstances.

This skill is demonstrated through an amazing story reported on National Public Radio that challenges our preconceptions about when submission, avoidance, assertion, or aggression might be called for. A young teen approached a man, pulled out a knife, and demanded his wallet. When telling this story, you may wish to pause here and ask your young friends to consider what they would have done in this situation. The most typical responses are that they would have reacted submissively or they would have reacted aggressively.

In this case, the man handed over his wallet. As the teen walked away, the man called out and offered his jacket, and then invited the teen for dinner. The teen accepted, paid for dinner with the man's money, and returned the man's wallet. The man then offered him twenty dollars in return for the knife. (To read this exquisite story in its entirety, visit http://www.npr.org and search for "a victim treats his mugger right.")

If you choose to share this story, use it as an invitation for inquiry. The intention of this discussion is to explore our habitual responses and skillful alternatives, not to imply that the man's response, or any particular response, is good or bad, right or wrong, better or worse. When I share this story, in all honesty, I also share that if I were in such a situation, I would still probably act submissively.

Putting It All Together: ABCs, STAR, and PEACE Practices (all ages)

As you may recall from the beginning of the book, my definition of mindfulness is "paying attention here and now, with kindness and curiosity, and then choosing your behavior." The entire course has been designed to support young people in applying this approach in their daily lives. Below are three practice mnemonics to support our young friends in doing this: ABCs, for children ages five to seven; STAR for children ages eight to twelve; and PEACE for tweens and teens.

ABCs (ages five to seven)

For young children, it's best to keep it very simple. Most children in this age group are familiar with the alphabet, or at least the first few letters. So you can simply say:

In life it helps to remember our ABCs. This is especially true when things are difficult. So when things are difficult, keep these ABCs in mind:

- *A is for attention. Sometimes it is helpful just to stop and pay attention to our*

- *B is for breath. Usually when we pay attention to our breath it is easier to*

- *C is for choose. When we stop and pay attention to our breath, then sometimes we can make a kind choice, a choice that is kind to us and kind to others.*

STAR (ages eight to eleven)

Every spring, all California public school students take assessments called the STAR (Standardized Testing and Reporting) tests. These assessments are often stressful for the students (and teachers), so at the request of some teachers I work with, I created the following practice. In addition to being helpful for stress reduction prior to or while taking the test, this mnemonic is useful in many other challenging situations:

You may find this simple STAR practice helpful when you are taking a test, doing homework, or dealing with any other difficulty. The practice goes like this:

- *S is for stop. When you are faced with a difficulty, like a question on the test that you don't know the answer to, or any difficulty in life, stop.*

- *T is for take a breath. Usually, taking a few slow, deep breaths relaxes the mind and allows us to…*

- *Accept. A is for accept. Accept that you're having difficulty, that you don't know the answer, and that you're a bit stressed. (One third grader remembered the A as "All's well.")*

- *R is for restart or resume. When you're ready, after you've taken some slow, deep breaths and accepted things, you can restart, trying the problem again or moving on to another problem.*

Remember, this practice can be used with a difficult problem on a test or homework, and with other difficulties in your life.

PEACE (ages twelve to eighteen)

PEACE practice is the most involved of the series of responsive practices. A spoken version of this practice can be found on the *Still Quiet Place: Mindfulness for Teens* CD. This is a detailed formal practice. As with other formal practices, it is best if it is guided slowly, and used repeatedly. Over time, teens naturally tune into the aspects of the practice that are most relevant to a particular situation, and eventually retain the basic elements of the practice.

If we remember to use it, mindfulness can help us deal with difficult situations, from ordinary everyday difficulties, like losing your cell phone, to more extreme difficulties like failing a class, breaking up with a girlfriend or boyfriend, having a friend go jail, or maybe even going to jail yourself, getting pregnant, or grieving a death in your family or community.

Mindfulness is much more than just watching the breath. For me, the power and beauty of mindfulness is that using it helps me when things are most difficult.

PEACE is an acronym for a practice that can be used in any difficult situation. Perhaps you can begin by practicing with small daily irritations. If you are dealing with more extreme circumstances, you may need to repeat the practice many times a day, and you may also want to get additional help from a friend, a parent, a counselor, or a doctor.

The practice goes like this:

P is for pause. When you realize that things are difficult, pause.

E is for exhale. When you exhale, you may want to let out a sigh or a groan, or even weep. And after you exhale you want to?… Inhale. Just keep breathing.…

A is for acknowledge, accept, and allow. As you continue to breathe, acknowledge the situation as it is. Your backpack with all your stuff is gone, your parents are getting divorced, your best friend is now dating the person who just became your ex. Acknowledging a situation doesn't mean you're happy about it. It just means that you recognize the situation is as it is, whether you like it or not.

A is also for accept: accepting the situation and your reaction to it, whether you're furious, devastated, heartbroken, jealous, or all of the above.

Finally, A is also for allowing your experience. Do your best to rest in the Still Quiet Place and watch the thoughts, feelings, and body sensations. Notice when you're tempted to suppress your experience by pretending that you're fine, or when you want to create additional drama by rehashing things in your head or with friends. And allow this, too (smile). See if you can discover a middle way—a way of having your thoughts and feelings without your thoughts and feelings having you, and making you act in ways you may regret.

C is for choose. When you are ready—and this may take a few moments, days, weeks, or even months, depending on the situation—choose how you will respond. At its best, responding involves some additional Cs: clarity, courage, compassion, and comedy.

Clarity is being clear about what you want, what your limits are, and what you're responsible for.

Courage means having the courage to speak your truth and hear the truth of others.

Compassion means being kind toward yourself and others, and understanding how incredibly difficult it sometimes is to be a human being.

As for comedy, I actually prefer the word "humor," but it doesn't start with C (smile). It's amazing how helpful it can be to have a sense of humor and not take ourselves too seriously.

Finally, E is for engage. After you have paused, exhaled, allowed, and chosen your response, you are ready to engage with people, with the situation, with life.

Remember, if possible, practice with small upsets first, and for extreme circumstances you may have to repeat this process over and over, and receive additional support. The more you practice, the more PEACE you will have.

Loving-Kindness Practice and Discussion (all ages)

There are several intertwined, equally important intentions for offering this exercise to children. A fundamental aspect of this practice is to facilitate people's experience of being loved, feeling worthy of love, and feeling lovable, just as they are. Of course, we all wish that every child and teen would have this experience frequently. Sadly, we know that often this is not the case. Developing a kind heart and extending loving-kindness toward oneself is a potent antidote to repeated negative messages from Unkind Mind, peers, parents, other important adults, and the media. Many young people hear negative messages so frequently that they come to believe and internalize them. Because loving-kindness practice fosters self-compassion, it's a powerful anti-dote to the repetitive negativity.

Kristin Neff, PhD, a pioneer in the field of self-compassion, emphasizes that self-compassion is distinct from self-esteem. Self-esteem is evaluative and reflects our sense of self-worth; it is frequently based on comparing ourselves to others, and on our perceptions regarding our recent "success" or "failure." I feel good about myself because I am in some way better than you, or I feel good about myself because I recently was successful at X.

In contrast, self-compassion is based on the understanding that all human beings, ourselves included, have difficulty and simultaneously deserve kindness. Unlike self-esteem, self-compassion is not dependent on our evaluations of ourselves, our successes or failures, or how we compare to others.

Dr. Neff and her colleagues (Neff, Hsich, & Dejitterat, 2005) delineate three components of self-compassion: kindness toward oneself, an understanding of our common humanity, and mindful awareness. Hopefully, at this point in this book, it is clear that the Still Quiet Place curriculum emphasizes the elements of mindful aware-ness and kindness. To paraphrase, Dr. Neff describes mindful awareness as a willing-ness to observe negative thoughts and emotions with openness and clarity, without either suppressing or indulging them; and self-kindness as the cultivation of kindness toward oneself, especially when we suffer, fail, or feel inadequate. The third element of self-compassion described by Dr. Neff is the recognition that suffering and feelings of personal inadequacy are part of the shared human experience—something we all go through, rather than something that happens to "me" alone. This element of self-compassion is touched on in many of the discussions in the Still Quiet Place curricu-lum, in both subtle and explicit ways.

According to Dr. Neff, self-compassion not only enhances well-being; it also increases resilience. In fact, her research demonstrates that self-compassion increases undergraduate students' ability to cope with perceived academic failure; and that it is positively associated with emotion-focused coping strategies and negatively associ-ated with avoidance-oriented strategies (2005, pp. 263–87). And, though research has yet to document the common experience that self-compassion enhances compas-sion for others and vice versa, two recent studies, one by Dr. Neff (Neff & Germer, 2013) and the other by Dr. Hooria Jazaieri and colleagues (2012) at the Stanford Center for Compassion and Altruism Research and Education (CCARE), have shown that self-compassion and compassion for others are correlated. Thus the self-kindness aspect of the loving-kindness practice is likely to enhance kindness and compassion for others indirectly.

Additionally, loving-kindness practice explicitly develops our young friends' capacities to offer kindness, caring, and love to others. They practice sending kindness, caring, and love to people they know well, to people they don't know well, to people they are having difficulty with, or to people who are no longer physically present in their lives. When added to the perspective taking of the difficult communication exercise, loving-kindness practice can enhance empathy and compassion for others. Over time, this practice can transform difficult relationships, even when the other person's behavior doesn't change. Kids who have felt animosity toward a particular individual or group for a long time are often surprised to discover that they feel less angry and aggressive toward the individual or group after doing this practice.

Thus, the loving-kindness practice below is intended to increase self-compassion, well-being, resilience, and compassion for others. It is intentionally described in somewhat vague terms. As mentioned in chapter 3, it's essential that you have an established practice before teaching mindfulness and loving-kindness to others. If you have not personally done traditional loving-kindness practice, please commit to a daily practice for at least two months before you share this practice with others. This practice is both joyful and rigorous, and if you aren't drawing on your own experience, you risk being removed or saccharine. A sample practice appropriate for all ages can be downloaded from http://www.newharbinger.com/27572. (See the back of the book for more information.) Age-specific versions of this practice can be found on the CDs *Still Quiet Place: Mindfulness for Teens* and *Still Quiet Place: Mindfulness for Children*.

Loving-Kindness Practice (all ages)

Let the participants settle into the Still Quiet Place, either sitting in chairs or lying on the floor. After a few moments of breathing, invite them to remember a simple moment when they felt cared for or loved by someone—a parent, a coach, a teacher, a neighbor, a friend, a brother or sister, or even a pet.... Let them know that moment could be as simple as a kind word or a pat on the back. Encourage them to remember the details of this moment—the time, the setting, the person's voice—and then to let the feeling of being cared for, or loved, fill them. Acknowledge that the feeling may be very small (subtle), or it may be big and powerful (intense), and that however it is, is fine.

Because life circumstances vary widely, it is important to make the descriptors of the caring or loving person very broad. Initially, you may want to add phrasing along the lines of "remember a time in the last week" or "bring to mind someone you see often." This can be particularly important when you are teaching the practice in a setting where there's a high likelihood of participants' caregivers being unavailable, absent, or perhaps even incarcerated or dead. Such phrasing minimizes the probability that a young person will initially choose someone who has moved away, been jailed, or died. In time, with practice, they may include people who are no longer physically present in their lives. Many children find the practice to be extraordinarily valuable, because it connects them with loved ones they no longer see.

Suggest they send caring or love to the person (or animal) they remembered. Encourage them to silently offer a kind wish to the person, such as "May you be happy," and once again feel the person's caring or love for them. Young children enjoy blowing kisses as they send their wishes. Before moving on to the next phase of the practice—extending loving-kindness to an unfamiliar, or neutral, person—suggest they send love to themselves and silently wish themselves well: "May I be happy."

This sequence can be repeated with two or three other people. They can experiment with sending caring or love to a person that they don't know well: the child who sits three rows back in math, the school janitor, a store clerk. Or they can send these feelings to someone they are having difficulty with: their "ex-best friend," their little brother.... After they send caring, love, and kind wishes to each person, have them send love and kind wishes to themselves.

With tweens and teens, I often add the phrase "just as I am" to their wishes; "May I be happy just as I am." "May I be peaceful and at ease just as I am." To counter Unkind Mind, I also encourage them to send caring, love, and kind wishes to an aspect of themselves they dislike or hate. "May my hair be happy." "May my anger be peaceful and at ease." " May my slow reading be filled with joy." Let them know that it is fine if it feels dorky or ridiculous. Encourage them, as the Nike slogan says, to "just do it," because it is these unliked or even hated aspects of ourselves that are most in need of our kindness. Let them know that they can play with phrases and discover what works best for them.

Close by having them send love to themselves and feel their love returning back to them, and then sending love to the whole world—the people, the animals, the plants, and the earth—and the sun, the stars, and the moon, and feeling the love of the whole world returning to them.

Loving-Kindness Discussion (ages eight to eighteen)

With children younger than eight, you can simply say, "Isn't it great to remember that we can send love and kindness to ourselves and others?"

With children eight and older you can explore the practice in more depth with the following questions. Be aware that some children and teens find this practice challenging or intense.

- *How was that practice for you?*

- *What were your feelings and thoughts?*

- *Did you find it easy or difficult to send love to, and receive love from, others? To yourself?*

- *Did you want to joke about it or blow it off?*

- *How did it feel in your body?*

- *How is it to know that you can practice sending and receiving love?*

- *Are you willing to play or work with this practice?*

- *Are you willing to try it with people you find difficult?*

- *Are you willing to use it as an antidote to Unkind Mind?*

Overview of Home Practice (all ages)

Finally, review the home practice. In keeping with this week's focus, the guided home practice is Loving-Kindness. The mindfulness in daily life practices include imagining yourself and the world from the other person's point of view during a difficulty or disagreement, and responding with Kind Heart rather than reacting out of Unkind Mind during stressful situations.

In the eight-week format, the next session is the final session. Thus, as indicated on the home practice sheet, I ask the participants to bring something to symbolize their experience of the course. Typically, I don't provide more guidance than what is written on the home practice sheet; I don't want to bias them, and I enjoy being surprised.

Also answer any questions participants may have about home practice.

Closing Mindful Listening Practice (all ages)

Close by allowing one or two attentive students to ring the bell for the closing listening practice.

Practicing at Home—Session 7

Mindfulness is a lifelong practice.

Practice makes practice.

Listen to the guided Loving-Kindness practice every day.

Practice mindfulness in daily life.

- *When you are having difficulty or disagreeing with someone, imagine yourself and the world from the other person's point of view.*

- *In stressful situations, respond with Kind Heart rather than reacting out of Unkind Mind.*

With kindness and curiosity, and without guilt, fill out the home practice log.

Next week is our last class. Please bring something that represents what the Still Quiet Place and mindfulness mean to you—such as a tangerine, a haiku, a picture, a short story, a favorite poem, a song….

If you have a mindful moment, questions, or difficulties you'd like to share, or if you won't be able to attend the next class, call or e-mail me.

session 8: the end of the out-breath

Intentions

The intentions for this session are to discuss the course participants' experiences with sending and receiving love, to remind them that with practice they can develop these capacities, and then to move toward "completion." The process of completion involves four primary components: creating the opportunity for them to share what the course has meant to them, both privately in the form of a "letter to a friend," and with the group during group discussion; discussing their thoughts and feelings about the course ending; sharing the variety of ways they can make the practice their own; and finally, reminding them that you will be available if they wish to connect in the future.

Outline: Practices, Exercises, and Discussions

- Mindful Listening practice*

- Mindful Eating practice*

- Home practice review

- Group choice practice or Flashlight practice*

- Letter to a Friend exercise

- Closing sharing*

- Ending of the course discussion*

- Closing Mindful Listening practice*

Mindful Listening and Mindful Eating Practice (all ages)

Because participants are now very familiar with these practices, you can let them know that you will be doing listening and eating practice in "silence." You can simply sound the chime, and then transition with a few brief words to eating in silence. As eating practice concludes, invite your young friends to rest in the stillness and quietness and attend to any thoughts or feelings they have about the course and the course ending.

Home Practice Review (ages six to eighteen)

Begin by asking participants about their experience with the loving-kindness practice. You may use the prompts from session 7. Make sure to elicit comments from those for whom it was neutral, unpleasant, or upsetting, and not just from those who enjoyed the practice or found it to be a positive experience. Remind them that their experience is fine just as it is, that the practice may change from day to day, and that they now have more skills for being with whatever arises.

Group Choice Practice or Flashlight Practice (all ages)

There are several options for the "last" guided practice of the course. Let your heart guide you. You may let the group choose a final practice from all of the practices they've done together: a Still Quiet Place breath-based practice, thought watching, feelings, the body scan, loving-kindness, and ABCs, STAR, or PEACE. Alternatively, you can offer the flashlight practice, described below. There is no magic ending practice, just what is chosen in the moment, and often it is magical.

Flashlight Practice (all ages)

This practice incorporates many of the primary elements offered during the course and provides an elegant final shared practice. It is a child-friendly version of adult choiceless awareness practice. A recorded version of this practice is on the CD *Still Quiet Place: Mindfulness for Teens*.

Simply invite participants to settle in and close their eyes, and rest the flashlight of their attention on the breath and the Still Quiet Place between the breaths....

After a minute or so, invite them to shine the flashlight of their attention on sound, listening to the sounds in the room, the sounds beyond the room, the sounds in their own body, their breath, their heartbeat, a ringing in their ears....

After another minute or so, invite them to shine the flashlight of attention on their bodies, noting where their bodies make contact with their chairs, their clothing, the air, areas of comfort and discomfort in their bodies....

Again, after some time, invite them to shine their flashlight of attention on their thoughts, noticing the thoughts as they come and go.

Then invite them to shine the flashlight of attention on their feelings, particularly any feelings about the course and the course ending, simply acknowledging whatever they are feeling in the moment....

Then have them shine the flashlight of attention on the breath, and then the Still Quiet Place itself.... Just breathing, and resting in stillness and quietness.

At the conclusion of the practice you can mention that it can be very helpful to know that we have a flashlight of attention, and that with practice we can learn to turn it on and choose where we focus it. We can expand the beam of our attention to include everything, or narrow it to just one thing: the ball and the hoop, the test question, the person in front of us, the taste of a tangerine.... This ability to expand and narrow (or focus) the flashlight of our attention can be very helpful when playing a sport or a musical instrument, taking a test, or having a difficult conversation.

Coming full circle, ask participants to return their attention to the breath and encourage them to rest in the Still Quiet Place. Pause here for a moment, then ask that they remain silent as you guide them in writing a Letter to a Friend.

Letter to a Friend Exercise (ages eight to eighteen)

Pass out paper and pens or pencils to all the participants. Then, invite them to write a brief letter to a friend who knows nothing about the Still Quiet Place or mindfulness, describing how it feels to rest in the Still Quiet Place, or rest in awareness, and how they use mindfulness in their daily life. If you like, you can photocopy and distribute the blank letter form at the end of this chapter (also available for download online at http://www.newharbinger.com/27572).

Explain that the friend can be anyone, including a pet or an imaginary friend. Reassure them that they do not need to put their names on their letters, and that unless they choose to they won't be sending these letters; it's just a way for them to share what the course has meant to them with you in a confidential way. Remind them that this is mindfulness, not English—(unless of course it is English)—and that they can just write what is true for them without worrying about spelling or punctuation. Also remember that there may be one or two students with learning differences for whom writing is difficult; you can offer to transcribe their letter for them. I usually keep the children's letters. If an individual wants to keep or send his letter, I ask permission to take a photo of the letter with my phone, or make a copy for my records.

Closing Sharing (all ages)

Encourage each person to share what they brought to represent their experience of mindfulness, and ask that they explain how or why it represents mindfulness. As with all the dialogues, comment or not, as you feel is skillful. Be aware of your attachment to participants liking the course and getting something out of it. Remember to allow participants to have their experience just as it is.

Children often bring food. One very shy fourth-grade girl brought apples, and the dialogue, which I have on video to share in my online course, went like this:

Me: Why do the apples remind you of mindfulness?

Sonia: The apples remind me of sweet. I don't know, my mom just "choosed" them.

Me:	Your mom just chose them?
Sonia:	(*Nod.*)
Me:	Did she know we ate apples often in here? Did you tell her that?
Sonia:	(*Nod.*)
Me:	Did you eat any apples mindfully with your mom?
Sonia:	(*Nod.*)
Me:	You did?! Did you teach her how to do it?
Sonia:	(*Nod.*)
Me:	What did she think?
Sonia:	She said it was too slow (*giggle*).
Me:	And what did you tell her about slowness?
Sonia:	That it was about the sweetness.
Me:	About tasting it, tasting the sweetness?
Sonia:	(*Nod.*)
Me:	And then what did she say? That is was still too slow (*giggle*)?
Sonia:	(*Nod.*)
Me:	She needs more lessons, Sonia….
Sonia:	She always hears the CD….

As students often do, this young Hispanic girl had brought the practices home to her family in multiple ways. She had shared eating practice, listening to the guided practices, and the hole and different streets story. And her family had used the story to resolve a recurrent conflict in their small apartment with many occupants in close quarters: Sonia wanted and needed to do her homework. Her younger sister wanted to play and often bothered her, leading to the hole of shared frustration. They agreed to take another street, and use a timer; they would set the timer for thirty minutes, and Sonia would do her homework, and her sister would play or color. Then Sonia would play with her sister for at least fifteen minutes. So, the apples Sonia shared actually represent an infusion of mindfulness into an entire low-income Hispanic household.

Ending of the Course Discussion (all ages)

I like to approach the discussion of the ending of the course by tying it back to the breath. I often say that the end of the course is like the end of the out-breath. Then there is a pause, and then the beginning of the in-breath. Each participant gets to choose if and how he will continue the practice. Some students will feel that the class was an interesting experience and leave it at that. Others choose to continue a daily practice and incorporate it into their lives. Others will return to it or fall back on it in times of stress.

Make room for questions, particularly about difficulties and uncertainties. At this point many participants express sadness that the course is ending and regret that they didn't practice more during the course. You can encourage them to allow these feelings and to use them to motivate them to begin practicing, again, now, in this new moment. Other participants worry that without the structure and support of the group, they will neglect their practice and forget their newfound wisdom. Again, you can encourage them to allow these feelings, and to choose if and how they wish to maintain their practice. Almost any concern can be responded to by suggesting they notice their thoughts and feelings with kindness and curiosity and then choose their behavior.

Also remind participants that while much of the course has focused on using mindfulness in difficult circumstances, you encourage them to continue to be mindful of the many pleasant moments in their lives. Congratulate them for completing the course and devoting time to developing the muscle (capacity) of paying attention to themselves, their experience, and others, with kindness and curiosity, and then choosing their behavior.

At the end of this discussion, I offer participants a reading list (see Resources) and a list of local resources to support their practice. Up-to-date lists of books and CDs for a given age group can be found on my website: http://www.stillquietplace .com. I strongly encourage you to let participants know that you are available by phone or e-mail anytime they wish to contact you. I've had participants e-mail me six to twelve months after a class concludes, usually asking how mindfulness might support them during a difficult time.

Closing Mindful Listening Practice (all ages)

If time allows and the participants agree to bring their full attention to each ring, I invite each participant to ring the tone bar once for the final closing Mindful Listening practice. With young children, the course often ends with the entire group joyfully surrounding the child ringing the bar, smiling and listening intently, as the sound fades into stillness and quietness.

***

Congratulations on completing the session chapters and devoting the time to developing your ability to share the Still Quiet Place and the practices of mindfulness with youth.

Now that you have also reached the end of the course, in this pause at the end of the out-breath, please take as much time as you need to be with the material and consider if and how you wish to proceed. As with the course participants, some readers will feel that this book was an interesting read and leave it at that. Others will choose the next sane and joyful step. More detailed suggestions for how to determine if you are ready to share the Still Quiet Place with children and adolescents, notes on preparing to teach, and several important cautions appear in the next two chapters.

If you have a mindful moment, questions, or difficulties you'd like to share, please call or e-mail me.

Practicing at Home—Session 8

Mindfulness is yours.

Make the practice your own.

Make a promise to yourself to practice for _____ minutes _____ times per week.

Put a reminder on your calendar (phone). Then, one month from now, with kindness and curiosity, check and see if you have kept your promise.

If you have kept your promise, choose whether you want to keep practicing.

If you have not kept your promise, choose whether you want to begin practicing again.

Practice mindfulness in daily life.

- *Just do it!*

If you have a mindful moment, questions, or difficulties you'd like to share, please call or e-mail me.

Letter to a Friend

Write a brief letter to a friend who knows nothing about mindfulness, describing:

- How it feels to rest in the Still Quiet Place, or rest in awareness.

- How you have used mindfulness in your daily life.

Just write what is true for you and don't worry about spelling or punctuation. If writing is difficult for you, you can tell me what you would like to say and I will write it down.

_____

_____

_____

_____

_____

_____

_____

_____

_____

_____

_____

_____

_____

_____

_____

_____

_____

_____

_____

12

am I ready? qualities and qualifications for visiting the still quiet place with children

As you have experienced through reading this book, during the course we revisit many themes with our young friends, deepening and expanding upon them over time. In this section we will revisit the recommendations regarding developing a personal practice, and the practice of facilitating, both of which were detailed in chapter 3. Now that you have a clearer sense of the course, it is essential that you bring your kind and curious attention to the question "Am I ready to share the Still Quiet Place with children and adolescents?" This chapter provides historical context and draws on the collective wisdom of pioneers in the Northern California MBSR community to express the qualities and qualifications for doing this work.

Although the heartfelt, rigorous dialogue described below took place almost 20 years ago, it is immediately relevant in the here and now. Developmentally, the field of mindfulness for youth is currently where the field of mindfulness in medicine was when the conversation below took place. There is tremendous interest and "buzz," which in turn creates both amazing opportunities and potential risks. More importantly, in this moment, the inquiry below is intimate and deeply personal: *Are you ready?* Following the inquiry, I describe the stages of my own journey through this inquiry and into teaching and teaching to youth.

Throughout the mid-1990s, a small group of MBSR teachers in Northern California—we eventually became known as the Northern California Advisory Group on Mindfulness in Medicine—met once a month to support one another, and to discuss the joys and challenges of teaching and facilitating mindfulness. Around this time, the Northern California Kaiser Hospital system decided to offer MBSR on a regional basis through its health education departments. Kaiser's model for health education was to give a trained health educator a standardized curriculum on a particular topic (smoking cessation, weight loss, MBSR) and have the health educator provide the curriculum more or less verbatim.

During this time, our group learned of several instances in which professionals with no mindfulness experience were hired to teach MBSR at various facilities throughout the region. One woman hired to teach wisely realized that mindfulness was distinct from the other health education curricula, and that she needed personal experience if she was to deliver MBSR authentically and effectively. To her credit, she approached one of the advisory group members for support. This woman's experience, among others, prompted the group to consider how we could support the administrators responsible for hiring the instructors, and the instructors themselves. Our aim was to ensure that MBSR was offered, in the Kaiser system and beyond, with the same exemplary degree of integrity and resultant high level of efficacy as it was at the Stress Reduction Clinic, at the University of Massachusetts.

Qualities and Qualifications

Our collective experience yielded a simple, clear certainty: a teacher or facilitator must have an "established practice" and teach from her experience. However, translating what this actually meant for ourselves, hospital administrators, and potential instructors turned out to be a mindfulness exercise in and of itself. Together, we spent almost a year discussing and refining the qualities and qualifications for MBSR instructors, and in 1996 we ultimately produced a document titled *Recommended Guidelines: Qualifications for Teachers of Mindfulness-Based Stress Reduction and Chronic Pain Programs*. The document itself is succinct and eloquently worded. It has tremendous power, in that it was written by a respected community of pioneers in the field of mindfulness in medicine, the majority of whom continue to be leaders in the field.

As with other elements in this book, I have retained the essence, clarity, and intention of the document. Simultaneously, I have included limited adaptations to speak to professionals working and playing with children and adolescents. The chosen modifications appear in italics. Given the vulnerability of young people, respecting the intention of these guidelines is perhaps even more important when teaching youth than when teaching adults.

Recommended Guidelines: Qualifications for Teachers of Mindfulness-Based Stress Reduction Youth Programs

More *schools and community settings* are developing mindfulness programs *for children and adolescents*. Based on our experience, those of us who are directing and teaching existing programs resolutely endorse the specific guidelines which appear below. These guidelines are offered in the spirit of filling a need, and maintaining the integrity of the work. These guidelines are not meant to be absolute, but rather to bring clarity to the process of (training and) hiring mindfulness instructors.

The primary role of an instructor of mindfulness practice is to offer an approach to *developing social, emotional, and academic competencies, and working with stress and suffering*. This is delicate work, and it therefore necessitates that instructors have a level of preparation that differs from and generally exceeds that of most other approaches to stress reduction.

This document describes both qualifications for and qualities of a mindfulness instructor. These guidelines represent the *minimum* qualifications and the ideal qualities. We wish to make explicit that the qualities are of primary importance. We are aware that there are individuals who meet the qualifications with regard to consistency, duration, and intensity of mindfulness experience, but who are not capable of teaching; and there are rare individuals who do not meet the specific qualifications, yet have developed the qualities of a teacher and are capable of teaching.

Qualities

- An ability to create a safe environment where participants are able to explore their physical, mental, and emotional territory.

- A *profound* ability to empathize with, and simultaneously maintain a non-judgmental perspective of, a participant's experience.

- A willingness to accept and engage with any participant's experience of physical sensation, emotion, or thought.

- Honesty about, and respect and compassion for, what it means to be human.

- A quality of unshockability.

- The discernment to make appropriate (*useful*) comments and suggestions to individual participants.

- An ongoing awareness of the evolutionary process of each individual and the group as a whole.

- A commitment to apply the principles of mindfulness to situations in daily life that the instructor herself finds personally challenging.

- The ability to model (*embody*) and convey self-acceptance and other principles of mindfulness.

- The (*consistent*) ability to inspire and maintain participant interest and adherence.

- A *love of, and willingness to connect with, youth.*

Qualifications

- A daily mindfulness practice.

- Five years of mindfulness experience.

- Extensive mindfulness retreat experience (multiple five- to ten-day, or longer, retreats recommended). This develops the instructor's essential experiential knowledge of the varied mind states that can arise during the process of mindfulness practice.

- An ability to translate mindfulness into ordinary, everyday language.

- Extensive experience teaching yoga or some other movement practice within the context of mindfulness. The essential elements of this context include nonstriving and honoring individual experience. The attention must be on the process itself and not on the results. This allows individuals to simultaneously investigate their limitations, and to gently challenge them.

- Professional experience (*teaching credential* or equivalent) working with *youth.*

- *Process-oriented* group facilitation skills.

- An ongoing affiliation with a community of mindfulness peers (teachers and practitioners) who encourage continued professional growth and development.

"Oh, Shit!" Moments

Perhaps as you read the guidelines you experienced what I fondly refer to as an "Oh, shit!" moment. Although the timing varies, "Oh, shit!" moments arise for almost all people committed to doing this work with integrity. When it arrives it sounds something like this: "Can I really do this work? Can I do it with skill, grace, vulnerability, devotion, and fearlessness? Am I equal to the responsibility and privilege of teaching?" Congratulations. This is a sign that you are committed to doing this work with authenticity. Keep breathing and trust that you will find *your* way.

The process of creating the Qualities and Qualifications was intense and provided me, and many of my colleagues, with our own "Oh, shit!" moments. My moments had to do with acknowledging that, although I was already teaching, I could not check two crucial boxes in the qualifications list—items 2 and 3: five years of mindfulness experience, and extensive mindfulness retreat experience. However, thanks to the rigorous life coaching I was participating in, the qualities had blossomed. So I continued to teach. And in my commitment to doing the work with integrity I continued my daily practice, and promptly participated in a guided silent retreat. Since then, for the last twenty years I have maintained an almost daily practice, and sat at least one annual silent retreat.

Further Notes

All of the qualities above must be held within a context of humility, as expressed in quality 4—honesty about, and respect and compassion for, what it means to be human—and quality 8: a commitment to apply the principles of mindfulness to situations in daily life that the instructor finds personally challenging.

None of us are able to embody all of the qualities all of the time, and if we think we can, we are most likely not paying enough attention (smile). The essential question is this: Can you commit to embodying the qualities and paying attention, and to being both rigorously honest and compassionate with yourself when you fall short? This is the essence of mindfulness. It is the primary measure of your own personal journey *and* your capacity to share this work with others.

So please pause here, take several slow deep breaths, and check in with yourself…. After having read this, what thoughts, feelings, and physical sensations are present?… Can you allow your experience to be exactly as it is in this moment, without needing to change or fix it?… Can you choose to start where you are and take the next sane and joyful step?… The intention of this chapter is to provide *you* with an "Oh, shit!" moment and compel you to ask yourself, "Am I *really* ready to teach?" Only you know. Live inside this question until the answer is clear and steady, at least most of the time. If you discover you are ready, go forth with chutzpah and humility! Please have fun and enjoy the journey! The views are spectacular and ever changing.

Remember, as Richard Bach (1977, p. 46) says, "Learning is finding out what you already know. Doing is demonstrating that you know it. Teaching is reminding others that they know just as well as you. You are all learners, doers, teachers."

My Story

There are many places to pick up the thread of anyone's story. While all threads can be traced back through childhood, and possibly through our parents' childhoods and beyond, I'll pick up my thread in the summer of 1989. I was recently married, a competitive bicyclist, and just about to start my second year of medical school. I had been considering working with a sports psychologist to improve the mental aspect of my cycling when a fellow racer invited me to attend a workshop with her transformational coach, Georgina Lindsey. Ms. Lindsey was a founding partner of the national transformational consulting firm Sports Vision. Simply put, that day changed my life. Although I didn't know it at the time, the day was my introduction to the precious domain of awareness that I would later come to know and love: the Still Quiet Place.

In the winter of 1990 I had two cycling "accidents" in short succession. The coaching enabled me to discover that things are not always as they seem, and that accidents are often, if not always, opportunities in disguise. During the time I was rehabilitating my knee, I picked up the strands of some neglected aspects of my life—both inner and outer—including finally joining the American Holistic Medical Association (AHMA). My AHMA membership materials included an announcement for their annual conference. Although I felt pulled to participate in this new world, the timing was such that I had missed the deadlines for registration, scholarships, and housing. Using the coaching distinction of "living from vision versus circumstances," I followed the thread, disregarded the circumstances, and sent in my application. As the thread would have it, another woman canceled at the last minute and I received her scholarship and housing!

As with my introduction to Ms. Lindsey, at the conference I had the undeniable experience of coming home, again. In contrast to my experiences in medical school, the physicians in the AHMA truly enjoyed their work; they treated their patients as whole human beings, rather than as diseases, and supported them in optimizing their health and well-being. Looking back, it was a combination of arrogance and zealous thread-following that prompted me to send a brief letter to the board of trustees with suggestions about how the AHMA might nurture the natural holism in medical students and residents. In June of that year, just four months after that conference, I miraculously found myself on the board of trustees of the AHMA.

The airing of Bill Moyers's PBS special *Healing and the Mind* in early 1993 was a pivotal event for the holistic medicine community and for me personally. After seeing the segment on the Stress Reduction Clinic at the University of Massachusetts, I had an undeniable urge to do this work. I read the book *Full Catastrophe Living* (1990), written by the clinic's director, Jon Kabat-Zinn, PhD, and immediately began a daily mindfulness practice.

Despite my minimal formal practice, an increasingly familiar mixture of arrogance, faith, persistence, and intuition compelled me to contact Dr. Kabat-Zinn at the Stress Reduction Clinic—*repeatedly*. Using the coaching distinction of "outrageous request," I asked to participate in comprehensive training in mindfulness-based stress reduction (MBSR). Again, life rewarded me for following the thread. The Stress Reduction Clinic accommodated my schedule, allowing me to attend half of what is now known as the eight-week practicum. The program director of my residency not only gave me a month to devote to studying mindfulness, she also gave me credit for attending the program and found funding to pay my tuition!

In 1993, I spent the gloriously vibrant month of October on the East Coast. I immersed myself in the practice and study of mindfulness, attending every class the Stress Reduction Clinic offered. These classes were the first through fourth classes of six separate but concurrent MBSR courses. Participating in six distinct courses made it absolutely clear that although the curriculum serves as a solid foundation, each teacher, each group, each moment, and therefore each course, is unique.

I came to understand at a core level what Jon Kabat-Zinn meant when he told me and my fellow prospective mindfulness teachers, "You can't teach 'my' course." Teaching out of one's own practice and life experience definitely requires more courage, faith, and humility than reciting a standardized curriculum. Yet, it is this way of teaching or facilitating—simultaneously honoring the foundational curriculum, one's own practice, and participants' experiences—that allows real transformation to occur both in ourselves and in those we serve.

Returning to California, I made arrangements to attend a colleague's entire eight-week MBSR course from beginning to end. The potent combination of the coaching, the month at the Stress Reduction Clinic, and the eight-week course opened my mind and heart, and intensified my desire to begin sharing these beneficial practices with others. In my final year of residency, still following the thread with my particular combination of chutzpah and devotion, I designed a $100,000 randomized, controlled trial to evaluate not only the individual benefits but also the cost-effectiveness of teaching mindfulness to patients with chronic pain and illness at Kaiser Santa Clara. The following year I was offered the opportunity to be chief resident in Internal Medicine. I accepted in large part because the position allowed me to teach several MBSR courses within the context of the clinical trial.

Fortunately, while following the thread has brought extraordinary opportunities, it has also tempered my personality (at least somewhat). I would be remiss if I didn't mention that following this thread has meant continually stepping through every preconceived notion of who I thought I was supposed to be as an athlete, doctor, wife, and mother. Initially, my commitment to bringing this work into my professional and personal life was challenged by many of the senior physicians in my residency, my friends, my family, my husband, and my own limited thinking. Despite these challenges, I didn't let go of the thread—or, perhaps more accurately, I realized the thread wouldn't let go of me.

Further Along the Thread:
More "Oh, Shit!" Moments

Since I began sharing the Still Quiet Place with children, I've had more "Oh, shit!" moments. The most unsettling of these came after a colleague asserted, "Jon Kabat-Zinn says you shouldn't teach mindfulness to children." Following this comment I watched waves of doubt arise. Then, because I wanted to be clear about what Jon *really* said, I went back and reread the chapter titled "Mindfulness in the Classroom: Getting to Know Yourself in School," in the book *Everyday Blessings* (Kabat-Zinn & Kabat-Zinn, 1997). In this chapter, Jon and his wife Myla write about Cherry Hamrick, a fifth-grade teacher in South Jordan, Utah, who incorporated mindfulness into her classroom—in a school in a predominantly Mormon community. The chapter ends with these two paragraphs:

> This is not to say that, as parents, we should teach our children how to meditate in any formal sense, although there are times when useful applications of meditation may naturally arise. In those moments, drawing on our own experience and practice, we might, for example, suggest to our young children to be aware of and look very closely at what "color" their pain is and how it changes from moment to moment when they have hurt themselves, or show them how to "float" on the waves of their breath as if in a little boat when they are having a hard time relaxing or going to sleep, or to see if they can think of times when their minds "waved" because of what other people did or said when their feelings have been hurt.
>
> It seems wise to take our cues from our children and their expressions of interest at different ages. Ultimately, the best teaching we can do is by example, through our own commitment to be present, and our sensitivity to them. When we practice formally, either sitting or lying down, we embody silence and stillness. Our children see us deeply focused and become familiar with this way of being. Many of the insights and attitudes that develop from our mindfulness practice will naturally filter into the culture of the family and affect our children in ways that they may in time find useful in their own lives. (p. 307)

After rereading the chapter, the wave of doubt subsided a bit. I had not set out to teach mindfulness to children. It is where the thread had led me. The practices that had arisen naturally—Feelings, Seaweed, Unkind Mind—were very similar to the examples Jon and Myla offered. And as with Cherry Hamrick's students, it seemed that the children I shared the practices with benefited.

Sometime later, I remembered Jon's story of being invited to present the work of the Stress Reduction Clinic to His Holiness the Dalai Lama. Some people had implied that the Dalai Lama would suggest that teaching MBSR wasn't wise or beneficial. As I recall Jon's telling of this teaching story, he was willing to listen respectfully to any concerns the Dalai Lama might express. And, the night before he was to make his presentation, Jon became clear that he would continue the work of the Stress Reduction Clinic, with or without the Dalai Lama's approval.

Recalling this story of Jon's discernment and thread-following brought a smile, along with some assurance. I, too, am willing to hear and carefully consider concerns. And, thus far, I have chosen to proceed with caution, faith, and courage, letting my experiences and the experiences of the children unspool the thread and guide me.

Looking back, it has become clear that my thread (with its strands of arrogance, devotion, courage, faith, and intuition) has led me to use the form of MBSR to bring the realizations I've experienced through my mindfulness practice and the coaching into the fields of medicine and education. Offering these practices to children is the truest form of preventive medicine I know. For me, the coaching and mindfulness are interwoven processes for

- Living in the full bloom of the reality of the present moment

- Becoming aware of habitual ways of thinking, feeling, and reacting

- Coming to understand that "I" am so much more than my limited thinking, feeling, and reacting

- Developing the capacity to respond, with wisdom and grace, to life's circumstances

- Treating myself and others with kindness and compassion

- Learning to dwell in awareness, otherwise known as the Still Quiet Place

May you find great joy in following your thread, and sharing the precious gifts of the Still Quiet Place with young people.

notes and cautions

In this chapter, I'll present considerations specific to those offering the curriculum to individuals, and to therapists and classroom teachers working with groups. In addition, I'll offer some cautionary tales, and close with a review of some overarching principles for presenting this curriculum.

Working with Individuals

Remember that while the exercises are presented here as a curriculum that builds sequentially, the offerings were initially created in response to ordinary moments with my children, students, and patients. Furthermore, when working with patients in my office, I often offer only selected portions of the curriculum, and frequently create new practices tailored to the individual. If you are a therapist, coach, allied professional, or parent working one-on-one with a child or teen, you may follow the course structure session by session as described, or tailor the program based on the specific needs of the young person you are supporting. For example, if a child you are working with has anger management issues, then you may emphasize Mindfulness of Feelings practice, basic emotion theory, watching the waves of emotion, and responding rather than reacting ("choosing a different street," in chapter 8). If a client is depressed, you may emphasize Thought Watching, with an emphasis on noticing Unkind Mind, and loving-kindness. If a client has ADD or ADHD (executive function deficits), you may focus on developing attention with breath-based practices, Flashlight practice, and noticing when the mind wanders. At a minimum, you are encouraged to offer every individual an experience of stillness and quietness, as well as guidance for observing thoughts, feelings, and physical sensations and choosing behavior.

A Note to Therapists

As a therapist you may find that some of the suggestions in this book are different from your usual therapeutic mode, and therefore uncomfortable. Please remember that while mindfulness may be therapeutic, it is distinct from therapy. The most important distinction is that mindfulness is about *being with* what is, rather than fixing things. If you realize you have shifted into fixing mode, take a breath, and then begin again, bringing agenda-less kindness and curiosity to the moment: "How is that for you?" "Can you breathe into that feeling?" " I notice that when you describe that situation, my body and jaw begin to tighten. What do you notice in your body?"

Also, at its best, mindfulness involves what my friend and colleague Sam Himelstein, who offers these practices to high-risk and incarcerated youth, calls "skillful self-disclosure," or "keepin' it real." Sharing these practices effectively depends on your ability to be a living example of mindfulness in its simultaneous reality and possibility. This means sharing the truth of your own practice—including where you fall short, react out of habit, or do something you regret—and the moments of grace and wisdom, when you manage to simply hold your tongue or respond with kindness for yourself and others.

You might say, for example, "Yeah, sometimes it is like that. The other day I was angry about an e-mail. My son came in the room and asked a simple question, and I snapped at him. That was a reaction. If I had it to do over again I would respond by saying, 'I am really angry right now; it doesn't have anything to do with you. Give me a minute and then we can talk.'" After such self-disclosure you can ask, "If you got a do-over, for your situation, how would you respond?" Like refraining from fixing, some therapists initially find skillful self-disclosure uncomfortable. Use your mindfulness practice to explore any discomfort that arises from the differences between the two approaches.

Additionally, mindfulness is about recognizing and honoring the essential wholeness of those we serve, rather than focusing on a diagnosis or difficulty. Do your best to nurture the natural stillness beneath the hyperactivity, and the peace beneath the depression. Talk to your clients about what is going well, their passions and small victories. Help them *realize* that they are so much more than their *DSM-5* diagnosis.

Lastly, most therapists have been trained to maintain strict boundaries with clients and may be reluctant to send mindful reminders and engage in between-class communication with clients and group participants. While it is not essential that you communicate between sessions, such communication definitely supports young people in establishing a daily or near-daily practice. I encourage you to remember that mindfulness is distinct from therapy, and to establish ways of offering it that simultaneously are true to the practice, acknowledge the distinctions, and feel authentic to you.

Distinguishing Between Mindfulness and Relaxation or Visualization

It is important to review how mindfulness is distinct from both relaxation and visualization, especially for those with therapeutic backgrounds trained in these modalities. Many people find that they feel more relaxed and happy when they practice mindfulness. However, mindfulness is not about relaxing or being happy. The only "goal" of mindfulness is to be with what is, internally and externally. If an adolescent is aware that she is angry or afraid, that is mindfulness.

In contrast, relaxation has a clear goal: to be relaxed. Thus, if due to some confusion, a child believes that the goal of mindfulness is to be relaxed and he isn't relaxed, he may feel that he has "failed," or that mindfulness doesn't work.

Similarly, visualization is often about going to a peaceful, happy place, like the beach. It can be helpful to use visual images when sharing mindfulness with children and adolescents. However, it is important to be clear that the intention in offering images is to support young people in connecting more fully with their present moment experience, rather than to have them mentally go somewhere else. When leading practices, do your best to ensure that there is no explicit or implicit goal, and that the images you use move the children toward, rather than away from, their here-and-now experience. An example of such an image is an otter wrapped in seaweed bobbing on the waves of the breath, feeling the sensation of rising up with the in-breath, and sinking down with the out-breath, and feeling the stillness and quietness at the top of the wave of the in-breath, and the stillness and quietness of the dip of the wave of the out-breath. An audio version of the practice is available on the *Still Quiet Place: Mindfulness for Young Children* CD.

A Note for Classroom Teachers

Like therapists, for many teachers, offering mindfulness may require a shift in perspective. If you are a classroom teacher, you've probably been trained primarily to manage your classroom, create lesson plans, and deliver content. While these are valuable skills that can be helpful in offering mindfulness to youth, they need to be balanced by being with and responding to what is happening in the moment: "Wow, I notice there is a lot of energy in the room. Do you notice it?" "Today I was planning to do a body scan, and I notice that there is a lot of upset about the changes in the cafeteria. So we are going to shift gears and do feelings practice, and then discuss ways to respond to the changes."

A wise woman who participated in my online course and who teaches English to low-income, high-risk high school students generously shared how she presents the distinction between teaching English and offering mindfulness to her students. She tells her students, "I know you see me as Ms. McDonald, your English teacher. For the next few minutes while we are doing mindfulness together, I am Caren. During our mindfulness time, I may let you do things and say things that I wouldn't let you do in English, like take off your shoes and write without worrying about spelling and grammar… I trust you to understand the difference and not take advantage of these freedoms." Even though she works with kids who push limits on a daily basis, she says that for the most part they have honored the distinctions and really appreciate the time for being somewhat more relaxed, personal, and informal.

Another distinction between teaching and sharing mindfulness has to with the difference between delivering content and *educating*. Educate comes from the Latin root *educere*, meaning "to lead out or draw forth." Most teachers I know are passionate about educating, despite the systemic challenges. For mindfulness, educating means drawing forth the essential wholeness and natural wisdom mentioned in the note to therapists above. Mindfulness is a flexible and responsive *process*, which looks and feels more like a Socratic seminar than a lecture. The intention is to have the students engage with kindness and curiosity in the practices, in the activities, and, ultimately, in life. Again, Caren beautifully captured this when she said, "The most effective mindfulness teacher is one who demonstrates her mindfulness practice in her interactions with her students in the classroom, and the text and the lab are the students and their experience."

Additionally, there are many ways to incorporate mindfulness into standard curricula. The discussion questions that follow the practices and exercises in this course can be used as writing prompts. Many passages in recommended literature, such as the opening passage in *Of Mice and Men*, exemplify mindful immersion in an experience. Students can explore how an author conveys a character's thoughts and feelings in terms of body language, facial expression, and language. They can consider characters' actions and plot outcomes in terms of responding and reacting. They can discuss or write about potential alternative choices that various characters could have made, and how these choices might have changed the story.

Similarly in social studies, both historical and current events can be looked at in terms of responding and reacting, choices, and outcomes. Science, at its best, is bringing kindness and curiosity to exploring the physical world. In math, sports, and the arts, as well as the other subjects, students can bring attention to *how* they engage with the processes of learning and performing. They can attend to their level of attention and their thoughts, feelings, and internal dialogue as they learn, do homework, practice, rehearse, take tests, compete, and perform. From math to social studies, many teachers who have training in mindfulness start each class with a brief practice, and after the first few weeks of the school year they often invite students to lead these practices. Many teachers have told me stories about being late to class or forgetting to offer a practice, only to have their students offer a reminder or spontaneously lead a practice. And relational mindfulness, applying mindfulness to interactions in and beyond the classroom, can enhance the learning environment and peer relations, and in some cases prevent suspension, incarceration, or death.

Proceed with Care

Please be aware that although you are holding a "finished" book in your hands, this curriculum remains a work in process. It is continually being refined by my joyful, and sometimes challenging, moment-to-moment interactions with the children and teens I am privileged to serve. As mindfulness *is* dynamic, present-moment responsiveness, it is essential that you also allow your interactions to continually refine your use of what is presented here.

While I can share experience, language, and suggestions, ultimately your teaching must come from the depths of your own practice. You must be able to hold whatever comes up, embracing it with both strength and tenderness. In any given classroom or therapy practice, there will be children who have lived through one or more of the following: neglect; divorce; illness; death of a family member; violence in their homes or communities; displacement from their homes; war; and emotional, physical, or sexual abuse. Unfortunately, in some settings, these experiences are the norm. These circumstances require that we stretch our capacity to respond to suffering with clarity and compassion. Even with the best of intentions, we can do harm if we expose wounds that we don't have the skill to attend to.

You may or may not be a therapist. However, regardless of your training, it is important that you identify local resources for issues that are beyond your expertise *before* sharing this curriculum with groups or individuals. If you are a classroom teacher or someone bringing mindfulness into school (or community) settings, it is important that you understand the institutional policies, the availability and limitations of any allied mental health services, and that you establish effective relationships with counselors and community mental health resources. If you are a therapist, hopefully you are already connected with one or more skilled child and adolescent psychiatrists whom you trust. If not, please establish these relationships *before* you begin teaching. When sensitive issues come up, it will be crucial that you accompany the child you are referring throughout the process of getting additional support. By "accompany," I mean providing mental, emotional, and in some cases action-oriented support such as taking initiative, walking the student to the counselor's office, speaking to caregivers, or making an appointment with a therapist.

Cautionary Tales

Some innocent missteps have taught me that, when bringing MBSR into a school setting, it is essential to clearly convey the secular and universal nature of mindfulness and to proactively elicit the support of parents, teachers, and administrators. One or two confused or frightened parents can end a program, and an unreceptive teacher can severely impact the children's experience. Below are two brief examples.

Parent Misunderstandings

When my son was in kindergarten, he began sharing mindfulness with his class. His teacher then asked me if I would offer mindfulness practices to her students once a week. We agreed that I would come for ten minutes on Wednesday mornings. At the same time, at the request of the preschool teacher, I was also sharing mindfulness with the preschoolers. The two teachers had very different ways of communicating with the parents. The preschool teacher sent an e-mail every day, informing the parents of the daily goings-on. The kindergarten teacher sent home a weekly note, and the ten minutes of mindfulness on Wednesday mornings never made the press.

At the time, the preschoolers were fascinated with colored glass bead droplets, using them to make artistic designs on lights boards and to create meandering paths throughout the classroom. Their fascination was the inspiration (pun intended) for a breath-based practice I called Jewel. In this practice the children placed colorful droplets on their bellies and felt the beads move up with the in-breath and down with the out-breath. The preschoolers loved the practice, and I subsequently transported this practice to the kindergarten classroom. A couple of kindergartners went home and reported that they were putting "crystals" on their bellies.

Two mothers became concerned and, to their credit, asked the principal if they could sit in on a session. After the session—which consisted of a short body scan and comments from the children—the parents, the principal, and I had a brief conversation. One parent indicated that she had concerns about mindfulness based on her religion. I tried to assure her that I had no intention of challenging anyone's religion and that I was simply teaching the children a special way of paying attention.

Then I started to discuss the benefits of mindfulness documented in adults. I began a sentence with "The research also shows that mindfulness changes the activity in the brain." One mother looked alarmed, grabbed my arm, and said, "I don't want my children's brain changed!" I could completely understand that, from her perspective, her children had been exposed to something that she didn't understand and that felt threatening. If I had gotten to complete the sentence, I would have said, "Mindfulness changes the activity in the brain to a more positive set point, increasing the activity in the areas associated with positive emotion and happiness."

I noticed the urge to defend and present a case for teaching mindfulness. Instead, I chose to use the aikido principle of stepping aside, rather than pushing back. My intention was to allow the fearful energy to dissipate. I agreed that I wouldn't teach the kindergartners until both the principal and the parents had a better understanding of mindfulness. During the spring of that year, I taught a six-week course to interested faculty, including the principal and assistant principal. At the conclusion of this course, most of the staff, including the principal and assistant principal, requested that I continue the sessions until the end of the school year.

Teacher Misgivings

The second cautionary tale comes from the same school the following year. With the full support of the principal and assistant principal, and after an introductory session for the parents on back-to-school night, I offered a mindfulness course to the two fifth-grade classes, alternating between the two classrooms each week. Both teachers were new to fifth grade, and working with new curricula. The experience in each of the two classrooms was entirely different.

In the first room, the teacher intuitively got the practice and said, "I did something similar as a child. I just didn't have a name for it." In the second room, the teacher's response was much cooler, and it wasn't until midyear that she fully verbalized her feelings. While I had sensed her feelings, I hadn't understood their depth. She said she resented me being in the room, that she felt mindfulness had been inserted into her curriculum, and that she wanted those forty minutes to teach. She also felt that the school as a whole was overly focused on social and emotional issues, communication, and children's stress and well-being. She said, "When I was a child, children just dealt with stress. The school is making too big a deal out of it."

The differing attitudes of the two teachers were reflected in the outcomes in the two rooms. In the first room, a majority of the children enjoyed mindfulness and found it beneficial. In the second room, many didn't enjoy it or find it beneficial. Those who did enjoy it let me know privately and told me that they were reluctant to express their enjoyment and experience of benefit in the presence of their teacher.

If I had those two experiences to do over again, I would have offered an introductory evening to the kindergarten parents, and I would have sought a clearer understanding of the resentful teacher's perspective earlier. It's notable that the next year, the school—an independent school in northern California—had a change in leadership and philosophy, "returned to their Christian roots," and chose, among other things, to discontinue the mindfulness program. My intention has always been to present mindfulness in a way that feels accessible, inviting, and safe to all. I offer these stories here as a reminder that once we trigger someone's fear, and they are in the refractory period, it can be difficult for them to understand the universal nature of mindfulness, or appreciate its documented benefits. Thus, it is crucial that you be *aware of and responsive to the most conservative listening in your community*. You never know where the line is, and once you cross it, it is difficult, if not impossible, to go back.

Working with Reluctance

Some children and young teens are initially reluctant to participate in the course. Kids, especially those who receive a variety of additional support—psychological therapy, speech therapy, tutoring, executive function coaching, and so on—may feel that this is just one more thing that they "have to" do. Understandably, they may see it as something that prevents them from participating in an activity they truly enjoy, such as sports or just hanging out with friends. It's important to acknowledge this view and allow their feelings. At the same time, let them know that life isn't always the way we hope it will be, and that part of this course involves exploring ways of dealing with these times in life. Explain the possibility that, if they participate fully, their new skills may make their preferred activities and the rest of their lives more enjoyable. Since they are attending the class, encourage them to see if they can find anything of value in the course. If, at the end of the course, they haven't found anything of value, they can choose to forget about the whole thing.

Working with Resistance

Please read this section slowly and allow yourself time to absorb what is being presented. In session 4, you will support participants in exploring how resisting things often increases their suffering. In preparation for that discussion, I'd like to revisit the topic of personal practice—specifically, how we work with our own resistance, aversion, and desire when it arises while sharing mindfulness with youth. When I'm speaking at conferences or sharing this curriculum during in-person or online trainings, the topic of resistance often comes up. Usually the question is phrased something like this: "How do you work with youth who are resistant to mindfulness?"

While there are thousands of possible in-the-moment responses to an individual or group who is expressing resistance, verbally or otherwise, I can offer a few guiding principles. First, resistance is a natural part of the human experience. It's helpful if we can observe it with kindness and curiosity and name it, preferably without judging it. Often it is enough to say, "With kindness and curiosity, notice if you are thinking this is ridiculous or a waste of time. Notice if you are choosing not to participate or to distract your classmate."

Second, participants' resistance is neither personal nor isolated to mindfulness. The majority of youth we label as "resistant" are engaged in the developmentally appropriate task of resisting almost everything until they discover its usefulness for themselves. This "resistance" is usually a healthy part of their development, and essential to the process of them discovering who they are in their own uniqueness. Unfortunately, many young people are so used to adults insisting that they know best that they are primed to fight back out of habit. To disarm that reaction, I often say, "Don't believe me. Don't take my word for it. Try it out. See what you discover. Report back. Share your experience. Disagree."

Naming resistance, not taking it personally, and not forcing the issue are most skillful when they can be done without judgment. And herein lies the rub. Often, there is an inherent contradiction contained within the question "How do you work with youth who are resistant?" Take a moment, and see if you can discover the contradiction for yourself... Breathe and be curious....

Often, underneath the question "How do you work with resistant youth?" is the questioner's subtle, or perhaps overt, resistance to the youth's resistance. Let that sink in.... Again, see if you can find how the question about a participant's resistance often contains the questioner's resistance—to the participant's resistance.

The question frequently implies that the youth should not be resistant, or that the facilitator should *do* something about the youth's resistance. This distortion of our best intentions is understandable. We choose to offer mindfulness to youth because we believe, and science demonstrates, that these skills benefit young people. In our zeal, we want them to participate, be engaged; in short, we want them to "get it." When they don't, we create suffering by resisting their resistance. We think, "They should be more participatory and respectful," or "I should be more engaging or clear." Then we either push harder or clamp down internally or externally. However, wisdom suggests meeting the resistance (theirs and ours) with humor or letting it be. Ironically, amazing shifts are possible when we simply open to what is and say, "How many of you are thinking 'This woman is crazy; I am not listening to her,' or 'This mindfulness stuff is useless'?" If you wish, you may add "I totally understand" or, with a smile, "That is just a thought."

It is our own moment-to moment practice that allows us to be aware of our resistance, aversion, desire, and judgment. Our practice helps us to catch the "should" thoughts, and the felt sensations of irritation, frustration, judgment, and anger as they arise in the moment.

When I am triggered by comments or behavior that I label as resistant and start judging, there is an internal tightening, which has a cold, metallic, clanging feel to it, like a steel door slamming shut. It is quite distinct. When I am aware of this particular constellation of thoughts, feelings, and physical sensations, I do my best to breathe, rest in stillness and quietness, and allow the wave to pass. Often, the spacious clarity of discernment follows in its wake, and I can find some skillful comment or question that acknowledges what is, thereby creating an opening. This verbal aikido of sharing mindfulness—with youth, or with anyone—was demonstrated in the "Head in the Game" and "Why the 'F'?" dialogues in session 3. In the beginning, the middle, and the end, it is our practice that allows us to *be* the teaching by paying attention to our thoughts, feelings, and physical sensations with kindness and curiosity, and then *choosing our behavior.*

teaching children and their parents simultaneously

This course can also be offered to children and their parents. While the course content and format are the same, some additional skills are taught, and a few modifications are required. I usually only offer child-parent courses to children twelve and under. For teens and parents, much of their stress comes from interacting with each other, and it is often difficult for them to speak about that honestly if they are all in the same room. If you are inclined to share mindfulness with teens and parents, I recommend that you partner with another teacher, with one of you teaching the teens and the other teaching the parents. And then, once both groups have some fluency in mindfulness, you can bring them together to explore common family holes (problematic situations and reactions) and difficult communications.

Letting Go

There are three important dynamics to be aware of when sharing mindfulness with child-parent pairs. In social settings, many parents feel obligated to manage their children's behavior. (If you are a parent, you may recognize this behavior in yourself.) Since mindfulness is about being with what is rather than managing, I encourage parents to allow me to be responsible for and responsive to the children and their behavior during the session. I say something like "As parents, we often feel that we have to modify, correct, manage, and generally control our children's behavior, especially in new group settings. To the best of your ability, see if for this hour and a half you can let that go and allow me to guide, redirect, set limits, create consequences. If I need your help, I'll let you know." Many parents find this both a challenge and a relief. The habits of intervening are ingrained, and the opportunity to simply be present with one's children in a group setting without feeling responsible for their behavior is rare.

Parental Attachment to Outcome

Perhaps the most challenging aspect of working with children and parents together is that, understandably, many parents have an agenda. Some parents sign their children up for mindfulness simply because they believe it is a valuable life skill. However, more often than not parents sign their children up because they're hoping mindfulness will benefit the children in some specific way. Put another way, as with adult MBSR, parents often enroll their children in a mindfulness course because either the child or the parent is suffering from the effects of the child's ADHD, anxiety, depression, physical illness, or from stress-induced physical symptoms, such as tension headaches, migraines, and stomachaches. Parents of some tweens may also be desperately seeking a remedy for ongoing self-destructive behavior, including eating disorders, cutting, substance abuse, acting out, and suicidal behavior.

These goals are understandable. Parents bring their children to class for exactly the benefits being documented in the research. However, parents can get quite attached to the outcome. In the third session of the first course in the child-parent study at Stanford, one parent asked, "What if my children don't want to come?" Based on how the question was asked and other interactions I had had with the mother, the question implied the hope that I would "make" the children come. This particular course was in the context of a research study, and research doesn't like dropouts. However, my response was "Mindfulness is about accepting what is, and not about forcing anything. Therefore, it's contrary to the practice to force anyone to participate."

The question prompted me to solicit suggestions from both the children and the parents about the class format, to help ensure that classes were appealing and inviting for the children. The children suggested more movement and less talk. As a group, we agreed that the suggestions would be incorporated into the upcoming classes; that the children who didn't want to continue would attend two more sessions; and if, at that point, they still didn't wish to participate, they would stop coming to class.

In the discussion with parents that followed, I shared the following thoughts: First, as parents, our practice is to notice when we want our children to be other than they are, and when we have an agenda. There is a distinction between supporting children in developing useful skills and trying to change or "fix" them. Once we realize our true intentions, we can make a wise choice about how to proceed. Perhaps living mindfully and being present with and responsive to our children moment by moment is more important than getting them to practice mindfulness.

Second, the first two sessions had provided children with an experience of the Still Quiet Place and vocabulary for sharing their experience. Before starting the course, the children didn't even know that they had a Still Quiet Place. By the time the children would be allowed to drop out, they also would have developed some capacity for observing their thoughts and feelings. Perhaps the benefits of experiencing the Still Quiet Place, learning to observe their thoughts and feelings, and developing a common family language were enough for now.

Third, introducing mindfulness to children and parents is like planting seeds, and seeds blossom in their own time. A child who is uninterested in mindfulness now may choose to apply this learning six months from now, before taking the SATs, or during a particularly difficult time in college. (As an aside, many colleges are now offering instruction in mindfulness to their students.)

In closing, I reminded the parents that although they may have enrolled in the mindfulness class "for Susie or Patrick," their children would benefit if the parents developed their own mindfulness practice. In fact, research indicates that parental stress significantly affects children's mental health. Thus parents may improve their children's well-being by using mindfulness to reduce their own stress, and providing a living demonstration of the value of mindfulness in daily life (Bakoula, Kolaitis, Veltsista, Gika, & Chrousos, 2009). I encourage parents to practice mindfulness "out loud," in front of their children, in the course of daily life. For example, a parent might demonstrate mindfulness of feelings and reactivity, and pausing to consider a more mindful response, in this way: "Wow! That e-mail from your coach really upset me. I'm going to take some time to notice my thoughts and feelings, and then choose what I want to say, before I write back."

These comments helped the parents remember that, in the first class, many of them had acknowledged that they were taking the mindfulness course not only for their child, but also to cultivate patience, kindness, clarity, gentleness, and wisdom within themselves.

Unique Opportunities and Challenges

When using the difficult communication exercise from session 6 with child-parent pairs, I encourage them to work with a partner who is *not* in their family or a friend of the family, and to share a difficult family communication. Something close to miraculous happens in this process as an event is reported, in a supportive setting, from the perspective of *a* child, rather than *my* child, or *a* parent rather than *my* parent. Participants usually report that they are able to share their feelings, desires, and needs clearly and simply and to hear and really understand what the other person felt, wanted, and needed. Then they are able to respond with kindness and compassion, rather than reacting out of habit, fear, defense, or the need to control.

In general, these role-plays tend to be much more skillful than the usual fraught communications on touchy subjects, and they tend to be characterized by mutual respect and trust—essential ingredients for mindful communication and positive outcomes. This kind of communication can help children convey what's important to them while also helping parents avoid long, drawn-out negotiations. The role-plays can help highlight the benefits of finding a neutral time to discuss problematic situations and make family agreements about how to handle them.

Adaptations

Within the context of the dynamics mentioned above, there are some simple procedural modifications for teaching child-parent pairs. In child-parent courses, both children and parents receive the same workbook and CD for home practice. The participants know that if a child picks up a "parent's" workbook or a parent picks up a "child's" workbook, they are exactly the same. This emphasizes that we are all in this together. At Stanford, I like to joke with the kids, telling them that Still Quiet Place is their first college course.

If the group is large, with twenty or more participants, encourage the children to be the primary speakers and have the parents take a secondary role, so that the discussions don't exceed the children's capacity for sitting and listening. If the kids are wiggly and need to do some movement, take them outside for a movement practice and leave the parents with a discussion question, such as: "What subtle feelings did you notice over the week?" "What are your common holes with your children?" or "What different streets are you discovering?"

For home practice, ask parents to choose an additional mindful activity that involves their children—for example, kissing them good-bye in the morning, greeting them after school, or tucking them in at night. During the last fifteen minutes of class, give the parents time to ask questions and have an adult discussion about applying mindfulness to the joys and challenges of parenting. Remember, this is a time to offer compassion for those moments when we are not the parents we intend to be, and, simultaneously, to encourage the parents to pay attention, here and now, with kindness and curiosity, and then choose their behavior, especially in challenging moments with their children. Parents really appreciate this time and often want to stay well past the end of class—and beyond their children's willingness to stay.

During this parent-focused time, the children can draw pictures of their experience of the Still Quiet Place, write haikus or poems, or play inside or outside. Inside games that engage mindfulness include pick-up sticks and Jenga, a game where blocks are placed in a stack, and then each player in turn pulls a block from the middle of the stack and places it on the top of the stack, with the object being not to topple the stack.

an academic perspective and research to date

As you read this academic chapter, please consider making the *process* of reading a mindfulness practice. Go slow; breathe; if you notice your attention has wandered, gently bring it back to the words, the page, the concepts.

As mentioned in the introduction, I began sharing mindfulness with my young son following his sweet request. I subsequently came to appreciate the distress that many of our young friends experience on an almost daily basis. Their longing for essential life skills to navigate their complex worlds is often expressed through unhealthy, problematic, and even destructive behaviors. Seeing many adults, and my own children, reap meaningful benefits from the practice inspired me to take a leap of faith and share these essential life skills with other children and adolescents.

Increasingly, research on executive function, emotional intelligence, and social development offers academic support for the leap of faith that I, and other pioneers in this field, took in bringing these practices to children. This chapter offers a brief overview of these interdependent developmental processes, which I will collectively refer to as essential competencies. The chapter concludes with a review of the preliminary evidence to date, demonstrating that mindfulness enhances these competencies.

From the intertwined perspectives of the essential competencies and mindfulness, the building blocks for choosing empathetic and compassionate behavior can be summarized as follows:

- *Pausing*, known as *inhibition* in the language of executive function, and *impulse control* in social development

- Developing and utilizing emotional self-awareness

- *Perspective taking,* which, according to pioneers in social development theory, provides a basis for both aggressive and empathetic action

- Activating moral rules or codes contained in working memory

- *Engaging cognitive flexibility*—specifically, switching between one's perspective and another's and considering multiple options, *and then choosing behavior*

Limitations of This Discussion—and of These Constructs

This discussion is by no means comprehensive. My aim here is simply to provide a broad framework within which to understand *some* of the benefits of mindfulness. Before moving on, it is important to note the limitations of these constructs. The majority of the research on executive function and social development has been done on children ages one through five. With proper support, during the preschool years, these essential competencies develop rapidly in young children. While I have offered basic mindfulness to preschool-aged children, this book is aimed at school-aged children. Thus, it is important to acknowledge that the children you work and play with will come to you with—and perhaps because of—particular deficiencies in some or all of these essential competencies. Another limitation of this framework is that until recently most of the research has examined each of the developmental competencies separately. Laboratory experiments designed to assess executive function, perspective taking, and social development are very specific and highly controlled, and rarely reflect the multiple, interrelated, emotionally charged complexities of a game of kickball on the playground, a group project in the classroom, or a heated argument with a friend or family member.

The authors of a paper titled "Executive Function and the Promotion of Social-Emotional Competence" (Riggs, Jahromi, Razza, Dillworth-Bart, & Mueller, 2006) state that "executive function is rarely considered in models of intervention programs that attempt to promote social and emotional learning" (p. 300). Conversely, I would add, the reverse is also true: until recently, social and emotional influences on executive function have seldom been addressed. However, recent research suggests that the development of these essential competencies, and their moment-to-moment manifestations in action, are intricately interdependent.

Historically, the role of emotions has been addressed within the context of emotional "inhibition," emotional "control," or emotional "regulation." For me, an essential quality that distinguishes mindfulness from other social-emotional curricula is that mindfulness is the practice of bringing kindness and curiosity to one's habits of thinking, feeling, and behaving. Thus, in the context of mindfulness, the terms *emotional awareness, emotional intelligence,* and *emotional responsiveness* are more apt. Having noted this distinction here, I will use the accepted terminology of executive function, emotion theory, and social development when drawing on these constructs.

Executive Function

Let's begin with some definitions. Executive function supports deliberate, intentional, goal-directed behavior. The three primary dimensions of executive function are inhibitory control, working memory, and cognitive flexibility. These skills are essential for learning to read, write, solve math problems, and participate in educational and social activities, such as mutual dialogue, engaged play, and collaborative projects. To quote what I will subsequently refer to as the "Brain Building" paper (formally titled "Building the Brain's 'Air Traffic Control' System: How Early Experiences Shape the Development of Executive Function," and jointly authored by the National Scientific Council on the Developing Child and the National Forum on Early Childhood Policy and Programs: "The increasingly competent executive functioning of childhood and adolescence enable children to plan and act in a way that makes them good students, classroom citizens, and friends" (Center on the Developing Child, 2011, p. 3). To that, I would add good family members and world citizens.

The following definitions and explanations of the components of executive function come from the "Brain Building" paper and a book chapter by Dr. Adele Diamond, titled "The Early Development of Executive Function," in *Lifespan Cognition* (2006, pp. 70–95).

Inhibitory Control

Inhibitory control, as defined by the "Brain Building" paper, is "the skill we use to master and filter our thoughts and impulses so that we can resist temptations, distractions, and habits, and pause and think before we act" (p. 2). The paper elaborates, stating that children use this skill to ignore distractions and stay on task, to wait until they are called on in class, and to prevent themselves from yelling or hitting when they feel they have been wronged (p. 2).

Working Memory

Working memory is the capacity to hold and manipulate information in the mind for short periods of time. It enables children to remember and connect information from one paragraph to the next, to solve complex math problems, to follow multistep instructions, and to participate in social interactions, like speaking with friends or playing a game (p. 2).

Cognitive Flexibility

Cognitive flexibility is the capacity to adjust to changed demands, priorities, or perspectives. It enables us to consider something from a fresh perspective, to "think outside the box," to apply different rules in different settings, to catch and correct "mistakes," and to change course when given new information. Children use this skill when learning exceptions to rules of grammar, using multiple strategies to solve a math or science problem, or considering options for resolving conflict (p. 2).

As described in the "Brain Building" paper, taken together, the three components of executive function provide the foundation for all educational and social activities. "Children who lack executive function skills," the paper states, "often struggle with the complexities of the school day routine, and group play; they get frustrated, act out, and are frequently isolated; such isolation can further decrease their opportunities to engage in activities which develop executive function" (p. 6).

Additionally, as we will explore later, it is likely that in combination with emotional intelligence these three components of executive function provide a fundamental foundation for perspective taking, which in turn supports moral behavior, including empathy, compassion, and altruism.

Emotion Theory and Emotional Intelligence

A brief review of emotion theory, based primarily on the work of Dr. Paul Ekman, and described in his book *Emotions Revealed*, provides a basic framework for understanding the bidirectional effects of executive function and emotion. Ekman's research demonstrates that emotions are natural, and serve an evolutionary purpose. Anger helps us overcome obstacles. Fear allows us to detect and react to danger. Sadness compels members of our tribe to comfort us. Happiness creates connection.

Ekman goes on to explain that both the body and the mind are hardwired to automatically appraise our environment, and that this hardwiring makes it difficult, but not impossible, to change our emotional reactions to various triggers. Importantly, in the context of executive function, emotional reactions rely on the more primitive parts of our brains and bypass the prefrontal cortex, the primary seat of executive function. Thus, during the height of an emotion—what Ekman calls the *refractory period*—executive function is essentially offline. In more colloquial terms, as we all know from personal experience, when we are in the grips of an emotion (at the height of the refractory period) we lose our ability to see the big picture, take in new information, understand another's perspective, and engage in creative problem solving.

Ekman suggests that despite the evolutionary hardwiring, it may be possible to learn to *respond,* rather than react, to emotional triggers. The essence of this possibility is captured in the quotes below:

> In order for us to be able to moderate our emotional behavior, to choose what we say or do, we have to know when we have become, or better still, are becoming emotional (p. 74).

> Learning about the sensations, the bodily feelings that distinguish each emotion should also help focus our attentiveness (p. 75).

> One method people can use to become more attentive to their emotions is to use the knowledge about the causes of each emotion.... By becoming more familiar with what triggers our emotions, we can increase our consciousness of when and why emotions occur (p. 75).

> The goal is not to be devoid of emotion, but instead to have more choice once we become emotional about [if and] how we will enact that emotion (p. 75).

As you learned in the session chapters, the Still Quiet Place curriculum teaches these skills explicitly. The Feelings practice offered in session 4 and the Emotion Improv exercise presented in session 5 support our young friends in becoming aware of the physiological (bodily) sensations associated with various emotions. The Holes and Different Streets and Hook Report exercises in session 5 and session 7, respectively, increase awareness of emotional triggers.

Social Development

Now, let's consider how executive function and emotional intelligence relate to and influence three components of social development: aggression, impulsivity, and moral behavior. The majority of the information below has been selectively and directly excerpted and paraphrased from Eleanor Maccoby's (1980) book *Social Development: Psychological Growth and the Parent-Child Relationship.*

As you read, it may be helpful to remember that according to Maccoby, perspective taking and understanding the connection between one's own actions and other people's emotional states provide the basis for both empathy and aggression (p. 124). Within the context of this book this statement could be expanded and refined as follows: Inhibitory control allows an individual to pause. A combination of emotional intelligence and working memory allow her to become aware of her emotional state, the emotional states of others, and how her actions may impact the emotional state of others, and then consider the social rules regarding behavior. Cognitive flexibility utilizes the "emotional awarenesses" and social norms activated in working memory to allow her to choose her behavior along the continuum from aggressive to compassionate. And with mindfulness this entire process is held within a context of kindness and curiosity.

Aggression

In social development theory, aggression depends on the knowledge that one's actions can cause others to feel distress. Aggression is defined as actions directed toward a specific person that are intended to hurt or frighten. "Aggression represents a complex pattern of behavior that calls for considerable processing—interpretation—of information concerning the feelings and behavior of other people, and the relation of the self to others" (Maccoby, 1980, p. 131). In social developmental theory, aggression is considered a stage; it is viewed as a form of self-reliance, which is more mature than frightened withdrawal to adult protection or passive yielding to another's assertions, and less mature than nonaggressive forms of self-defense and self-assertion (p. 149).

Maccoby states, "Children four years and older know a variety of ways to hurt others. Whether a child carries out these actions depends...on whether the child *chooses* to use the elements in his or her repertoire" (p. 125). She adds that a child's ability to behave in nonaggressive ways depends upon her understanding and sharing of others' feelings, "experiencing positive affection for others, and having a desire not to hurt them" (p. 150). These motivations must be combined with effective social skills. Over time, "children learn how to discover what each wants from the other and what each will concede in the interests of mutual satisfaction" (p. 149).

Thus, Maccoby's conclusions support the explicit teaching of skills for pausing, cultivating empathy, and choosing behavior. As you may recall, the Difficult Communication exercise in session 6 of this curriculum explicitly supports course participants in practicing these specific skills.

Impulsivity

The definition of impulsivity in the context of social development is essentially a lack of the inhibitory control function. Children who have developed impulse control demonstrate the ability to delay actions, concentrate, and block out extraneous irrelevant stimulation; to "manage" emotional states, rather than experience tantrums, consider future consequences, find solutions, choose from alternatives, and maximize the input of information needed for execution of the chosen plan (p. 163).

In contrast to much of the literature on executive function, Maccoby emphasizes the role of "managing" emotions in developing impulse control. She states,

> The management of emotional states occupies a central place in the development of children's capacity to maintain and improve the level of organization of their behavior.... Children must learn to "inhibit" the strong feelings that previously disorganized their behavior; they must learn to cope with circumstances that interfere with immediate or complete satisfaction of their needs and wishes" (pp. 164, 177).

She goes on to state that the ability to not become strongly upset over frustrating events, and to not have an emotional storm when genuinely upset, are major achievements in a child's emotional development (p. 178). Her conclusions mirror and support Ekman's. Importantly, she concludes that children must establish some "control" over their emotions in order to be able to plan, or choose, their behavior.

Perspective Taking and Moral Behavior

In sharing the Still Quiet Place with youth, it is my experience that as young people develop increased emotional self-awareness via Feelings practice, their awareness of others' emotions is also enhanced. In addition, the Difficult Communications exercise directly develops awareness of others' feelings. Interestingly, as previously mentioned, according to social development theory, awareness of others' feelings underlies both aggressive and empathetic behavior.

Ultimately, the interdependent processes of executive function and emotional intelligence form the underpinnings for perspective taking and thus for ethical, moral, empathetic, compassionate, and altruistic behavior. In the context of executive function, ethics can be thought of as social rules governing behavior; these rules are maintained in long-term memory, and subsequently activated in working memory. As described by Maccoby, most societies have rules regarding safety, control of aggression, truth telling and promise keeping, self-reliance, work, and respect for authority. The rules provide guidelines for individual behavior in a social context. Usually, the welfare of each person and society as a whole depends on people following the agreed-upon rules and conventions (Maccoby, 1980, pp. 297–99).

According to Maccoby, "a morally socialized child has been taught, and learned, to resolve the conflict between self-interest and the interests of others" (p. 300). A child's "progress through the developmental levels of moral judgment requires an increasingly sophisticated understanding of other people's [feelings,] wants and needs" (p. 317). To resolve conflicts, "a morally advanced individual must be able to take the perspective of others" (p. 317). Ultimately, perspective taking enhances children's ability to communicate effectively and cooperate with others (p. 317).

Using experimental designs, such as having children describe landscapes from another person's perspective or offer instructions to a blindfolded partner, researchers have outlined the typical, chronological development of perspective taking—known as "theory of mind," in the lexicon of executive function. Again, it should be noted that, when compared to many highly emotionally charged daily interactions, the experimental designs are essentially emotionally neutral. These extremely neutral experiments have demonstrated that second graders understand that others have perspectives different from their own; and that, between the ages of seven and sixteen an enormous improvement takes place in the ability to appreciate the implications of these differences, and use this knowledge in communication.

Maccoby notes that a well-developed intelligence—which, in her lexicon, is roughly equivalent to executive function—seems to be necessary but not sufficient for mature moral behavior (p. 317). Additionally, Maccoby emphasizes that moral development in children is the achievement of control over their own behavior in situations where no outside agent is present to enforce the rules (p. 300). (This principle is portrayed in the teaching story of the school master offered in session 6.)

Compassionate Action and Altruism

Compassionate action and altruism are perhaps the highest forms of moral behavior. As noted previously, Maccoby states that perspective taking underlies the behavioral continuum moving from aggression to altruism. She concludes that:

Moral maturity in thinking and behavior is enhanced by techniques that:

1. Build children's perspective taking skills enabling them to understand how their own actions will be experienced by others, and to take into account others' needs, information, and expectations

2. Foster children's empathy, making possible both the understanding and sharing of emotions

3. Give children a reasonable amount of control over their own actions and emphasize that they have this control (p. 362)

Ultimately, her view supports the hypothesis that compassionate action depends upon a combination of executive function and emotional intelligence, which allows for perspective taking and choice making.

Interdependent Competencies

Fascinating studies using brain imaging, genetic mapping, and molecular analysis have recently provided high-tech evidence demonstrating the interdependent nature of the essential executive, emotional, and social competencies. A paper titled "Biological Processes in Prevention and Intervention: The Promotion of Self-Regulation as a Means of Preventing School Failure" (Blair & Diamond, 2008), states that in preschoolers executive function and emotional arousal are inversely related. The authors emphasize that "self-regulation development can be characterized as balance or interaction between processes of emotional-motivational arousal and cognitive control processes" (p. 4). This paper describes intriguing research demonstrating that genetic variations, determining the rate at which the neurotransmitter dopamine is cleared from the prefrontal cortex, have a complex influence on executive function. Furthermore, the authors cite additional research showing that a specific region of the brain, called the anterior cingulate cortex, plays a central role in integrating and balancing the emotional reactive and cognitive control networks.

Related fMRI research with adolescents offers further support for the contention that emotional processing interferes with executive attention. This brain imaging study identified distinct neural networks for attentional (executive) and affective (emotional) processes. The research demonstrated that the separate networks for cognitive regulation and affective regulation affect each other at a neural level (Crone, 2009). Thus, we now have brain imaging evidence to support the theory that when a child, adolescent, even an adult is emotionally aroused, and in the refractory period, he is unable to optimally utilize his executive function!

The corollary conclusion that executive function is directly implicated in children's social-emotional development is supported by a growing number of studies (Riggs et al., 2006). These studies suggest that executive function is a precursor to theory of mind, or perspective taking—which, as Maccoby has demonstrated, is the foundation for empathetic behavior. Thus an intervention such as mindfulness, which simultaneously improves executive function, enhances emotional intelligence, encourages perspective taking, and emphasizes choice making, is likely to promote empathetic action.

While the focus of this chapter has been on social and emotional development, it is important to note that executive function (most likely in combination with emotional intelligence) also enhances academic development. The "Brain Building" paper emphasizes the academic benefits of interventions that improve executive function: "Current research shows that self-regulation—often called executive function—has a stronger association with academic achievement than IQ or entry-level reading or math skills" (p. 5).

Not surprisingly, the paper titled "Biological Processes" states that "consideration of the depth and breadth of developing self-regulation in young children can help to establish a framework for interventions to promote self-regulation as a means of preventing school failure" (Blair & Diamond, 2008, p. 2). Thus, although rigorous studies assessing the effects of mindfulness on academic performance have yet to be done, the research on executive function suggests potential important academic—as well as social-emotional—benefits.

Before moving on to a review of the research on the benefits of mindfulness for youth, it is important to note again that, for me, what distinguishes mindfulness from other social-emotional learning curricula is the attitude of kindness and curiosity one brings to oneself and others.

Research on the Benefits of Mindfulness for Children

The integrated framework presented above can help us understand the benefits of mindfulness documented by the research to date. For those without a background in scientific research this next section offers a simplified overview. Two documents cover most of this research in more depth: "Integrating Mindfulness Training into K-12 Education: Fostering the Resilience of Teachers and Students" (Meiklejohn et al., 2010), and *PBS Teachers Guide*. Both documents can be downloaded from http://www.stillquietplace.com, under the "Resources" tab via the "Research" and "Press" links respectively. It can be extremely helpful to provide copies of these articles to decision makers when you are working to establish a mindfulness program for youth in your school, clinic, hospital, or community setting. However, because many decision makers are busy and overwhelmed and may not read these longer articles, in Appendix A you will find a sample letter to a school principal, summarizing the benefits of mindfulness for youth on a single page.

Medicine has long been evidence based. Education and therapy are becoming increasingly evidence based. As you read about, promote, and implement mindfulness programs for youth, it will be important for you to understand the strengths and weaknesses of various research designs and conclusions. The gold standard for determining the effectiveness of a program is a randomized controlled trial with a large number of participants, using validated self-report and objective measures, and with long-term follow-up.

Research on mindfulness for youth is in its infancy. To date, no studies meet all of the gold standard criteria. Fortunately, early results are encouraging and the field is evolving rapidly. Below, the preliminary studies with children and adolescents are presented in order of increasing scientific rigor. However, this section will quickly be out-of-date. For information that's more up-to-date, please visit my website, http://www.stillquietplace.com, and subscribe to the newsletter *Mindfulness Research Monthly*, at http://www.mindfulexperience.org/newsletter.php.

I invite you to consider the data below in the context of the discussion above, and encourage you to continue reading mindfully—breathing, going slow, and when you find your attention wandering, gently returning it to the section or sentence you are reading.

Young Children

In a study of a twelve-week mindfulness-based cognitive therapy intervention, twenty-five clinic-referred nine- to twelve-year-olds experienced significant reductions in attention problems; those with elevated anxiety at pretest had decreased anxiety. Parents noted reductions in behavioral and anger management problems (Lee, Semple, Rosa, & Miller, 2008).

A pilot study compared a control group of twenty-four sixth graders to twenty-eight fifth graders in public schools in Madison, Wisconsin. The fifth graders received the mindfulness-based Learning to BREATHE (L2B) program. Students in one of the fifth grade L2B classes were primarily Spanish-speaking. The L2B students' performance on a computerized task of spatial working memory showed statistically significant improvements in strategy use and reductions in error rate. The L2B students also demonstrated fewer symptoms of depression and anxiety and a greater internal locus of control after program completion.

Qualitative reports from teachers indicated that the L2B students were more focused and better able to deal with stressful situations. The reports indicated improvements in social competence, noting that the students learned to pause, if only briefly, and "acknowledge their thoughts and feelings, something that set L2B apart from most social skills programs." Students became more aware of helpful and unhelpful thoughts and actions. The classroom environment was more relaxed and less stressful. Overall, the mindfulness lessons had a strong impact on the classroom climate and individual students' stress levels (P. C. Broderick, personal communication, 2011).

A wait-list controlled study of fourth- through sixth-graders and their parents, which I conducted in collaboration with the Department of Psychology at Stanford, showed that the thirty-one children who participated in seventy-five minutes of mindfulness training for eight consecutive weeks had decreased anxiety. Further, their written narratives indicated they experienced decreased emotional reactivity, increased focus, and ability to deal with challenges (Goldin, Saltzman, & Jha, 2008).

In a wait-list controlled study, students in six elementary classrooms received a mindfulness education training consisting of four teacher-delivered components: quieting the mind, mindful attention (mindfulness of sensation, thoughts, and feelings), managing negative emotions and thinking, and acknowledgment of self and others. Students in the ME classrooms reported increased optimism, but not improvements in self-concept or affect. Teachers reported improvements in teacher-rated behavior and social competence (Schonert-Reichl & Lawlor, 2010).

In a randomized controlled trail with thirty-two second and third graders who engaged in Mindfulness Awareness Practices for thirty minutes twice a week for eight weeks, Lisa Flook, PhD, and her colleagues at the Mindfulness Awareness Research Center at UCLA documented that children who began the study with poor executive function had gains in behavioral regulation, metacognition, and overall global executive control. Analyses also showed significant effects for specific executive function capacities, such as attention shifting, monitoring, and initiating. These results demonstrate that Mindfulness Awareness Practice training benefits children with poor executive function (Flook et al. 2010).

In a randomized controlled trial conducted by Maria Napoli, PhD, and colleagues, 194 first, second, and third graders who participated in a biweekly, twelve-session mindfulness and relaxation program showed significant increases in attention and social skills and decreases in test anxiety and ADHD behaviors (Napoli, Krech, & Holley, 2005). (Note: Decreased ADHD behaviors basically translate into increased executive function.)

A randomized controlled trial of the Mindful Schools curriculum to 915 elementary school children in the high-crime areas of Oakland found that after four hours of mindfulness training the students demonstrated an increase in their abilities to pay attention and self-calm, and show care for others, as well as an increase in social compliance (Mindful Schools, n.d.).

Adolescents

In a feasibility study, which offered mindful awareness practices and psychoeducation to a mixed group of adults and adolescents with ADHD, combined population findings included improvements in self-reported ADHD symptoms, anxiety, depressive symptoms, and working memory (Zylowska et al., 2008).

In a study of thirty-two adolescents with learning disabilities (LD) at a private residential school, participants were led in mindfulness meditation for five to ten minutes at the beginning of each class period, five days per week, for five consecutive weeks, by two classroom teachers. Students' self-reports revealed decreased state (short-term) and trait (long-term) anxiety. Teacher ratings showed improvements of students' social skills and academics, and decreases in problem behaviors (Beauchemin, Hutchins, & Patterson, 2008).

A study using mindfulness-based cognitive therapy (MBCT) with a clinical population of fourteen adolescents, eleven to eighteen years of age, found improvements in sustained attention, self-reported behavior, personal goals, subjective happiness, and mindful awareness (Bögels, Hoogstad, van Dun, de Schutter, & Restifo, 2008).

In a study of a nine-week MBSR program for thirty-three urban youth, age thirteen to twenty-one, 79 percent of the youth attended the majority of the MBSR sessions and were considered "program completers." Among program completers, eleven were HIV-infected, 77 percent were female, and all were African American. Quantitative data shows that, following the MBSR program, participants had a significant reduction in hostility, general discomfort, and emotional discomfort. Qualitative data shows perceived improvements in interpersonal relationships (including less conflict), school achievement, physical health, and reduced stress. Interview data from an HIV-infected subgroup revealed improved attitude, behavior, and self-care (including medication adherence), and decreased reactivity (Sibinga et al., 2011), with transformative experiences of variable levels described by all participants (Kerrigan et al., 2011).

A six-session intervention—which included MBSR, insomnia treatment, and cognitive therapy—for fifty-five substance abusers, thirteen to nineteen years of age, with current sleep disturbances found improvements in sleep and reduced worry and mental distress (Bootzin & Stevens, 2005).

When compared to 30 control students, 120 senior high school girls who participated in the mindfulness curriculum Learning to BREATHE (L2B; mentioned previously) experienced reductions in negative affect, tiredness, aches and pains and increases in emotion regulation, feelings of calmness, relaxation, and self-acceptance. The students who participated in L2B were more able to recognize their emotions and to label them. They reported that the greatest overall advantage for them was the ability to let go of distressing thoughts and feelings (Broderick & Metz, 2009).

In a randomized controlled trial, 102 adolescents participated in a mindfulness course for two hours a week for eight weeks. The teens reported reductions in perceived stress; in symptoms of anxiety, depression, and somatic (physical) distress and interpersonal problems; and increased self-esteem and sleep quality. Independent clinicians documented a higher percentage of diagnostic improvement and significant increases in global assessment of functioning scores in the mindfulness group, versus the control group. In layperson's terms, this means that adolescents who were initially diagnosed as clinically depressed and anxious no longer met clinical criteria for depression or anxiety (Biegel, Brown, Shapiro, & Schubert, 2009). Further analysis found that statistically significant increases in mindfulness were present and were significantly related to positive changes in mental health (Brown, West, Loverich, & Biegel, 2011).

Before a randomized controlled trial with 400 students in five middle schools in Flanders, Belgium, both the mindfulness group (21%) and the control group (24%) had a similar percentage of students reporting evidence of depression. After the eight weekly 100-minute mindfulness sessions, the number of students with symptoms of depression was significantly lower in the mindfulness group: 15% versus 27% in the control group. This difference persisted six months after the training, when 16% of the intervention group versus 31% of the control group reported evidence of depression. The results suggest that mindfulness can lead to a decrease in symptoms associated with depression and, moreover, that it protects against the later development of depression-like symptoms (Raes, Griffith, Van der Gucht, & Williams, 2013).

Cautious Optimism

While the results above are encouraging, it is important to note that most of the studies described involved relatively small numbers of participants, used few objective measures, and had limited follow-up. Therefore, as encouraging as these preliminary results are in demonstrating that mindfulness enhances executive function, emotional intelligence, social development, and compassionate action, it is important not to overstate the current research. To assess the full impact of such programs, we need randomized controlled trials with large numbers of participants, using validated subjective and objective measures, and long-term follow-up. In the meantime, the current data provides a sufficient foundation for you to begin. It is equally important to remember that there are benefits of mindfulness that are profoundly transformative, and difficult—if not impossible—to quantify, especially in children and adolescents. For example, can we ever really quantify the benefits of experiencing, even just for a moment, one's own natural stillness and quietness?

appendices

presenting or pitching
the program

As suggested in the foundational chapters of this book, when presenting this program to schools and other organizations, it's crucial that you emphasize the secular and universal nature of mindfulness, and that you clearly demonstrate how mindfulness fulfills the needs of children and the community.

In these times of tight budgets, most schools, hospitals, clinics, community centers, and religious organizations are looking for cost-effective tools to increase the well-being of the young people they serve. Schools are seeking to improve students' attention and to address their social and emotional needs, so that they arrive in class ready and able to learn. Hospitals and clinics are looking to provide patients and clients with skills to decrease the suffering caused by physical, mental, and emotional pain. Community centers are particularly interested in offering participants life skills and supporting them in making wise choices. Religious institutions want to provide their young members with these same skills, and often find that mindfulness enhances and supports their offerings. Athletic coaches and art, music, and theater directors recognize that mindfulness can decrease anxiety and enhance performance.

As you present or pitch the program, remember that most decision makers are overworked, underpaid, and underappreciated—in other words, stressed out and short on time. Therefore it can be helpful to provide a one-page letter, like the sample letter below, that clearly and succinctly states the proven benefits of mindfulness. Feel free to use the letter below as a template, and then tailor it to your setting. It is helpful to provide decision makers with this summary, and a copy of the paper *Integrating Mindfulness into K-12 Education*, and perhaps the *PBS Teachers Guide*. These documents can be downloaded

" and "Press" links via the Resources tab on my website (http://
ace.com).

working to bring mindfulness into a particular setting, you probably
ve connections with one or more individuals. However, if you want to have
atest chance of children reaping the benefits of the practice and the program
shing, it is essential that you create an opportunity for administrators, staff, and
rents to *experience* mindfulness and ask questions, so that misconceptions don't
arise and gain momentum.

Insurance

If you are working in a setting other than your usual work setting, that would not be
covered under any existing insurance, it is wise to purchase at least some general
liability insurance. Many schools will require that you obtain a rider from your liability insurance to cover any issues that may arise while teaching.

Fees and Funding

When determining fees for afterschool, hospital, clinic, or community programs, I
suggest that you familiarize yourself with your market. Price your program in line
with other offerings of similar duration, such as eight weeks of chess or Italian
cooking. My policy is that I always offer a limited number of partial scholarships.
Those requesting scholarships are asked to provide some basic financial information,
including household annual income, number of people in the household, and any
extenuating circumstances, such as accumulating educational debt, prolonged unem-
ployment, volunteering or working in extremely underserved areas, family illness or
death, costly legal procedures, and so on.

In our society, an exchange of money is usually how we demonstrate the value of
something, and paying even a small amount helps people value what they receive.
Thus, except in very underserved areas, I always have people pay something, even if
it is just a five-dollar fee for materials. That said, there have been many occasions
when I have taught for free; I've even provided kids with inexpensive CD players,
understanding that the equipment may not be returned and being grateful when it is.
Conversely, if I'm speaking or teaching in an extremely affluent setting, I charge their
going rate. This "Robin Hood" method allows me to be of service in a wide variety of
settings.

When determining your fees, consider your expenses—including gas, room
rental, materials, and child care—and set an hourly wage that allows you to pay your

rent and buy groceries. Do your best to find a middle path between greed and under-valuing what you are offering.

Consent

When I teach mindfulness to individual patients in my medical office, the patient and parent complete a comprehensive intake form, and the parent also provides consent for treatment. When I teach to groups in community settings, each participant completes a simple intake form, and the parents provide consent. A copy of the simple intake form is provided at the end of this appendix.

Most schools consider in-class mindfulness a part of their curriculum, like math or language arts, and choose not to request consent. In this case, the only information I have about a child is what the child shares during class and any insights offered by the teacher. Some schools consider mindfulness more like drug and alcohol education or sex education and request parental consent. In that case, I use the intake form provided. If you work in research settings, you know that any formal research *must* be approved by your institutional review board. When offering the Still Quiet Place curriculum in research contexts, the teams I've worked with have requested both parental consent and child assent. If you are not formally trained in conducting research and you want to collect meaningful data regarding outcomes, you are strongly encouraged to partner with a university-affiliated research colleague who can guide you in adhering to proper methodology, selecting relevant measures, and analyzing the data.

The Value of Persistence

Please know that if you are working to bring mindfulness to a new setting, it will probably take time to have the needed collaborative dialogues, agree on the details, make the community aware of the offering, and enroll participants. Do your best not be discouraged if it is slow going. This is often the way of it. I have had "sure" things fall through, and opportunities I've let go of have reappeared. As Jon Kabat-Zinn once said, "There is a lot of schlepping involved in offering mindfulness." Remember that the Center for Mindfulness was once the Stress Reduction Clinic, and it was in the basement of the hospital. When I trained there, I carried mats and cushions from one location to another alongside Jon, Saki, Santorelli, and the other teachers. And today it is much the same. So enjoy the schlepping!

One-Page Letter for Decision Makers

Dear Mr./Ms. Gray,

It was a pleasure speaking with you this morning, and I look forward to sharing mindfulness with the Hoover School community. As we discussed, below is a brief summary of the proven benefits of mindfulness. Attached are two articles that review these results in greater detail.

Research demonstrates that children who practice mindfulness experience the following benefits*:

- Increased attention

- Increased executive function (working memory, planning, organization, and impulse control)

- Decreased ADHD behaviors—specifically hyperactivity and impulsivity

- Fewer conduct and anger management problems

- Increased emotional regulation

- Increased self-calming

- Increased social skills and social compliance

- Increased care for others

- Decreased negative affect, or emotions

- Decreased anxiety in general and text anxiety in particular

- Decreased depression

- Increased sense of calmness, relaxation, and self-acceptance

- Increased self-esteem

- Increased quality of sleep

Please let me know if you or members of the committee have any additional questions. I look forward to our ongoing collaboration.

* Journal articles available upon request.

Sample Program Flier for Eight- to Eleven-Year-Olds

Mindfulness for Everyday Life

LEARN HOW TO FOCUS THE FLASHLIGHT OF YOUR ATTENTION

TO IMPROVE YOUR SCHOOLWORK AND TEST TAKING

 ATHLETIC PERFORMANCE

CREATIVITY

 AND RELATIONSHIPS

In this eight-week course you will learn a specific way of paying attention to your breath, your body, your thoughts, your feelings, and the world around you. This way of paying attention is very powerful because when you can observe your thoughts and feelings, then you can *choose* what you say and how you act. And choosing your words and actions can improve your life! Children who have taken this course have found it has helped them with their friends, parents, brothers, sisters, schoolwork, sports, and other activities.

More than twenty-five years of research have proven that mindfulness increases attention and focus; reduces stress, anxiety, and depression; and increases well-being. Mindfulness is used by professional athletes, artists, musicians, business people, teachers, healthcare professionals, lawyers, and military personnel to enhance their performance.

Who: 3rd–5th graders

When: Tuesday evenings beginning February 1st, 7:00 to 8:00 p.m.

Where: Hoover Elementary School Library

Costs: $_____ A limited number of partial scholarships are available.

Registration: Amy Saltzman, M.D., 885 Oak Grove Ave., #204, Menlo Park, CA 94025. Please mail your check and registration form by January 10th and include your child's name, your phone # and e-mail address. Spaces are limited so sign up early. If you have questions, please contact Dr. Saltzman: 650-575-5780, dramy@stillquietplace.com

Dr. Saltzman is trained in internal medicine and is a founding diplomate of the Board of Holistic Medicine. She served for eight years as a trustee on the Board of the American Holistic Medical Association. She is the director of the Association for Mindfulness in Education. She speaks at educational and medical conferences and to parent and teacher organizations. She also offers individual mindfulness coaching and holistic medical care to adults and children.

Consent Form

Still Quiet Place
Mindfulness in Daily Life

Participant name: _____ Age: _____

Phone number: _____ E-mail: _____

Emergency contact: _____ Phone number: _____

Physician: _____ Phone number: _____

Therapist: _____ Phone number: _____

Physical/ Psychological conditions:

_____

Medications:

_____

Please answer the questions below as honestly and completely as possible, so that I can help you as much as possible.

1. What do you find stressful, difficult, annoying, upsetting?

2. How do you deal with stressful, difficult, annoying, upsetting situations?

3. Are the ways you deal with stress helpful to you? Please explain.

4. What would you like to learn from taking this course?

Is there anything else you would like me to know about you, your school, friends, family?

_____

Confidentiality and Commitment

All forms and discussions will be considered confidential to the extent that there is no immediate concern of harm to myself or to others. I give permission for you to call my health provider if such harm is a concern. I commit to attend the eight weekly sessions, and practice the home assignments to the best of my abilities. I further understand that after the end of the first class, refunds are granted only for extenuating circumstances.

PARTICIPANT SIGNATURE: _____ DATE: _____

PARENT SIGNATURE: _____ DATE: _____

course outline

Session	Elements	Intentions	Home Practice
Introductory Evening	Parents only Mindful eating Review data Rationale for the course Commitment Questions	Provide an experience of mindfulness Review data to date for children and teens, and selected data for adults Review the rationale for offering MBSR to children Discuss the course structure and time commitment Answer questions	
Class 1	Mindful listening (tone bar) Introduction to Mindfulness Group agreements and class guidelines Individual introductions Mindful eating Breath-based practice: Jewel/Treasure/Rest Introduce Still Quiet Place Define mindfulness—paying attention, here and now, with kindness and curiosity, and then choosing our behavior Daily life practice—mindful toothbrushing Mindful listening (tone bar)	Create a safe, welcoming environment Introduce participants to each other and to the Still Quiet Place/mindfulness Provide an experience and working definition of Still Quiet Place/mindfulness Give examples of mindfulness in daily life (informal practice)	Jewel/Treasure Rest Toothbrushing

Class 2	Review class 1 and experience with home practice Discuss barriers to practice, generate solutions Seaween movement practice Jewel/Treasure/Rest Pleasant Events exercise Investigate how often our attention is in the past or the future Daily life practice—mindful shoe tying Answer questions Encourage home practice	Explore experience of CD and daily life practice Support the children in establishing a daily practice with the CD	Jewel/Treasure Rest Shoe tying
Class 3	Review class 2 and experience with home practice Action Circle movement practice Bubbles/Thought Watching Introduce concept of Unkind Mind (critical internal dialogue) Nine dots	Discuss experience with CD and daily life practice Cultivate the capacity to observe thoughts Nine dots Perception—how we view ourselves, others Thoughts during a difficult task Introduce the concept of Unkind Mind (critical internal dialogue)	Bubbles/Thought Watching Notice Unkind Mind

Class 4	Review class 3 and experience with home practice Unpleasant Event exercise Suffering = Pain x Resistance Mindful Dance Party Finger Yoga practice Mindfulness of feelings Discuss that this is the halfway point in the course, and a new moment to recommit to the practices Daily life practice—mindful showering	Examine the thoughts and feelings associated with unpleasant experiences Resistance Wanting things to be different Examine how resistance/wanting circumstances, ourselves, others to be different creates upset/suffering Develop emotional fluency	Feelings Haiku/poetry/art depicting a feeling Play with $S = P \times R$ Watch how we create suffering Showering
Class 5	Review class 4 and experience with home practice Emotion theory and Improv "Autobiography in Five Short Chapters" Yoga	Introduce basic emotion theory Explore common "holes" and "different streets" Use holes and streets to discuss reacting vs. responding Yoga Self-talk/Self-compassion Balance as dynamic Explore how often Unkind Mind is inaccurate/negative/looking for trouble	Mountain/Stretch and Balance Notice "holes" and "different streets" Continue to notice Unkind Mind
Week 5 Vacation	*School schedules often contain vacations. Although it is not always possible, it is best to schedule the course so that vacations fall after week 4, when the students have some momentum.*	Maintain practice without support of weekly class	Alternate Feelings and one of the other practices each day Notice "holes"(difficult situations) and practice choosing "different streets" (responding)

Class 6	Discuss falling in and staying out of holes Body Scan Communication dyads exercise (one person describes one difficult communication, the other listens and then reflects, then the roles are reversed) Walking Introduce possibility of Kind Heart as an antidote to Unkind Mind	Continue developing the capacity to respond rather than react Bring attention into the body Enhance capacity to observe thoughts and feelings Practice using mindfulness during difficult communications Moving our practice into the world Introduce Kind Heart	Alternate Body Scan/Being in the Body, and Walking Thoreau/nature walk Practice responding (with Kind Heart) to both Unkind Mind and in difficult situations
Class 7	Share examples of responding; and role-play new responses to situations when the students reacted Aikido Loving-kindness ABC, STAR, and PEACE practices Discuss that next week is the last class Request that students bring something for the last class that symbolizes their experience with the course	Continue to develop the capacity to respond (with Kind Heart) rather than react Introduce loving-kindness as a specific practice for developing Kind Heart	Loving-kindness Continue responding (with Kind Heart) to both Unkind Mind and in difficult situations Bring something symbolic to share for the last session
Class 8	Discuss experience with loving-kindness Group choice Letter to a friend Completion/beginning Making the practice their own	Discuss the natural capacity to send and receive love Share what the course has meant to them Discuss variety of ways they can make the practice their own Discuss the completion of the course Remind them they can always call or e-mail	Your choice Sit/Flashlight Make a commitment (or not) as to how you will continue the CD and daily life practice

It cannot be emphasized enough: your own solid personal practice is an essential prerequisite for you to offer mindfulness to others!

Although it has not been listed, to conserve space, every class starting with session 2 will begin and conclude with Mindful Listening, and Mindful Eating always follows the initial Mindful Listening practice.

It is important that you attend to participants' natural need for movement.

In the discussions, use the children's real-life experience to demonstrate how mindfulness can be applied in daily life: test anxiety, playground interactions, disagreements with siblings, romantic breakups....

resources

Books and Resources for Children

Baylor, Byrd. 1974. *Everybody Needs a Rock*. New York: Aladdin Paperbacks.

Baylor, Byrd. 1997. *The Other Way to Listen*. New York: Aladdin Paperbacks.

Buckley, Annie. 2003. *The Kids' Yoga Deck*. San Francisco: Chronicle Books.

Despard, Brian. 2011. *You Are Not Your Thoughts: Mindfulness for Children of All Ages*. Chicopee, MA: New Life Design Studio.

Dr. Seuss. 1996. *My Many Colored Days*. New York: Knopf.

Kung Fu Panda. 2008. DreamWorks Animation. Redwood City, CA: Paramount Pictures.

Leaf, Munro. 1936. *The Story of Ferdinand*. New York: Viking.

McKinley, Cindy. 2002. *One Smile*. Kirkland, WA: Illumination Arts Publishing Company.

Muth, Jon. 2005. *Zen Shorts*. New York: Scholastic Press.

Muth, Jon. 2008. *Zen Ties*. New York: Scholastic Press.

Rice, David. 1999. *Because Brian Hugged His Mother*. Nevada City, CA: Dawn Publications.

Rose, Betsy. 2007. *Calm Down Boogie: Songs for Peaceful Moments and Lively Spirits*. Albany, NY: A Gentle Wind.

Thomas, Marlo. 2004. *Thanks & Giving All Year Long*. New York: Simon and Schuster Books for Young Readers.

Viorst, Judith. 1972. *Alexander and the Terrible, Horrible, No Good, Very Bad Day*. New York: Atheneum Books for Young Readers.

Wood, Douglas. 2002. *A Quiet Place*. New York: Simon and Schuster Books for Young Readers.

Wood, Douglas. 2005. *The Secret of Saying Thanks*. New York: Simon and Schuster Books for Young Readers.

Books and Resources for Teens

Biegel, Gina. 2010. *The Stress Reduction Workbook For Teens*. Oakland, CA: New Harbinger Publications.

Carlson, Richard. 2000. *Don't Sweat the Small Stuff For Teens*. New York: Hyperion.

Gordhamer, Soren. 2001. *Just Say Om!: Your Life's Journey*. Avon, MA: Adams Media Corporation.

Levine, Noah. 2003. *Dharma Punx*. New York: HarperCollins.

Winston, Diana. 2003. *Wide Awake: A Buddhist Guide for Teens*. New York: The Berkeley Publishing Group.

Shils, Judi. 2003. *The Diary Deck: About Teens by Teens*. San Francisco: Chronicle Books.

Books on Sharing Mindfulness with Youth

Brady, Richard, and Irene McHenry. 2009. *Tuning In: Mindfulness in Teaching and Learning*. Philadelphia, PA: Friends Council on Education.

Freedom Writers, with Erin Gruwell. 1999. *The Freedom Writers Diary: How a Teacher and 150 Teens Used Writing to Change Themselves and the World Around Them*. New York: Broadway Books.

Greco, Laurie, and Steven C. Hayes. 2008. *Acceptance and Mindfulness Treatments for Children and Adolescents: A Practitioner's Guide*. Oakland, CA: New Harbinger Publications.

Kaiser Greenland, Susan. 2010. *The Mindful Child: How to Help Your Kid Manage Stress and Become Happier, Kinder, and More Compassionate*. New York: Free Press.

Lantieri, Linda. 2008. *Building Emotional Intelligence: Techniques to Cultivate Inner Strength in Children*. Boulder, CO: Sounds True.

Nhat Hanh, Thich. 2011. *Planting Seeds: Practicing Mindfulness with Children*. Berkeley, CA: Parallax Press.

Schoeberlein, Deborah. 2009. *Mindful Teaching and Teaching Mindfulness: A Guide for Anyone Who Teaches Anything*. Somerville, MA: Wisdom Publications.

Willard, Christopher. 2010. *Child's Mind: Mindfulness Practices to Help Our Children Be More Focused, Calm, and Relaxed*. Berkeley, CA: Parallax Press.

Books for Establishing and Deepening Your Practice

Kabat-Zinn, Jon. 1990. *Full Catastrophe Living: Using the Wisdom of Your Body and Mind to Face Stress, Pain, and Illness.* New York: Delacorte Press.

Kabat-Zinn, Jon. 1994. *Wherever You Go, There You Are.* New York: Hyperion.

Kabat-Zinn, Jon. 2012. *Mindfulness for Beginners: Reclaiming the Present Moment—and Your Life.* Boulder, CO: Sounds True.

Palmer, Parker J. 1998. *The Courage to Teach: Exploring the Inner Landscape of a Teacher's Life.* San Francisco: Jossey-Bass.

Santorelli, Saki. 1999. *Heal Thy Self: Lessons on Mindfulness in Medicine.* New York: Bell Tower.

Siegel, Daniel. 2007. *The Mindful Brain: Reflection and Attunement in the Cultivation of Well-Being.* New York: W. W. Norton & Company.

Stahl, Bob, and Elisha Goldstein. 2010. *A Mindfulness-Based Stress Reduction Workbook.* Oakland, CA: New Harbinger Publications.

Books and Resources for Parents

Bailey, Michelle. 2011. *Parenting Your Stressed Child: 10 Mindfulness-Based Stress Reduction Practices to Help Your Child Manage Stress and Build Essential Life Skills.* Oakland, CA: New Harbinger Publications.

Bertin, Mark. 2011. *The Family ADHD Solution: A Scientific Approach to Maximizing Your Child's Attention and Minimizing Parental Stress.* New York: Macmillan.

Farber, Adele, and Elaine Mazlish. 1990. *Liberated Parents, Liberated Children: Your Guide to a Happier Family.* New York: Avon Books.

Goleman, Daniel. 1995. *Emotional Intelligence: Why It Can Matter More Than IQ.* New York: Bantam Books.

Gore, Ariel. 2000. *The Mother Trip: Hip Mama's Guide to Staying Sane in the Chaos of Motherhood.* Seattle: Seal Press.

Kabat-Zinn, Jon. 1994. *Wherever You Go, There You Are.* New York: Hyperion.

Kabat-Zinn, Jon. 2012. *Mindfulness for Beginners: Reclaiming the Present Moment—and Your Life.* Boulder, CO: Sounds True.

Kabat-Zinn, Jon, and Myla Kabat-Zinn. 1997. *Everyday Blessings: The Inner Work of Mindful Parenting.* New York: Hyperion.

Kaiser Greenland, Susan. 2010. *The Mindful Child: How to Help Your Kid Manage Stress and Become Happier, Kinder, and More Compassionate.* New York: Free Press.

Kettmann, Steve. 2010. "Why He's Our Freak—Not Anyone Else's." *Modern Luxury San Francisco Magazine,* June 18. http://www.modernluxury.com/san-francisco/story/why-hes-our-freak-not-anyone-elses

Lantieri, Linda. 2008. *Building Emotional Intelligence: Techniques to Cultivate Inner Strength in Children*. Boulder, CO: Sounds True.

Lerner, Harriet. 1998. *The Mother Dance: How Children Change Your Life*. New York: HarperCollins.

Levine, Madeline. 2006. *The Price of Privilege: How Parental Pressure and Material Advantage Are Creating A Generation of Disconnected and Unhappy Kids*. New York: HarperCollins.

MacKenzie, Robert. 2001. *Setting Limits with Your Strong-Willed Child: Eliminating Conflict by Establishing Clear, Firm, and Respectful Boundaries*. New York: Three Rivers Press.

Martin, William. 1999. *The Parent's Tao Te Ching: Ancient Advice for Modern Parents: A New Interpretation*. New York: Marlowe & Company.

Nelson, Portia. 1993. *There's a Hole in My Sidewalk: The Romance of Self-Discovery*. 3rd ed. Hillsboro, OR: Beyond Words Publishing.

Nhat Hanh, Thich. 2011. *Planting Seeds: Practicing Mindfulness with Children*. Berkeley, CA: Parallax Press.

Pope, Denise. 2001. *"Doing School": How We Are Creating a Generation of Stressed Out, Materialistic, and Miseducated Students*. New Haven, CT: Yale University Press.

Riera, Michael, and Joseph Di Prisco. 2000. *Field Guide to the American Teenager: Appreciating the Teenager You Live With*. Cambridge, MA: Perseus Publishing.

Roy, Denise. 2001. *My Monastery is a Minivan: Where the Daily Is Divine and the Routine Becomes Prayer*. Chicago: Loyola Press.

Roy, Denise. 2007. *Momfulness: Mothering with Mindfulness, Compassion, and Grace*. San Francisco: Jossey-Bass.

Siegel, Daniel. 2007. *The Mindful Brain: Reflection and Attunement in the Cultivation of Well-Being*. New York: W. W. Norton & Company.

Stahl, Bob, and Elisha Goldstein. 2010. *A Mindfulness-Based Stress Reduction Workbook*. Oakland, CA: New Harbinger Publications.

Willard, Christopher. 2010. *Child's Mind: Mindfulness Practices to Help Our Children Be More Focused, Calm, and Relaxed*. Berkeley, CA: Parallax Press.

Online Bibliographies

http://www.mindfulexperience.org

http://www.umassmed.edu/cfm/research/index.aspx?linkidentifier=id&itemid=42066

references

Bach, Richard. 1977. *Illusions: The Adventures of a Reluctant Messiah*. New York: Dell Publishing.

Bakoula, C., Kolaitis, G., Veltsista, A., Gika, A, & Chrousos, G. (2009). Parental stress affects the emotions and behaviour of children up to adolescence: A Greek prospective, longitudinal study." *Stress, 12*(6), 486–498. doi: 10.3109/10253890802645041.

Beauchemin, J., Hutchins, T. L., & Patterson, F. (2008). Mindfulness meditation may lessen anxiety, promote social skills, and improve academic performance among adolescents with learning disabilities. *Complementary Health Practice Review, 13*(1), 34–45. doi:10.1177/1533210107311624.

Biegel, G., Brown, K., Shapiro, S. & Schubert, C. (2009). Mindfulness-based stress reduction for the treatment of adolescent psychiatric outpatients: a randomized clinical trial. *Journal of Consulting and Clinical Psychology, 77*(5), 855–866.

Blackwell, L. S., Trzesniewski, K. H., & Dweck, C. S. (2007). Implicit theories of intelligence predict achievement across an adolescent transition: a longitudinal study and an intervention. *Child Development, 78*(1), 246–263.

Blair, C., & Diamond, A. (2008). Biological processes in prevention and intervention: the promotion of self-regulation as a means of preventing school failure. *Development and Psychopathology, 20*(3), 899–911.

Bögels, S., Hoogstad, B., van Dun, L., de Schutter, S., & Restifo, K. (2008). Mindfulness training for adolescents with externalising disorders and their parents. *Behavioural and Cognitive Psychotherapy, 36*(2), 193–209. doi:10.1017/S1352465808004190.

Bootzin, R. R., & Stevens, S. J. (2005). Adolescents, substance abuse, and the treatment of insomnia and daytime sleepiness. *Clinical Psychology Review, 25*(5), 629–644.

Broderick, P. C., and Metz, S. (2009). Learning to BREATHE: A pilot trial of a mindfulness curriculum for adolescents. *Advances in School Mental Health Promotion, 2*(1), 35–46.

Brown, K., West, A., Loverich, T., and Biegel, G. (2011). Assessing adolescent mindfulness: Validation of an adapted Mindful Attention Awareness Scale in adolescent normative and psychiatric populations. *Psychological Assessment, 23*(4), 1023–1033.

Center on the Developing Child at Harvard University. (2011). Building the brain's "air traffic control" system: how early experiences shape the development of executive function. (Working Paper No. 11.) Retrieved from http://www.developingchild.harvard.edu.

Crone, E. (2009). Executive functions in adolescence: inferences from brain and behavior. *Developmental Science, 12*(6), 825–830.

Davidson, R., Kabat-Zinn, J., Schumacher, J., Rosenkranz, M., Muller, D., Santorelli, S. F., Urbanowski, F., Harrington, A., Bonus, K., & Sheridan, J. F. (2003). Alterations in brain and immune function produced by mindfulness meditation. *Psychosomatic Medicine, 65(4)*, 564–570.

Diamond, A. 2006. The early development of executive functions. In E. Bialystok & F. I. M. Craik (Eds.), *Lifespan Cognitions: Mechanisms of Change*. New York: Oxford University Press.

Ekman, Paul. (2003). *Emotions Revealed: Recognizing Faces and Feelings to Improve Communication and Emotional Life*. New York: Henry Holt and Company.

Evans, G. W., & Schamberg, M. A. 2009. Childhood poverty, chronic stress, and adult working memory. *Proceedings of the National Academy of Sciences, 106*(16), 6545–6549.

Flook, L., Smalley, S. L., Kitil, M. J., Galla, B. M., Greenland, S. K., Locke, J., Ishijima, E., & Kasari, C. (2010). Effects of mindful awareness practices on executive functions in elementary school children. *Journal of Applied School Psychology, 26(1)*, 70–95.

Garofalo, M. (2008, March 8). A victim treats his mugger right. In NPR (Producer), *Weekend Morning Edition*. Retrieved from http://www.npr.org/2008/03/28/89164759/a-victim-treats-his-mugger-right

Goldin, P., Saltzman, A., & Jha, A. (2008, November). Mindfulness meditation training in families. Paper presented at the *42nd Annual Association for Behavioral and Cognitive Therapies (ABCT) Convention*, Orlando, FL.

Hölzel, B., Carmody, J., Vangel, M., Congleton, C., Yerramsetti, S. M., Gard, T., & Lazar, S. W. (2011). Mindfulness practice leads to increases in regional brain gray matter density. *Psychiatry Research: Neuroimaging, 191*(1), 36–43.

Jazaieri, H., Jinpa, G. T., McGonigal, K., Rosenberg, E. L., Finkelstein, J., Simon-Thomas, E., Cullen, M., Doty, J. R., Gross, J. J., & Goldin, P. R. (2012). Enhancing compassion: a randomized controlled trial of a compassion cultivation training program. *Journal of Happiness Studies, 14*(4),1113-1126. doi:10.1007/s10902-012-9373-z.

Kabat-Zinn, J. (1982). An outpatient program in behavioral medicine for chronic pain patients based on the practice of mindfulness meditation: Theoretical considerations and preliminary results. *General Hospital Psychiatry, 4(1)*, 33–47.

Kabat-Zinn, J. (1990). *Full Catastrophe Living: Using the Wisdom of Your Body and Mind to Face Stress, Pain, and Illness*. New York: Delacorte Press.

Kabat-Zinn, J., Lipworth, L., & Burney, R. (1985). The clinical use of mindfulness meditation for the self-regulation of chronic pain. *Journal of Behavioral Medicine, 8*(2), 163–190.

Kabat-Zinn, J., Lipworth, L., Burney, R. and Sellers, W. (1986). Four-year follow-up of a meditation-based program for the self-regulation of chronic pain: Treatment outcomes and compliance. *Clinical Journal of Pain, 2(3)*, 159–173.

Kabat-Zinn, J., & Chapman-Waldrop, A. (1988). Compliance with an outpatient stress reduction program: Rates and predictors of program completion. *Journal of Behavioral Medicine, 11*(4), 333–352.

Kabat-Zinn, J., and Kabat-Zinn, M. (1997). *Everyday Blessings: The Inner Work of Mindful Parenting*. New York: Hyperion.

Kerrigan, D., Johnson, K., Stewart, M., Magyari, T., Hutton, N., Ellen, J. M., & Sibinga, E. M. (2011). Perceptions, experiences, and shifts in perspective occurring among urban youth participating in a mindfulness-based stress reduction program. *Complementary Therapies in Clinical Practice, 17*(2), 96–101.

Lee, J., Semple, R. J., Rosa, D., & Miller, L. F. (2008). Mindfulness-based cognitive therapy for children: Results of a pilot study. *Journal of Cognitive Psychotherapy, 22*(1), 15–28.

Luthar, S. S. (2003). The culture of affluence: Psychological costs of material wealth. *Child Development, 74*(6), 1581–1593.

Luthar, S. S., & Barkin, S. H. (2012). Are affluent youth truly "at risk"? Vulnerability and resilience across three diverse samples. *Development and Psychopathology, 24*(2), 429–449.

Maccoby, E. E. (1980). *Social Development: Psychological Growth and the Parent-Child Relationship.* New York: Harcourt Brace Jovanovich.

McCown, D., Reibel, D., & Micozzi, M. (2010). *Teaching Mindfulness: A Practical Guide for Clinicians and Educators.* New York: Springer.

Meiklejohn, J., Phillips, C., Freedman, M. L., Griffin, M. L., Biegel, G., Roach, A. et al. (2010). Integrating mindfulness training into K–12 education: Fostering resilience of teachers and students. *Mindfulness, 3*(4), 291-307.

Napoli, M., Krech, P. R., & Holley, L. C. (2005). Mindfulness training for elementary school students: The attention academy. *Journal of Applied School Psychology, 21*(1), 99–125.

Neff, K. D., Hsieh, Y. P., & Dejitterat, K. (2005). Self-compassion, achievement goals, and coping with academic failure. *Self and Identity, 4*(3), 263-287.

Neff, K. D., & Germer, C. K. (2013). A pilot study and randomized controlled trial of the mindful self-compassion program. *Journal of Clinical Psychology, 69*(1), 28-44. doi:10.1002/jclp.21923.

Raes, F., Griffith, J. W., Van der Gucht, K., & Williams, J. M. G. (2013). School-based prevention and reduction of depression in adolescents: A cluster-randomized controlled trial of a mindfulness group program. *Mindfulness.* doi:10.1007/s12671-013-0202-1.

Riggs, N., Jahromi, L., Razza, R., Dillworth-Bart, J., & Mueller, U. (2006). Executive function and the promotion of social-emotional competence. *Journal of Applied Developmental Psychology, 27*(4), 300–309.

Saltzman, A., & Goldin, P. (2008). Mindfulness-based stress reduction for school-age children. In S. C. Hayes & L. A. Greco (Eds.), *Acceptance and Mindfulness Treatments for Children, Adolescents, and Families.* Oakland, CA: Context Press/New Harbinger Publications.

Santorelli, S. (1999). *Heal Thy Self: Lessons on Mindfulness in Medicine.* New York: Bell Tower.

Schonert-Reichl, K. A., & Lawlor, M. S. (2010). The effects of a mindfulness-based education program on pre- and early adolescents' well-being and social and emotional competence. *Mindfulness.* doi:10.1007/s12671-010-0011-8.

Sibinga, E., Kerrigan, D., Stewart, M., Johnson, K., Magyari, T., & Ellen, J. (2011). Mindfulness-based stress reduction for urban youth. *Journal of Alternative and Complementary Medicine, 17*(3), 213–218.

Zylowska, L., Ackerman, D. L., Yang, M. H., Futrell, J. L., Horton, N. L., Hale, T. S., Pataki, C., & Smalley, S. L. (2008). Mindfulness meditation training in adults and adolescents with ADHD A feasibility study. *Journal of Attention Disorders, 11*(6), 737–746. doi:10.1177/1087054707308502.

Amy Saltzman, MD, is a holistic physician, mindfulness coach, scientist, wife, mother, devoted student of transformation, longtime athlete, and occasional poet. Her passion is supporting people of all ages in enhancing their well-being and discovering the *Still Quiet Place* within. She is recognized by her peers as a visionary and pioneer in the fields of holistic medicine and mindfulness for youth. She is founder and director of the Association for Mindfulness in Education, an inaugural and longstanding member of the steering committee for the Mindfulness in Education Network, and a founding member of the Northern California Advisory Committee on Mindfulness. She lives in the San Francisco Bay Area with her husband and two teenage children. For more information, visit www. stillquietplace.com.

Foreword writer **Saki Santorelli, EdD, MA**, is executive director of the Center for Mindfulness in Medicine, Health Care, and Society at the University of Massachusetts Medical School and author of *Heal Thyself.*

Index

Session 8 of SQP course, 149–156; closing
sharing, 152–153; ending of the course
discussion, 154; Flashlight practice,
151–152; group choice practice, 151;
home practice assignment, 155;
intentions of, 149; Letter to a Friend
exercise, 152, 156; Mindful Eating
practice, 150; Mindful Listening
practice, 150, 154; outline of, 150, 210;
review of home practice, 150
showering mindfully, 39–40
shy yoga discussion, 96
Sideways Stories from Wayside School
(Sachar), 130
signals, 38
social development, 185–189; aggression
and, 186; impulsivity and, 187; moral
behavior and, 187–188; perspective
taking and, 187–188
Social Development (Maccoby), 185
space bubble, 50–51
Stahl, Bob, 24
STAR practice, 140–141
State of America's Children report, v
Still Quiet Place: author's stories about,
2–4, 164–165; children's description of,
32–33; physical sensation of, 1; sharing
with youth, 29–45, 164–165. *See also*
mindfulness
Still Quiet Place practice audio, 60, 70
Still Quiet Place (SQP) course: age-
appropriate adaptations to, 30–32;
author's development of, 4; beginning
sessions in, 34–35; books/resources
related to, 211–214; child-parent pairs in,
177–180; consent form used in, 199,
202–203; conversations engaged in,
36–37; distilling mindfulness for, 8–12;
do-overs used in, 41; essentials of
teaching, 32–33; fees and funding for,
198–199; home practice in, 38–41;
individual instruction based on, 167;
instructor qualities/qualifications for,
159–160; introductory evening for, 34,

206; language and languaging in, 37;
leading and practicing in, 36; letter for
decision makers, 200; liability insurance
for, 198; listening practice in, 35; MBSR
compared to, 13–19, 20; mindful
reminders used in, 40–41; movement
allowed in, 38; notes and cautions about,
167–176; outline of sessions in, 206–210;
practice log used in, 40; practice of
facilitating, 42–45; practices/exercises
offered in, 35; presenting to schools/
organizations, 197–203; program flier
example, 201; reluctance to participate
in, 174; responsive improv in, 20–21;
room environment for, 34; signals used
in, 38; training available for, 25;
transitions facilitated in, 37–38. *See also
specific course sessions*
Still Quiet Place: Mindfulness CDs, 35, 60,
141, 144, 151
stillquietplace.com website, 26, 191
stress: childhood, 5–6; discussing with
youth, 20; research on mindfulness and,
191
Stress Reduction Workbook for Teens, The
(Biegel), 26
submissive response, 137
suffering, equation for, 16, 85, 90–92

T

teachers. *See* classroom teachers
Teaching Mindfulness (McCown, Reibel, and
Micozzi), 25
team players, 51
teenagers. *See* adolescents
theory of mind, 188
therapy vs. mindfulness, 168
Thought Watching practice/discussion,
77–78, 79, 80
thoughts: mindfulness of, 14–15, 27, 76–78;
Unkind Mind and, 78–79, 93
toothbrushing, mindful, 59, 60
transitions, course, 37–38

Register your **new harbinger** titles for additional benefits!

When you register your **new harbinger** title—purchased in any format, from any source—you get access to benefits like the following:

- Downloadable accessories like printable worksheets and extra content

- Instructional videos and audio files

- Information about updates, corrections, and new editions

Not every title has accessories, but we're adding new material all the time.

Access free accessories in 3 easy steps:

1. Sign in at NewHarbinger.com (or **register** to create an account).

2. Click on **register a book**. Search for your title and click the **register** button when it appears.

3. Click on the **book cover or title** to go to its details page. Click on **accessories** to view and access files.

That's all there is to it!

If you need help, visit:

NewHarbinger.com/accessories

new harbinger
CELEBRATING
40 YEARS